2/96

When Indians Became Cowboys

When Indians Became Cowboys

Native Peoples and Cattle Ranching in the American West

By Peter Iverson

UNIVERSITY OF OKLAHOMA PRESS : NORMAN AND LONDON

By Peter Iverson

The Navajos: A Critical Bibliography (Bloomington, 1976)
The Navajo Nation (Westport, 1981; Albuquerque, 1983)
Carlos Montezuma and the Changing World of American Indians
  (Albuquerque, 1982)
(ed.) *The Plains Indians of the Twentieth Century* (Norman, 1985)
The Navajos (New York, 1990)
(ed., with Albert L. Hurtado) *Major Problems in American Indian History*
  (Lexington, 1994)
When the Indians Became Cowboys: Native Peoples and Cattle Ranching in the
  American West (Norman, 1994)

"Raisin Eyes" is reprinted from *Sáani Dahaataał/The Women Are Singing: Poems and Stories*, Sun Tracks, Volume 23, by Luci Tapahonso, by permission of the University of Arizona Press, copyright 1993 Luci Tapahonso. Portions of the following articles by Peter Iverson have been incorporated in this book and are used with permission: "Cowboys, Indians, and the Modern West," *Arizona and the West* 28, no. 2 (Summer 1986):107–24; and "The Cowboys Are Indians: Indian Cattle Ranching in the American West," special issue on The American Indian Today, *Storia Nordamericana* 5, no. 1 (1988):115–24.

Published with the assistance of the National Endowment for the Humanities, a federal agency which supports the study of such fields as history, philosophy, literature, and language.

Iverson, Peter.
   When Indians became cowboys : native peoples and cattle ranching in the American West / by Peter Iverson.
      p.   cm.
   Includes bibliographical references (p.   ) and index.
   ISBN 0-8061-1867-9 (alk. paper)
      1. Indian cowboys—West (U.S.)   2. Ranches—West (U.S.)   3. Indians of North America—West (U.S.)—Domestic animals.   4. West (U.S.)—History.   I. Title.
E78.W5I94   1994
978—dc20   94-10314
                                                                CIP

The paper in this book meets the guidelines for permanence and durability of the Committee on Production Guidelines for Book Longevity of the Council on Library Resources, Inc. ⊚

1 2 3 4 5 6 7 8 9 10

To Kaaren

Contents

Illustrations

FIGURES

MAPS

Preface

I GREW UP IN TOWN. IN COMMON WITH AN INCREAS-
ing percentage of children in the American West in the years
that followed the Second World War, I knew basketball courts and
baseball diamonds far more intimately than I did open range.

Yet in keeping with many in my generation, I became interested in cowboys and Indians at an early age. At some level, it ran
in the family. My father had been on the early Lone Ranger radio
shows in Buffalo, New York, and that item on his résumé always
impressed me more than some of his more mundane academic
credentials. In the days before television, I gained a proper
appreciation of radio and thus the adventures not only of the
Lone Ranger but of the Cisco Kid and other characters as well.
My mother's father had worked in Indian Service schools, toiling
in relative obscurity in places such as Keams Canyon and
Toadlena. Given his influence and that of others in my mother's
family, I developed an interest in Indian history that has only
grown as the years have gone by.

Teaching on the Navajo Nation and in Wyoming and getting

to know ranching families in the northern plains provided the foundation for this book. Most recently, I have returned to residing in a more urban setting. Yet living in Arizona continues to offer frequent opportunities for open spaces and for an ongoing appreciation of rural life. Teaching about Indian history and the history of the American West also has encouraged me to think about change and continuity in the region.

Over the past generation, cowboys and Indians have rapidly lost the prominence they once enjoyed as symbols of American life. I used to tease my students at Wyoming that they didn't know the difference between a Hereford and a Holstein and that they didn't much care; I don't even bother to bring the matter up in Tempe. As many observers have noted, we have moved on in our culture to other frontiers; space rather than the OK Corral has become the location for duels. Despite the recent success of the television adaptation of the Larry McMurtry novel *Lonesome Dove*, the day of the television western appears to be over. One thinks of the diverging routes taken by the stars of the old show, *Bonanza*: Lorne Green became enmeshed in the Battlestar Galactica; before he died, Michael Landon took a highway to heaven; and Pernell Roberts went to medical school. More generally within the context of contemporary western America, Indians and cowboys have become more a part of the scenery than of society. They increasingly have been flown over, driven by, ignored. Although many of us would prefer to define the West in rural terms, there is no getting around the fact that most of us live and work in an urban environment. One of the casualties of that transformation, for better or worse, is that most kids no longer grow up playing cowboys and Indians.

With the exception of the three years in the Midwest devoted to completing my graduate studies, since 1969 I have lived in Arizona and Wyoming. That time has afforded me the chance to come to terms with those old symbols of the West: cowboys and Indians. I finally understood that while the old image consisted of cowboys versus Indians in the Old West, the New West of the past century had witnessed these two groups as people who were not entirely different from one another. Rather, with the passage of time and in the environment of a changing region, they have had more in common than either group often realized and the general urban public could possibly perceive.

This book has been cast in several forms over the course of its gradual emergence. Initially I intended for it to be more equally a book about non-Indian ranchers and their relationships with neighboring Indian communities. For a variety of reasons I decided to change the main focus of the study to that of Indian participation in cattle ranching. In a larger sense, of course, I hope to be saying something about how non-Indian cowboys (and ranchers) have become increasingly like the Indians of old—surrounded by a society that does not understand them and has other priorities for their land. And I hope to tell of how the Indians, many of them at least, are cowboys now. While I do not want to paint an overly romantic portrait, this canvas should reflect the kind of respect, affection, and admiration I have for the people portrayed here. Although this book is primarily about Indian cattle ranching, it mirrors a more general concern for all people in the West who have known, worked, and loved a particular piece of land.

In the field of western history today, there is a particular and understandable concern about definitions and labels. Historians argue about the geographic boundaries of the West and about the principal influences on western development. They fret over terms applied to that experience. "Frontier," "conquest," "colonialism," and other words are affixed, scrutinized, and sometimes erased. "Cowboys," "Indians," and "Native" or "Native Americans" are additional cases in point. I have chosen not to worry unduly about distinguishing between "cowboys" and "ranchers" or between "cowboys" and "cowgirls." Clearly there is a difference between working for and owning the ranch, and men and women do not always have the same roles in the operation of a ranch. Nonetheless, given the power of the symbol of cowboy, as it is generally understood, I use it in umbrella fashion, to cover all those people who have worked in the cattle business. This is more a book about ranching than cowboying, but I see the rancher as a person who usually has the skills of a cowboy, especially in the past century since the end of the era of long cattle drives and open range.

"Indians" is also a misnomer, and yet, again, hundreds of years of popular usage have given it a power and a clarity that "Native Americans" does not provide. We all know that terms for racial and ethnic communities vary over time, but most "Indian" people I know still prefer this term to "Native American," and, as with "cowboy," even with its inadequacies, I will employ it in the pages that follow. "Native" is, if anything, more problematic. Generally I do not use it to describe Indian individuals or communities, other than for the sake of linguistic variety. I do employ "Natives" for that same reason and because it is a term in common usage in Alaska, where the absence of the accompanying "American" seems to offer less offense.

At the same time, I take seriously the often-voiced claim by old non-Indian farming and ranching families that they are native to a particular locale. Indeed, one of the central arguments of this book is that both Indian and non-Indian rural history in the West has involved migration and change and thus the process of the creation of cultural homelands. This does not mean that Indians and non-Indians have gone about that process in precisely the same way, socially, economically, or culturally. But as the writings of Mari Sandoz and Wallace Stegner, for example, have made apparent, the evolution of a sense of place and the emotion and tradition that become a part of one's life through generations in a particular location cannot be considered the exclusive province of only one group in the region. Indians and some non-Indians have become "native" (with a small "n") westerners. The sad and ironic story of western history is that the two groups have found it difficult to observe the shared dimensions of their experience.

We can give some of the credit for continuing dichotomy to Hollywood and the popular media, which continue to focus on the years before the twentieth century and on a conflict almost always portrayed in melodramatic and incomplete fashion. Even if we recognize the miserable job done by the mythmakers and pulp producers, we cannot deny their influence. The enduring nature of the lines they have drawn make it difficult for Indians as much as whites to step back from the power of old labels and easy contrasts. Joe Medicine Crow, the Crow historian, may say with a smile that "cowboys and Indians go together like doughnuts and coffee," but not all share his vision.[1]

"Cowboys ain't Indians; buffalo ain't cows," reads the headline for a recent piece by Arapahoe reporter Debra Thunder. She quotes Native American Rights Fund staff attorney Walter Echo-Hawk: "The ranchers haven't been here in the American West long enough to establish a set of cultures or customs within the meaning of federal laws that are intended to protect culture." Thunder adds, "If supposed similarities are so evident, why are Indians and buffalo either destroyed or herded onto reservations and national parks to make way for cowboys and cows? It is because they represented a way of life and a culture that could not be tolerated."[2]

Thunder's article attests to the long shadow of the last century. As the following discussion will reflect, one cannot deny the role white ranchers played in reducing Indian landholdings and limiting Indian power. What she does not mention is the degree to which Indians, including her own tribe, turned to cattle ranching in the years that followed. And what her article fails to discern is the degree to which the non-Indian ranchers' economic and social status has been altered. It is harder to perceive an urbanized West from Wyoming, where cities may be illegal by state statute. However, most westerners now reside in city and suburb. Much as Thunder may resent the notion that "Indians should now join forces with the descendants of those who forced us off the land," that seemingly unlikely alliance may have more promise and potential than other alternatives, even with its attendant ironies.[3]

I have tried to indicate through straightforward chapter titles the general direction of the book. In the first two chapters, I briefly tell of the introduction of cattle into the world of American Indians. In chapter 3, I emphasize the central role played by Indian lands in the growth of the western cattle industry following the Civil War. Then I examine the decision of Indian communities in the northern plains, Oklahoma, and the Southwest to enter cattle ranching and the results they achieved. In chapter 6, I delineate the impact of John Collier and his commissionership of Indian affairs on Indian cattle ranching. Then the attempted reversal of the Collier era and the emergence of the modern era of Indian cattle ranching are depicted. An epilogue reviews the overlapping world of white ranchers and Indians, including a discussion of Indians and rodeo and environmentalists versus the cattle ranchers.

This volume is a collection of essays. In addition to my own research, I have built from the foundation constructed by many other writers. Although I first presented the contours of this work in a paper given at the annual meeting of the Western History Association in 1984, I have tried to keep up with the current scholarship and have cited the recent work of others even if I had already come to comparable conclusions. Inevitably, I will have missed a few sources. And it almost goes without saying that there are other works I could have cited to supplement these citations. Nonetheless, the notes should make clear my debt.

I have also chosen to write in this form because, as is the case with nearly all of my published work, I am interested in reaching more than a scholarly audience. I hope that the subjects of these pages will find what follows approachable and, at least at times, engaging. It should be evident that I have had a good time writing this book and that it is a subject about which I care a good deal.

Residents of some sections of the West may feel neglected by the main focus of these essays. In choosing to concentrate my attention on the Plains and the Southwest, I am acknowledging in part the central Indian presence in these areas. I could have written about other Indian communities in the Great Basin or the Northwest. However, a decade in Wyoming and slightly more than a decade in Arizona have surely shaped how I see this subject in general and the West in particular. By narrowing my vision, of course, I have been able to write a shorter book but one whose general conclusions should be applicable to other sections of the region. Additional studies are needed not only of the parts of the West less examined here but also of individual Indian communities. The specific histories of cattle ranching on different reservations will allow for greater detail than I could provide in this book. I know such work will be forthcoming and I look forward to it.

Acknowledgments

I HAVE THOUGHT ABOUT THIS BOOK FOR TWENTY years and have tried to work on it over the past ten. Throughout this time many people and institutions have helped me. Sabbatical leave from the University of Wyoming and a fellowship for independent study and research from the National Endowment for the Humanities in 1982–83 allowed me to start; sabbatical leave from Arizona State University in autumn 1992 permitted me to finish. Indian students at Navajo Community College, the University of Wyoming, Arizona State University, and elsewhere allowed me to learn more about their communities, traditions, and values. Students from ranching families who attended the University of Wyoming taught me a lot, too. For many years, members of a ranching family in the northern plains permitted a town kid to learn about a tradition, a culture, and the dilemmas of the present. I remember their kindness.

As I moved toward completion of my research, Arizona State University graduate students Kathy Evans and Paivi Hoikkala helped me find materials in the Hayden Library of Arizona State

University and the archives of the Arizona Historical Foundation. Myla Carpio assisted in a search for appropriate photographs. Pat Etter, Chris Marin, Ed Oetting, and Richard Pearce-Moses at the library and Evelyn Cooper, Dick Lynch, and Susie Sato at the foundation were unfailingly gracious in providing assistance.

At the University of Wyoming, such colleagues and good friends as Bill Gienapp, Debby Hardy, Bob Righter, Dave Robson, and Roger Williams encouraged me. More recently, at Arizona State University, Roger Adelson, Shank Gilkeson, Susan Gray, Al Hurtado, Beth Luey, Steve MacKinnon, Steve Pyne, Jim Rush, Bob Sutton, Miguel Tinker Salas, Bob Trennert, Phil VanderMeer, and others too numerous to mention provided friendship, support, and camaraderie.

I have been very fortunate to work with gifted and dedicated undergraduate and graduate students who have made me feel lucky to be a teacher. Staff members Marlene Bolf, Sharon Brockus, Sharon Melton, Linda Moss, Pat Nay, Alice Valenzuela, and Joyce Walker at Arizona State University were as generous and helpful as Diane Alexander and Irene Walker had been at the University of Wyoming. I would like to thank Pat Nay in particular for her help in typing a final copy of the manuscript and for additional assistance with other manuscripts over the past several years.

In one way or another a large number of colleagues helped strengthen my understanding of American Indian history. Bob Bonner and Cliff Clark gave me the opportunity to return to Carleton College to teach. Fred Hoxie and his associates brought me to Newberry Library conferences. Markku Henriksson made it possible for me to come to Finland on two separate occasions. Ken Coates invited me to the University of Victoria to contribute to an international conference on indigenous communities. Gary Holthaus allowed me to witness another such gathering in Alaska. Lillian Turner and others at the Buffalo Bill Historical Center in Cody, Wyoming, let me come up to Park County to teach and talk there.

Through direct or indirect assistance, through the example of their own fine work in American Indian studies, Marjane Ambler, Robert F. Berkhofer, Bahe Billy, Leonard Bruguier, Colin Calloway, Leonard Carlson, Ken Coates, Robin Cutler, Ray DeMallie, Dave Edmunds, Don Fixico, Loretta Fowler, Markku Henriksson, Herb Hoover, Fred Hoxie, Tom Hagan, Tom Hall, Clara Sue Kidwell, David Lewis, Ron Lewis, Clyde Milner, George Moses, Peter Nabokov, Paul Prucha, Jim Ronda, Steve Schulte, Bill Swagerty, Margaret Connell Szasz, Mark Trahant, Herman Viola, Richard White, and John Wunder have improved what I have tried to say here.

John Drayton, editor-in-chief of the University of Oklahoma Press, has offered unfailing counsel. I am grateful for his patience and for his friendship. I hope this work fulfills his expectations. Managing editor Sarah Nestor helped me improve the final version of the manuscript. The readers for the Press offered thorough, perceptive criticism.

Finally, I am happy to thank once again my parents, William and Adelaide Iverson, my brothers, David and Paul, and their families for all they have given me. Thanks especially to my father for showing me the value of stories and to my mother for teaching me the importance of history. To all the Gonsoulins, thank you for making me a part of your family. To Erika and Jens, Tim and Scott, thanks for your patience and love. Kaaren has endured the slow creation of this volume with her usual blend of understanding and encouragement. This book is for her, with love, always.

When Indians Became Cowboys

Map of Indian lands. From *Historical Atlas of the American West*, by Warren A. Beck and Ynez D. Haase. Copyright © 1989 by the University of Oklahoma Press.

CHAPTER ONE

Horses, Cattle, and Indian Identity

THE CATTLE CAME FROM ELSEWHERE. SO DID THE horses. These animals, so prominent in the history and imagery of the American West, arrived with the Europeans when they made those long and remarkable journeys to what they termed a new world.

As James Merrell has suggested in his work about the Catawbas of the southeastern United States, the advent of the Europeans and all they brought with them signaled a new world as well for the original peoples of the Americas. Columbus and Cabot and Cortés came, and that old world of the American Indians, as they would be called, could never again be the same.[1]

Of course, this is not to observe or even imply an old world characterized by sameness, where change was unknown. On the contrary. From the moment these first peoples intruded on the continent, whether they emerged from a world below or pushed across the Bering Strait or arrived by raft, they knew change. Indeed, they created change. They wanted change. To survive and eventually to prosper in their new environment demanded innovation.

How can we hunt? What can we grow? Where can we build? The ancient peoples asked these and other fundamental questions as they began to come to terms with the world around them. Rather than staying put in an unproductive environment, they moved on. Rather than trying to hunt the same animals with the same weapons, they sought better ways of getting the job done. Rather than limiting themselves to certain foods or certain songs, they were willing to try, to learn, to fail and to succeed.

There is an understandable tendency to see American Indians prior to Columbus in a very different light. From first incursion to the present day, intruders of European descent have argued and have generally believed that Indians were stolid occupants of an unproductive land. Their inertia, their lack of imagination or technological aptitude, so they concluded, led inevitably to a limited existence. The Indians failed to take advantage of the land; they failed to obey the exhortation to subdue the earth. From this perspective, European and later American settlement and control of the continent could be easily justified.

This common view misses the mark on at least two central counts. The Indians, of course, did take advantage of the earth and the sky. They were farmers as well as hunters. Over the course of the centuries they learned a great deal about living off and with the land. Such knowledge was not gained easily or quickly. Instead it was learned from mother to daughter and from father to son, as well as from uncles and aunts, grandfathers and grandmothers.

In addition, the arrival of the Europeans presented opportunity for continuing innovation as well as obvious dangers to ways of life. The Europeans brought material items that could be incorporated over time and given new means, eventually made "traditional." Livestock represented one important case in point, although hardly the only example one could cite.

Before the white people came, before the label "Indians" had been affixed, the native inhabitants of North America made their own migrations. These journeys sometimes involved trips on a seasonal basis; in other instances, they involved a complete uprooting and an effort to create a new homeland hundreds or thousands of miles away. These movements, of course, were sometimes quite involuntary. Rival groups vying for territory or resources could force opposing populations to move. Warfare could occasion flight. Disease could force exile. Climatic changes, volcanic eruptions, or other natural phenomena could encourage gradual or immediate departure. Internal disagreements or power struggles within a particular community might also lead to a portion of the group choosing or being forced to leave.

Yet Indian groups also often left quite freely to improve their lives. In hunt or in war men could cover a great span of territory and learn of new options in other sites. Migrations could occur over generations, with intermediate stops made along the way. Indian populations generally proved flexible in what cultural baggage they brought along—discarding no longer relevant items and adding new dimensions to their repertoire. Over time they could redefine who they were or who they could become.

Thus, contrary to popular imagination or convenient historical memory, we need to see Native populations prior to 1492 as flexible, creative entities. To them truly belongs the appropriate sobriquet, "pioneers." One should not diminish the courage, fortitude, and determination of later arrivals, Euro-Americans who more frequently have had that honorable title bestowed on them. But we should have no doubt about who initially saw things, let alone—to use a verb we heard a million times in 1992—discovered them. The Indians first climbed the mountains, crossed the deserts, and all the rest. They gave names to flora and fauna.[2] They irrigated; they used fire; they altered the land in order for their peoples to lead more comfortable or varied lives.[3]

It is instructive to realize that many of the great Indian communities of the present day not only live in different locations from their general boundaries of one hundred or two hundred years ago but reside in entirely different areas from where they had been situated five hundred or eight hundred years ago. Quite apart from the relatively self-evident point that the "tribes" of today were often formed in response to Euro-American intrusions and definitions, Indian groups have been quite fluid in their location and self-definition since before the Norman conquest. When we recall how relatively recent a development has been European nationalism and that even after the creation of European nation-states local peasants and regional enthusiasts clung stubbornly to old loyalties and identities, it is not at all surprising that in many significant ways change as much as continuity characterized pre-Columbian life on the continent.[4]

To be sure, there are continuities worth noting. One of central importance was embedded in the segregation generally between the work men did and the work women did. While there inevitably were exceptions, almost always the men carried out the tasks of war and of the hunt. Even in more sedentary societies, the men traveled great distances from the villages to bring in meat for all to share. The women also enjoyed the seasonal movements to harvest nature's bounty: grasses, fruits, and other crops that ripened with the season. When one visits the sites of ancient communities or simply views the dioramas set up in countless museums, one is reminded that these were people whose lives were focused in the outdoors. Housing provided shelter, but life was to be lived under the sky rather than under the roof.

The remarkably far-flung trade networks also suggest another vital continuity. Native societies traded over thousands of miles for items not available within the immediate vicinity of their homes. This trade primarily involved ceremonial items—feathers, shell, and so forth. Without essential self-sufficiency, indigenous groups obviously were in a lot of trouble. Yet surpluses could be swapped to bring in a welcome addition to a predictable diet or even material items, such as pottery or baskets, that would make daily life a little easier. Again, over time, various items could be reproduced or grown or imitated and made a part of tribal life. These communities may have chosen carefully what they added to their cultural inventory, but it is abundantly clear that most constantly shifted, selected, and discarded.

Equipment, food, and other elements added to a particular tribal society usually did not alter how that society operated. Rather, a community made every effort not to disrupt social organization and social operation. Ideally people tried to fit a particular item into a way of life rich with tradition and meaning. They wanted to maintain what worked. They wanted to honor the ways that had been learned from first memory. All segments of the community had roles to play, from the elders to the young children. It was crucial for all to contribute; it was vital for all to be valued and to value themselves for their contributions.[5]

The arrival of the Europeans posed, sooner or later, a challenge of unprecedented dimensions to these native peoples in terms of how to accommodate both directed and nondirected change. Some of the dimensions of what has properly been termed by the anthropologist Edward Spicer as a culture of conquest proved especially problematic. If the would-be conquerors found themselves in a position to dictate what language one spoke, what gods one worshiped, and what languages one did not speak and what gods one did not worship, fundamental crises quickly developed within the social order. As many recent historians have noted, disease struck at the center of tribal life. Disease killed the elders, the storehouses of community knowledge and ritual. It called into question the fragile harmony the tribal shamans had attempted to maintain. It reduced or eliminated military opposition to European expansion. And it provided an entrée for the white man's shamans, who seemingly had power to control the diseases, for these religious leaders never seemed to be sick.[6]

Other components of European culture in some instances appeared less immediately difficult for Indian cultures to absorb or come to terms with in the first decades of contact. In the same sense, as Alfred Crosby has illustrated in *The Columbian Ex-*

change, certain components of Indian cultures also found their ways in varying degrees and with varying speeds into European cultures. One of the least threatening and most pervasive examples of such international exchange may be found within the realm of food.

Just as Marco Polo's venture to China brought spaghetti to Italy, so, too, the voyages of the early European venturers brought a number of now-familiar vegetables and other foods to Europe. At the same time, early Spanish sojourners—padres, ranchers, settlers, all—brought with them foods to feed themselves and soon thereafter to introduce to natives of the New World.[7]

Within what became known as Mexico and what eventually became known as the southwestern United States, the Spanish padres embarked on the challenging assignment of establishing a mission system. Such an enterprise needed to become relatively self-sufficient in a relatively short time. The padres were among those Spaniards who tried the hardest to commandeer Native labor and to harness that labor for what they deemed an essential job: feeding the mission. In this manner, significant new crops were added to the indigenous staples of melons, squash, and maize.

Most Spaniards were not vegetarians. Even the most embattled padre tended to be a meat eater, and, of course, cattle and other livestock could be utilized for labor as well as lunch. Horses and cattle were introduced to the Americas even before the first days of the fifteenth century. In the year before Cortés concluded his long campaign against the Aztecs, the first cattle came to the continent. From that first arrival in 1521 under the direction of Gregorio de Villalobos, the Spanish cattle holdings promptly expanded in Mexico. Cortés himself took an active interest in the business. With his approval and under his command, Mexican ranchers impressed Indian labor to work on their lands. Indian farmers lost their lands to the growing Spanish enterprise. Within the first generation of the arrival of cattle, the Spanish frontier knew rustling, boundary disputes, and other familiar hallmarks of the American West in centuries to come.[8]

That first famous intruder into Arizona and New Mexico, Francisco Vásquez de Coronado, began his journey in 1540 with hundreds of cattle; few, if any, actually made the thankless trek all the way to the Gila River. In 1598, Juan de Oñate as well brought livestock with him into the valley of the Rio Grande. As the Spanish ranching empire expanded inexorably north and westward toward what became the United States, the foundation was established for the growth of the livestock enterprise in the northern reaches of New Spain.[9]

That expansion of the Spanish cattle industry included the concomitant introduction of the horse to this northern country. Spanish vaqueros depended on the horse to round up cattle, and horses were invaluable for transportation in regions where alternative forms of travel would not be available for a very long time. The utility for both cattle and horses naturally could be observed by local Indian communities. At some point in the early 1600s, tribes of northern New Spain such as the Apaches and the Comanches began to acquire horses. Although it would be later in the 1600s that other Indian groups in the southwestern United States became more acquainted with the possibilities of raising cattle, the horse transformed immediately the potential of these small Indian populations. In war and in peace, they never would be the same. Horses quickly became objects to be stolen, traded for, fought over, dreamed about.

What eventually transpired for cattle began with horses. Over time and in due course, the horse became integral to tribal identity. Wrapped in the strands of people's stories and ceremonies, it eventually became impossible to imagine the people themselves without livestock. Thus the Navajos and other southwestern Indian groups eventually gave thanks not to the Spaniards for introducing the horse or the sheep but to their own holy beings.

The Navajos (Diné) told instead the story of the two boys and coming of the horses. After the boys had learned the necessary ceremonial chants, the White Bead Woman said, "The Diné shall have horses." She sang:

> From the East comes a big black mare.
> Changed into a maiden.
> She comes to me.
> From the South comes a blue mare.
> Changed into a maiden.
> She comes to me.
> From the West comes a sorrel mare.
> Changed into a maiden.
> She comes to me.
> From the North comes a white mare.
> Changed into a maiden.
> She comes to me.[10]

After White Bead Woman's chanting, four stone fetishes became transformed into living horses. She put them on the white bead plain, the turquoise plain, the white bead hill, and the turquoise hill. Then she put medicine into four baskets of white bead, turquoise, white shell, and black jet. The medicine would cause the horses to drop their colts. White Bead Woman chanted again, and then the horses descended from the hills. There were more than four horses now, and after they licked the medicine they ran way.

White Bead Woman taught the boys more chants to help the horses. She also explained that the parts of the animal related to the elements. The horses' hooves were *hada'huniye*, the banded male stone. The hair of the mane and tail was *nltsa'najin*, the little streaks of rain. The ears were heat lightning and the eyes the big stars; their faces were the various growing plants.[11]

Later a man came who had seen a vision of a horse and was told to visit the home of his father, the Sun. And the man chanted a prayer of thanks:

> I am the Sun's son.
> I sat on the turquoise horse.
> He went to the opening in the sky.
> He went with me to the opening.
> The turquoise horse prances with me.

> From where we start the turquoise horse is seen.
> The lightning flashes from the turquoise horse.
> The turquoise horse is terrifying.
> He stands on the upper circle of the rainbow.
> The sunbeam is in his mouth for his bridle.
> He circles around all the peoples of the earth
> With their goods.
> Today he is on my side
> And I shall win with him. [12]

The Sun instructed the man to go in the four directions and offer a gift to four different plants that he would find, saying that then he would find the horse. And so the man did. And in a chant, stunning even in its translation, he sang. He sang to link the horses with turquoise and white shell, with the black clouds and the rainbow, with sheep, with the earth, and with the holy people:

> I came upon it.
> I came upon it.
> I came upon it.
> I came upon it.

The white bead horses stood toward the basket from the four directions,

> As I came upon it.
> All the beautiful flowers are its pollen,
> Black clouds are the water they have in their mouths,
> As I came upon them . . .
> The rainbow for its gate,
> As I came upon it.
> The sun closes its entrance . . .
> As I came upon it.
> The white bead horses pour out,
> As I came upon them.

The turquoise horses pouring out,
As I came upon them.
The white shell horses pouring out,
As I came upon them.
The male banded stone horses pouring out,
As I came upon them.
All mixed horses, together with the sheep, pouring out,
As I came upon them.
All the horses pour out with the beautiful goods,
As I came upon them.
The earth's pollen (dust) rises as they pour out,
The shining dust of the earth covers their bodies,
As I came upon them.
To multiply and not to decrease,
As I came upon them.
Like the Most High Power Whose Ways Are Beautiful are my
    horses,
As I came upon them.
Before my horses all is beautiful.
Behind my horses all is beautiful.
As I came upon them.
As I came upon them.[13]

Beginning in the 1600s, livestock—first horses, then sheep, cattle, and goats—began to become integrated into the societies and economies of southwestern American Indians and later all over North America. That process of socioeconomic integration laid the foundation for Indians, in time, to become cowboys. Ultimately this process involved means through which Indian communities defined and maintained themselves.

When we ponder the reasons that Indians in the southwestern United States incorporated horses and later sheep or cattle into their cultures, we cannot consider the matter solely in economic terms. Economic reasons were not insignificant, but one must approach the question more broadly. The arrival of Europeans and the demands that Europeans promptly and often successfully or partially successfully placed on Indian communities challenged group esteem and self-esteem. In the context of a fluid, unprecedented era, ways had to be found to maintain or in some cases regenerate esteem and identity.

Identity may be defined as "the sum total of feelings on the part of group members about those values, symbols, and common histories that identify them as a distinct group."[14] Many historians have tended to swallow the whole notion that a time period including bad policies and negative effects on Indian communities must be perceived in only negative terms. While not minimizing the deleterious effects of any period, one needs to move beyond the casual assumption that bad policies yield only bad results.[15]

Social scientists have noted for a great many years that individuals and groups may respond in a variety of ways to prejudice and discrimination; one of the responses can be a strengthening of loyalty or ties to the very group that is the object of that prejudice or discrimination. In a related sense, students of African tribal groups in the 1950s and 1960s have stressed that increased interaction between groups promoted ethnic identity rather than discouraged it.[16] Contact with new peoples and new situations thus could heighten tribal identity, if not create opportunities for innovation and change as well as present the possibility of deterioration and despair. The adoption of horses and cattle may properly be seen in this way.

As does Loretta Fowler, the anthropologist who has written about the Northern Arapahoes and the Gros Ventres, I believe it is useful to employ some of the key ideas of Clifford Geertz. To understand change over time, she suggests, we need to look at "the interaction, the reciprocal interplay, between cultural and social forces." As societies change, they invent, discard, or reinterpret new symbols. A new element may become incorporated into a society and over time centrally reflect the identity of this community.[17] Following the work of Anya Peterson Royce and Abner Cohen, I see symbols as "objects, acts, concepts, or linguistic formations that stand ambiguously for a multiplicity of disparate meanings."[18] All societies have symbols; flags, anthems, languages, churches, foods, music, and other examples come readily to mind. "The Star Spangled Banner" may not be the world's greatest musical composition, but once established as a national anthem, it becomes a symbol for the country and over time becomes progressively more entrenched in the workings of the culture.

Minority ethnic and racial groups within larger nations always need some flexibility in how they define themselves.[19] They must have strategies to maintain their sense of themselves. Over time some item brought in from the outside may become "traditional." Look at the sheep, the silverwork, and, perhaps, the weaving of the Navajos, or Diné. Such features of Navajo culture have not always been present, or certainly evolved over centuries. But it does not matter from whence they came. What matters is how the people perceive and define them.

In the nineteenth century, Indian cattle ranching fully emerged as a strategy to confront changing times. It became part of the tradition of many western Indian communities. While the outcome of this transition can be analyzed in economic terms, the importance of this pastime must be seen as well in a social and cultural context. Just as later observers would be ill-advised to dissect the value placed on cattle ranching by non-Indian ranchers strictly on the basis of dollars and cents, the same perception should be applied to the gradual adoption of cattle ranching by Indians. Cattle ranching could contribute to tribal identity and individual self-esteem. Cattle ranching emerged, therefore, as a symbol for a new day. But that new day was long in coming, following an extended period of non-Indian expansion, Indian resistance, and the drawing of reservation lines. What preceded this era was also significant. In the time from when the Spaniards first introduced cattle on the North American continent until the later years of the nineteenth century, Indians at different rates of speed gradually added livestock to their way of life.

CHAPTER TWO

Livestock Enters
the Indian World

WHEN WE THINK TODAY OF THE CATTLE KINGDOM IN the American West, we generally draw our images from a very narrow span of time. In little more than a generation, the golden era transpired and then expired with the close of the American frontier about a decade before the first days of the twentieth century. When Joseph McCoy chose Abilene, Kansas, in 1867 as an appropriate spot to drive cattle to and from Texas, to ship beef via the railroad to a ready marketplace, he unleashed the forces that came to dominate a large portion of the West. The Anglo-American cattle kingdom suddenly swept from the Red River to the Milk River, leaving a permanent imprint on American folklore.

That remarkable period came after a far more extended and much less publicized era. The eventual socioeconomic structure of modern cattle ranching developed slowly and from various sources. Texas did contribute in a significant way, and California also provided a vital and productive environment for the growth of Hispanic ranching. Key elements in the material culture and vocabulary of the industry—chaps, saddle, rope, brands, and positions of brands—developed here. Yet with due respect to Walter Prescott Webb and other chauvinistic Texan (to repeat myself) historians, the Anglo-American antecedents must also be noted. Although the woodland East and South differed in geographic character from most of the trans-Mississippi West, these regions—and eventually the Midwest—also were important.[1]

Given the Anglo-American cast of the eventual American economic order, it is hardly surprising that English elements also contributed to the development of ranching. The Texas longhorn proved to be a useful and hardy breed, well suited for survival and some degree of prosperity in marginal terrain. But if it had been the perfect animal in all respects, it would have dominated the industry for all time. It was not, and it did not. Other kinds of cattle that did dominate the late-nineteenth-century western scene came indeed from the British Isles and then to the eastern stretches of what became the United States. Originally employed as draft animals, noteworthy for their stamina and for their ability to gain weight and produce beef more tasty to the Anglo tongue, breeds such as the Hereford found their way into America.

Early Anglo-Americans who owned livestock rarely merited the label "rancher." Instead, they were almost always farmers who used a portion of what they raised on their land to feed their livestock. Their cattle could be kept primarily for dairy products or for beef as well as for assistance in plowing or clearing the land. For the first couple of centuries of the Anglo presence on the continent, there appears to be little evidence to suggest that the Indians saw cattle as other than problematic. English settlements in New England, for example, often adjoined older, well-established Indian settlements. Indian farmers frequently had to contend with English cattle determined to feast on their crops, trampling vegetables they did not actually consume. While it may be a bit overstated to see this maneuver as part of an Anglo-American conspiracy to force Indians off their lands and while English courts may have attempted to curtail such developments, there can be little doubt that the English cattle provoked tension and unhappiness among Indian communities.[2]

The rapid dispossession of Indian landholdings that characterized New England in the seventeenth and eighteenth centuries afforded little opportunity for Indians to acquire significant numbers of livestock. In the Southeast, where the presence of sizable Indian communities—including the famous Five Tribes, the Cherokees, Chickasaws, Choctaws, Creeks, and Seminoles—combined with a different socioeconomic picture, Indians had more of a chance to add livestock to their lives. Eventually, before the removal period cut down these great Indian nations and forced most of their citizens to vacate the region, Indians were able to build up their herds.[3]

That increase was accompanied by federal encouragement. Federal officials promoted agriculture as a key ingredient in the process of Indian assimilation. George Washington, Thomas Jefferson, and others linked agriculture to progress from the forest to the field. Washington, for example, urged the Cherokees in 1796 to continue to increase their numbers of cattle and hogs; by the turn of the century the Creeks also raised livestock, and the Choctaws and Chickasaws also benefited from federal funds to purchase livestock for their use.[4]

As always, federal expectations accompanied such promotion. Jefferson particularly and predictably thought agriculture would prompt sweetness and light rather than Indian intransigence, just as well-meaning missionaries believed their churches and schools would yield acquiescence rather than resistance.[5] Yet because of such innovation, the major tribes of the Southeast became all the more determined to maintain their homelands. The familiar story of removal need not be retold here. What is more important for our purposes is to note that livestock assisted in the very difficult transition to the West.

Even within the decade following the various trails of tears, Indians from the Five Tribes used cattle as part of their overall strategy of coming to terms with their new surroundings. Cherokee farmers sold beef to nearby Fort Gibson; Choctaw farmers raised enough beef for themselves and for Creek contractors as well. Creeks owned, in agricultural historian Douglas Hurt's words, "a large number of cattle" by the early 1830s. By the following decade, Creek cattle had gained the interest of midwestern drovers who purchased hundreds of head from these Indian farmers. Thus, the days of large-scale ranching in the Indian territory following the Civil War had been preceded by a period demonstrating the potential of the land for profitable raising of cattle.[6]

This transition, far more pronounced in the Southeast than elsewhere in Indian communities east of the Mississippi, marked significant alterations within the Indian world. For Indians to become involved in the raising of livestock, they had to alter quite simply how they saw animals. As William Cronon has suggested, Natives in New England had hunted certain animals such as deer, moose, and beaver, but they had never thought they owned them. The kind of ownership the English claimed over their livestock represented a sort of control and a type of relationship with animals that had never before appeared in Native life. In addition, that ownership was by the individual rather than by the group. Livestock as well demanded a particular, large space for themselves—much more than the percentage of acreage required by the various crops.[7]

When livestock did enter into the economic world of Indians, it also indicated generally a shift in the overall working of that economy. Livestock clearly were not raised solely for internal consumption and with the single goal of self-sufficiency. Rather, livestock were tied to the workings of a larger marketplace. The raising of livestock offered a usually predictable source of cash, for the product could be sold either to urban people or in salted form to more distant peoples, such as those in the Caribbean region.[8]

Richard White has remarked that "domesticated animals made a new way of life possible; they did not make it inevitable." Writing about the Choctaws of the Southeast, he observed that livestock "became important only in the context of this larger economic and social breakdown." The people who moved into the Choctaw border regions were hardly traditionalists but rather intermarried whites and mixed-bloods less interested in old ways than in establishing new ones that would work in these altered circumstances.[9]

Thus, in the early nineteenth century it can be argued convincingly that livestock "did not just enter the lands of the Choctaws; it entered their culture as well and made pastoralists of many who had been hunters." Beef and cattle entered into ceremonies and special occasions such as the birth of a child. They thus began to matter not only as a means of economic exchange but also as a means to feed one's family. They began to become an essential, natural, integral part of events. They helped facilitate the gatherings that brought meaning to the rituals that symbolized important life events. In this manner, the Choctaws anticipated the kind of role that cattle would soon play elsewhere in the West. Again, one sees the significance of cattle in more than economic terms.[10]

Within the Southwest, cattle raising became important over time to many Indian communities. Introduced early in the period of contact between the Spaniards and the Pueblo villages of the Rio Grande valley, cattle did not represent a significant alteration to their way of life. Already sedentary, with agriculture at the heart of their seasonal patterns, the Pueblos merely added livestock as a useful but rather peripheral element to their economy. Spicer argues convincingly that the impact of livestock proved far more dramatic on more nomadic native peoples of the region.[11]

While less directly under Spanish rule and relatively little touched by the missionaries, the Apaches and the Navajos, by contrast, had their lives dramatically altered by the introduction of livestock. As already has been suggested, the horse became centrally important to both Athapaskan peoples. By the beginning of the eighteenth century they had acquired enough horses to change their vision of what territory they could use or occupy and what they could acquire or control in the process of that expansion. The Apaches obtained more cattle than the Navajos, who were quickly absorbing the herding of sheep into their culture. Neither people developed into cattle raisers at this time. The Apaches raided for cattle, without question, but had less interest in raising them and more interest in immediately consuming them. However, in the case of both tribes, the transition of this era once again made the possibility of cattle ranching in a later period not only possible but probable. Given the country they came to occupy and given their love of horses and movement within their homelands, the Apaches and Navajos would emerge as prime candidates for livestock raising in the latter part of the nineteenth century.[12]

Among the Piman-speaking communities of the Sonoran desert region of the Southwest, the incorporation of cattle proved somewhat more complete in the Spanish period. The famous Jesuit missionary Eusebio Kino established many missions in southern Arizona and northern Sonora during the late 1600s and 1700s. Kino used cattle and other livestock as gifts to the Indians he intended to convert to Catholicism. His missions held livestock — cattle, sheep, and goats — and Pima and Papago men learned about the animals at these locations.

According to a study by the anthropologist Ruth Underhill, Kino's work in the era did not have the full effect that the industrious padre had intended. The movement to give cattle to the Indians lost momentum after his death, and by the time the Jesuits departed the country, to be replaced by the Franciscans who had no comparable interest in livestock, the Indians were on their own. Northern bands of the Pimas and Papagos (today called the Tohono O'odham) had few cattle or horses, while their southern counterparts — less affected by Apache raiding — were able to maintain more animals. The cattle that remained were more wild than contained and similar to the longhorns of

Texas fame. Desert fed rather than corn fed, they yielded beef not easily chewed. But, like the people themselves, they adapted to the Sonoran desert. They survived. The people no doubt admired their ability to do so; the Tohono O'odham particularly have allowed a place for cattle in the overall workings of their culture ever since these early days.[13]

The overlap between Hispanic and Indian in the raising of cattle could be seen elsewhere in New Spain. As noted by Richard W. Slatta in his panoramic *Cowboys of the Americas*, Kino's counterparts were not unimportant in the establishment of the industry in Texas and in California. Texas missions had little luck in converting Natives, who were far more likely to steal the livestock than help raise it within the confines of mission lands.[14]

But in California, of course, Junípero Serra and other missionaries established a string of missions along the coast. Here as in the territory we today call Mexico, Indian vaqueros were very much a part of the picture. They herded cattle and roped and branded them. In this instance, the early experience did not leave the same kind of lasting impression. Devastated by disease and overrun by the eventual flood of Anglo-American migrants to the state, California Indians, unlike the Indians of Arizona and New Mexico, would not become cattle ranchers to the same extent. With few exceptions, by the mid-nineteenth century they had been reduced to small rancherías with very limited potential for ranching.

Their initial role in the development of cattle ranching in the state has been generally ignored. At San Gabriel and other large mission estates, very large herds of cattle were kept. Nora Ramirez notes that at the time of secularization of missions in 1834, 31,000 mission vaqueros oversaw 396,000 head of cattle. Many of those vaqueros were Indians. With the end of mission domination in California, the great mission herds were broken up, and the Indian cowboy soon was eclipsed by others willing to take his place. The vital hide and tallow industry continued after secularization, but given the agricultural promise of the ranchos, some Anglos converted these lands to farming purposes in the decades to come.[15]

The war with Mexico in the 1840s, concluded by the Treaty of Guadalupe Hidalgo in 1848, opened a vast new portion of the West to Anglo-American use. Early Anglo-American arrivals in California had already perceived the potential of the land. By the end of the decade, gold had been discovered in California, the boundary lines between Canada and the northwestern United States had been established, and the Mormons had migrated to the valley of the Great Salt Lake. As more Anglo-Americans surged westward, they began to recognize the true potential of the land in a region once dismissed as the great American desert. With the conclusion of the Civil War in 1865, U.S. policymakers turned their full attention to the interior of the region. In a few remarkable, fleeting decades, the days of open range, the golden era of American cattle ranching came and disappeared.

During that same time, the powerful and less powerful Native peoples of the region confronted the undisguised ambition of this still new nation. When the cattle industry reached and receded from its zenith in the late nineteenth century, the Lakotas, the Cheyennes, the Apaches, and other extraordinary Indian nations had been forced to sign treaties, to be confined on reservations that looked and felt like prisons. The Anglo-American rancher, had he even read the plaintive words of Seattle of the Suquamish, could not have imagined that they could possibly have been applied to him. The future appeared as boundless as the sky, as the land itself. How could he see commonality with a people whose best days appeared to be in the past rather than in the future?

Seattle's words are in translation, and there is considerable doubt about their precise nature. In any event, his people claim him and claim his words. When one visits that small community on the edge of the Olympic peninsula in Washington, one can enter the tribal museum. And in that small, well-presented mirror of the tribal past, I obtained a slim volume about the

Suquamish. This man's words are quoted here, as they are quoted in one context or another all over Indian America to this day. His remarks to Territorial Governor Isaac Stevens, delivered in 1855, developed resonance and poignance anew in the decades that followed. In 1855, though, the Anglo-American cattleman hardly saw himself as part of a tribe, could hardly know that more difficult days would ever come.

Seattle noted that the white people were "like the grass that covers vast prairies," while the Indians were few in number, though they had once been otherwise. "Your God," he told Governor Stevens, "makes your people wax strong every day. Soon they will fill all the land. Our people are ebbing away like a rapidly receding tide that will never return." "How then can we be brothers?" Seattle asked.

He argued that Indians and whites appeared to have little in common. "To us the ashes of our ancestors are sacred and their resting place is hallowed ground. You wander far from the graves of your ancestors and seemingly without regret." The white man's dead seemed soon "to be forgotten and never return. Our dead never forget the beautiful world that gave them being."

But if the Indians were to disappear, if the memory of the Suquamish would become a myth in white American history, the whites should not imagine themselves by themselves. The invisible dead of the Suquamish and other Indian nations would remain. "When your children's children think themselves alone in the field, the store, the shop, upon the highway, or in the silence of the pathless woods, they will not be alone."

Moreover, if the Indians were to vanish, it should be remembered that history was cyclical rather than linear.

> But why should I mourn at the untimely fate of my people? Tribe follows tribe, and nation follows nation, like the waves of the sea. It is the order of nature, and regret is useless. Your time of decay may be distant—but it will surely come, for even the White Man . . . cannot be exempt from the common destiny. We may be brothers after all. We will see.[16]

The day of reckoning for non-Indian farmers and ranchers would be distant, indeed. The mid-nineteenth century offered few signs that they would ever be endangered. The Homestead Act soon would be passed; America would always be an agrarian nation dominated by rural interests. Wouldn't it?

CHAPTER THREE

Indian Lands and the Expansion of the Cattle Industry

THE DAYS OF OPEN RANGE LASTED LITTLE MORE than a generation. From Joseph McCoy to *Lonesome Dove*, they have been chronicled, rehashed, and told again. It is a grand story, full of drama, humor, grit, and failure. We do not need to tell it one more time. What we do need to understand is the relation of Indians and Indian lands to the growth of that empire and the triumph of what became tradition and then legend.

Cattle ranching is a story usually told and nearly always understood in one color, and that color is white. Slatta is only the latest person to remind us of the importance of people of other skin colors in the expansion of cattle ranching. He breaks more new ground in his rendition of the cattle business south of the Rio Grande, for that is a tale less often told.[1] And there the cowboys are indeed vaqueros, and they are indeed not Anglos. To

25

the north, the southwestern cattle enterprise was widely participated in by Mexican and Hispanic cowboys. To the north, black
men in smaller numbers rode on cattle drives. Other than those
few like Jesse Chisholm, who could claim, in part, an Indian
heritage, Indians are not linked to the expansion of cattle raising
other than in one way: they resisted it.

That resistance, even if portrayed in hackneyed Hollywood
ways, did take place and is a central element in the developments
of this time. We need to comprehend that expansion in a broader
context. We need to see that the ranches of the late-nineteenth-
century American West could not exist and could not expand in
a vacuum. One should recall the role of two other entities: the
federal government and the Indians themselves.

Despite the image of individualistic and independent cattlemen,
the rapid expansion of the industry in the late nineteenth century
owed much of its speed to federal intervention and support. Just as
the national government provided railroad magnates with land and
subsidies to build the framework of a national transportation
system, federal officials also were committed to a continuation of
westward expansion. Laws and policies combined to allow the new
farmers and ranchers to use the land.

Public policy prior to the Civil War had clearly favored
moving lands into private ownership. Although the system of
land distribution as much favored land speculators as pioneers,
the bias of an agrarian nation argued for a continuation of this
practice. The Homestead Act of 1862 promised cheap land. And
many migrants began to pour into the West to take advantage of
it. Still, federal support for railroads, federal provision of forts,
federal development of roads, and other forms of national commitment had to occur for individuals and corporations to make
much headway.

It almost goes without saying that these people and these
financial entities did not defeat the Indians militarily, did not
sign effective treaties with them, did not confine them to
reservations. There were, of course, examples of citizen action,
and nearly all of them proved ill-fated, unfortunate, or worse.

The Sand Creek massacre in southeastern Colorado in 1864 demonstrated the potential for violent vigilantism that state militias and other such bodies tended to carry out. Obviously we do not want to portray George Armstrong Custer as an ambassador par excellence of cultural pluralism and military restraint. The blue coats included their fair share of hotheads and bigots. But the army regulars for the most part appear no better and no worse than the average non-Indian of the day, doing the bidding of a nation with poor pay, poor shoes, poor housing, and poor food.

The United States sought expansion with honor.[2] But above all, it sought expansion. Only when the Indians were defeated and only when they were limited severely in where they could live could the economic potential of the interior West be realized. As the Cherokees and other peoples who had been praised and blessed with the label "civilized" had discovered during the presidency of Andrew Jackson, it mattered little what label had been applied. If you went to a Christian church on Sunday, if you spoke English, and even, in the ways of the "civilized" South, if you held slaves, you were still in the way. And you would have to move, some day.

The days following the Civil War thus were especially poignant for those "civilized" Tribes of Indian Territory but equally painful for all. Again, the tragedy of the West, to paraphrase Richard Slotkin, was that of the evolving frontier, that regeneration of one person's fortune too often was accompanied by or achieved through violence. And if not with violence, then at least at the expense of another person's fortune.[3]

For contrary to what so many Americans wished to believe, then and now, American Indians not only occupied but used the land. Not always in the same way or for the same reasons, at one level, but ultimately of course for common cause: personal satisfaction, family well-being. When McCoy and others began to expand the horizon of the cattleman's West, the Indians stood in the way. The buffalo, however, had largely disappeared, and with that disappearance northern and central plains life teetered on the verge of major cultural and economic change.

When one looks back at this time, just yesterday in the Indian memory, one cannot help but be impressed by the apparent arrogance of the newcomers. Buoyed by their own needs and their own cultural assumptions, these intruders hardly ever seemed to recognize that they were, in fact, intruding. They did not see it as Indian land, just land. Empty land. That is what the government or railroad brochures and circulars said. They did not need much convincing.

For the Indians, the convictions were of another kind. They fought, resisted, wondered about the future. If the golden era of the cattlemen lasted only a generation, the final chapter of Indian resistance could not be more protracted. The dates of the more celebrated stands and points of confrontation extend for two decades. Not long. Not long for sacred mountains to be wrested away from control over even access, for means of obtaining glory or meat to be surrendered, for daily life to be altered from sunrise to sunset. No wonder they fought. No wonder the treaties could not be fully understood or accepted. No wonder the boundaries of the new reservations seemed so arbitrary and confining.

The reservations "opened" the lands to new people and new dreams. The loss of Indian land took a variety of forms. Treaties forced reduction of lands customarily used. Passage of the General Allotment Act of 1887 splintered and reduced reservations that already represented but a portion of the former Native estate. Negotiated cessions after 1887 also carved away chunks of the reservations. Thus, in these years another old pattern reasserted itself. Despite the enormity of their loss, it was not enough. Whether or not they had fought, whether or not they had provided scouts to the American military, whether or not they were willing to send their sons and daughters to boarding school, whether or not they were willing to go to church, it was not enough. The better their land, the more concentrated or ambitious the surrounding population, of course, the more pressure could be applied. Americans prided themselves on being people of laws, of the sanctity of contracts, of the importance of keeping one's word. Somehow, the treaties fell outside of this framework. Agreements with individual tribes did not have to be honored. As they had in previous generations, non-Indians muttered that the Native peoples did not deserve the lands they claimed. Unfortunately for the Indians, officials within the federal government agreed. As the lands in the West became harder to obtain, as much of what we might call a frontier began to be closed, pressure inevitably grew to sacrifice these protected enclaves—in the name of progress, in the name of opportunity, in the name of preference. In one of many ironies, the descendants of these newcomers would often emerge as bitter critics of affirmative action, equal opportunity, or other compensatory programs. They could not or would not acknowledge the kinds of assistance their ancestors had obtained.

In his aptly named analysis of federal Indian policy, *A Final Promise*, Frederick Hoxie argues convincingly that the squeeze on Indian lands grew tighter as the nineteenth century drew to a close. The much-maligned General Allotment Act of 1887, also known as the Dawes Act, after its congressional sponsor, Sen. Henry Dawes of Massachusetts, is blamed customarily for the massive loss of land the Indians suffered during the next several decades. The Dawes Act surely may be called ill-advised at best. Modeled after the Homestead Act of 1862, the Allotment Act parceled out 160-acre, quarter-section plots to individual Indians. Indians could not boycott these proceedings. Government agents were empowered to make the selection for Indians who chose initially not to take advantage of this arrangement.[4]

It is convenient to paint all the assigned allotment agents as evil, sneaky people. However, this is not always accurate. Take Alice Fletcher as an example. Dispatched to the Nez Perce reservation in northern Idaho to divide up the tribe's lands, she participated in what she saw as an inevitable process. Fletcher had helped shape the form of the Dawes Act and served as an allotment agent at Omaha and Winnebago. As an ethnologist, she cared about the past and the future of Indian life, and she did her best during her summer forays to try to get the Nez Perces to make wise choices of the allotments. She had once been an unabashed advocate of allotment and had spoken unequivocally in favor of it at gatherings of the so-called Friends of the Indian at Lake Mohonk in New York. But her experience as an allotment agent on the Omaha reservation had reduced her ardor for the process. Perhaps she should have boycotted the whole business at Nez Perce altogether. One can make the same sanctimonious argument that she simply should not have taken part at all, but one could apply the same line of reasoning to teaching in boarding schools, serving as an agent on a reservation, or working in some other capacity under the federal aegis. However, for individuals who recognized the seeming inevitability of allotment — using the language of the Navajo treaty of 1868, that children would be "compelled" to attend school — one defensible option could be the choice to make a difficult situation somewhat more humane. Fletcher concluded that in the absence of allotment, the land base would be entirely sacrificed. It was too crucial a transition to be left solely to the hacks who had no other choices or the zealots whose frothy assimilationism left no room for any remnants, let alone meaningful portions, of tribal cultures.[5]

Many reservations, especially in the Southwest, avoided the fate of allotment. As one would anticipate, the law affected the tribes with the best lands in the perception of turn-of-the-century non-Indians. Southwestern Indians lived in too remote and too inhospitable a region to be as threatened as their counterparts to the north. Allotment did take place in the vicinity of the budding Phoenix metropolitan area, spurred more by the agrarian potential of the Salt River valley than by urban dreams.

Thus, allotment occurred in the northern Plains more fully than in any other location. Yet even there the reduction of the Indian estate proved incomplete. Even if they held the land in divided form, tribal members still controlled significant acreages. Nonetheless, the allotment put individual Indians in an untenable position. They did not have enough land to farm or raise livestock in a manner that permitted self-sufficiency. Inheritance only complicated an already unhealthy scenario. Denying the virtue of primogeniture, Native families tended to divide meager portions into still smaller, even less adequate ones. Such division discouraged the very agrarian initiative the idealists who supported the Dawes Act had hoped to foster.

For others who backed the Allotment Act, this predicament bordered on the providential. These folks generally are described in the literature by various unseemly labels, "land-hungry" probably the most popular of them. They applauded Henry Dawes, for his efforts achieved just what they hoped: the availability of more land. Western farmers and ranchers of the era did not have access to information made possible by today's technology, and they likely would not have taken advantage of it even if they could have. They worked hard, and most of them lived on the ragged edge of desperation. They witnessed the failures of neighbors who also worked hard. They could not control hailstorms; they could not deny drought. The railroads and other creatures of eastern industrialism brought more problems than they solved. As the business of farming and ranching became steadily just that, it became more expensive. Industrialism improved productivity and somewhat eased physical demands, but it came at an escalating cost. The only way out, or so it seemed, was to produce more. And the best way to produce more was to have more land.

Thus, the expansion of the ranching industry among non-Indians may be perceived as occurring in two stages: from immediately after the Civil War and then from the drive to open more Indian lands during the final years of the nineteenth century and the first years of the twentieth. Obviously, other forces helped fuel the effort to defeat the Indians and confine them to reservations. However, especially in the northern plains, cattlemen played a major role in this process. The rapid demise of the frontier, then, led inevitably to an assault on the reduced yet somewhat safeguarded Native enclaves.

The Allotment Act did not fully please any of the peoples who hoped to benefit from it. Philanthropists who saw in private property a magic elixir whose contents would alter Indian behavior tended to be disappointed at the residual tribalism they witnessed. The Indians themselves were caught in a terrible dilemma, for allotment surely did not propel them to new economic heights. And the "surplus" land thrown to the Anglo farmers and ranchers who lingered like coyotes to snap up the portions tossed their way proved not enough to curb their appetite.

The answer, then, had to come in the form of further land cessions combined with direct access to the lands the Indians still claimed. The *Lone Wolf v. Hitchcock* decision by the U.S. Supreme Court in 1903 epitomized the limits on Native sovereignty. Even the names of the protagonists symbolized the dichotomy. A Kiowa man, Lone Wolf, objected to the opening of his reservation in southwestern Oklahoma. Lone Wolf was just that—a solitary figure outmanned by the forces allied against him, personified by Ethan Allen Hitchcock, secretary of the interior, who represented those who believed staunchly that Indians had too much land. Did the government need the permission of a certain percentage of the tribe to justify this kind of abrupt expropriation of the Indian estate? Black-robed men a very long way away from Kiowa country ruled in the negative. The government could do what it pleased, regardless of Native sentiment.

It pleased federal officials to carve off hunks of several reservations at this time: Rosebud in South Dakota, Flathead in Montana, Wind River in Wyoming, Crow in Montana, Uintah in Utah. Not coincidentally, they all were places where cattle interests sought more land. These cessions generated far less publicity in the historical literature than the Dawes Act. However, in these instances we are talking about millions of acres lost and for the most part not to be regained, unless non-Indian interest did not live up to expectations and outsiders could not be lured in sufficient numbers. Wind River typified the kind of relentless pressure faced by many Indian communities in the late nineteenth century and early twentieth century. The Shoshones and Arapahoes who shared the Wyoming reservation worried that they might be moved or that they would be left with little acreage. Created by the Fort Bridger Treaty of July 3, 1868, Wind River initially served as home for the Shoshones, who objected strongly to the placement of the Arapahoes there a decade later. Even before the Arapahoe arrival, the Shoshones had been forced to relinquish the southern portion of their lands in 1872, following mineral discoveries in that area. Washakie and other Shoshones obtained money and cattle for their surrender of this section. In 1891, both tribes gave up half of the remaining reservation, but ironically the agreement failed to take effect when Congress chose not to ratify it, believing that the Indians had not given up enough land. Unhappy with the whole business, the tribes would not hear of any alternative agreement in 1893, when other emissaries came to urge a new option of land reduction.

Predictably, three years later, a federal representative, James McLaughlin, surfaced to engineer the separation of the hot springs area, the site of present-day Thermopolis. Some of the proceeds went for cattle for the Arapahoes and more cattle for the Shoshones. In April 1904, fresh on the heels of *Lone Wolf v. Hitchcock*, McLaughlin made an encore performance, telling the tribes they had to let go of most of their reservation. In this instance, although the Shoshones and Arapahoes reluctantly agreed to cede much of their lands, a change in federal policy made the deal contingent on outsiders coming in and paying the Indians for the acres they purchased. Botched attempts at irrigation by private companies and the finite agricultural potential of Wind River meant a trickle rather than a flood of folks. The tribes held on through the remainder of the assimilation era; the coming of the Indian New Deal eventually spelled a guarantee that the reservation would remain.[6]

Even the cessions were not enough. They could not be wrenched from many reservations. Leasing, however, could be justified on just about any reserve. In contrast to the Dawes Act, leasing offered something satisfactory to several parties. For non-

Indians, it provided the opportunity to put checkerboarded bits of land together into a workable economic unit and at very inexpensive rates. For Indians, it offered the chance to have small landholdings yield at least a minimal return. And for bureaucrats in the Indian Office, it satisfied their firm convictions that Indian lands must be put to use. The post-*Lone Wolf* period marks an escalation of pressure and a change in philosophy by the Bureau of Indian Affairs (BIA). Leasing itself undercut allotment; it promoted passivity on the part of the Indians rather than that prized commodity, individual initiative. The Dawes Act had called for a trust period with government protection of allotments; by the time the Indian Appropriations Act of 1902 had passed, inherited trust allotments could now be sold. By decade's end, 775,000 of these acres had been lost.[7]

Leasing may have offered something for everyone, but it also presented confusion and misunderstanding time and again. Several problems compounded the situation on most reservations. The matter of language perhaps was most vexing. Few Indians on the affected reserves spoke English well, and not many more understood it easily. Just as in treaty negotiations, the translator had an unenviable assignment and even with the best of intentions, could not always convey precise meanings or subtle details. Occasionally a veteran federal representative, such as the ubiquitous McLaughlin, would "understand sufficient of the Sioux language to get the general meaning," but general meanings were not always enough to forge firm and fair arrangements.[8]

In addition, the reservations were new institutions, often either on lands that the people had not occupied previously at all or on particular pieces of which they had not resided. Discussions over leasing reflect a clear sense of people groping toward accommodation in what was still a new world. The people kept asking such questions as how are we to live? how are we to make the land work for us? how are we to get along with our white neighbors? how can we please these federal officials who always seem to want something else? If outsiders asked for access to lands that few or no one occupied or used, they said, then perhaps we can agree to it. However, if it is truly our land, do we not have the right to say no? And if we are to increase our own herds of cattle, how can we allow others to use the land instead?

The proceedings of the Standing Rock reservation in North Dakota in May 1902 contain just these sentiments. Here we have the prominent cattleman Ed Lemmon attempting to gain a mammoth lease. Samuel Brosius of the Indian Rights Association (IRA) telegrammed his advice to the Standing Rock council to accept it as a "liberal compromise." Herbert Welsh of the IRA and George Bird Grinnell, the well-known student of Cheyenne life, were both on hand. The Reverend Philip Deloria, of what would become a prominent Lakota family, was present to monitor the discussion. And, of course, McLaughlin was there. Standing Rock representatives Red Fish and Mad Bear and Rosebud wrestled with what to do. They looked to the demands of the present. They remembered the indignities of the recent past. They pondered the prospects of their children. They knew they might possibly have some room to maneuver, but only so much.

As *Lone Wolf* would make evident in the following year, it may be their land, but it was not theirs alone. Federal officials neither saw it generally as theirs on a permanent basis nor theirs for their exclusive use. It may be useful to think of Indian reservations as not entirely dissimilar to forest reserves, soon to be known as national forests. John Muir fought the good fight to keep sheep out of those lands. He labeled sheep "hoofed locusts" and suggested none too cheerfully that as sheep advance, plenty and poetry vanish. Muir lost. The guiding principle became what we today call multiple use and what Muir no doubt would call multiple opportunities for degradation. Mining, timbering, grazing, and other interests could be accommodated within the boundaries of the national forests. Why could they not be accommodated as well on these other national lands, the Indian reservations?[9]

So here is Rosebud talking to McLaughlin and others assembled in the late spring of the second year of this century.

You were our agent here and you have instructed us to learn the ways of the white people and make a living. It is your wish that we should look forward to the coming generations, . . . we that are progressing in such a way as to benefit ourselves. You have told us to put in crops, but we could not do it. Since we have failed in raising crops, you instructed us to try stock raising. We have tried that, but if there is no rain and the ground is dry the cattle are lost just the same. For this reason the Indians on the Grand River—there is not one there that does not own at least one head of stock—the reason why they could not spare this land is that we see our cattle are increasing— also our children, and I have been wondering how it is when you see us in this state that you allow these cattlemen to use our land for their stock. And for this reason I am displeased.[10]

The Lakota word Rosebud employed might have been stronger than "displeased." Regardless, we can imagine the range of emotions that he and his colleagues felt: anger, frustration, puzzlement, uncertainty. As with their predecessors on earlier frontiers, they did not know when this bargaining would resurface; they only knew, based on experience, that one agreement, one arrangement never settled everything for the white people. They kept coming back. They always wanted more.

Janet A. McDonnell has documented the failures of the leasing program during the first three decades of the twentieth century. Leasing was a central ingredient in a recipe for dispossession.[11] Rather than repeat most of McDonnell's discussion, what can be added here is more detailed illustration of how Anglo use of Indian grazing lands affected those involved. What needs to be understood is that the impact of this entanglement reverberates to our own day. Because of allotment, cession, and sale, many reservations became checkerboarded with white inholders and individual Indian landowners. That complex legacy haunts contemporary efforts at economic development.

Over this period, then, non-Indian cattle ranchers developed stakes in Indian country. They saw such land as necessary to their survival, and they saw it as theirs because they were the ones who had "developed" it. They resembled the residents of

Salamanca, New York, who expressed outrage when the ninety-nine-year lease on the town came due a few years ago to the Senecas of western New York. They had paid almost nothing on the land and had thought almost not at all about the equity of the arrangements. When the Senecas reminded them about the obligations of history, they portrayed themselves in the best American tradition as creatures of the present rather than as prisoners bound by the past. Why should a dusty lease from a distant past be their problem? A somewhat more equitable compromise was reached eventually, thanks in large degree to people of goodwill on both sides. The peacemakers, you can be sure, caught hell for their troubles.

They were also like the ranchers of today dependent on leases through the Bureau of Land Management and other federal agencies. These leases have also been minimal, and any change in them is perceived as an insult to one's ancestors who struggled to make a go of it in inhospitable country. If you up the ante, we cannot stay in the game, they say. Moreover, it is really our land. We have established that right by years of hard work, of commitment through generations. How can you change the rules after the game has been played for so long?

In 1900 and 1910 and 1920, the Anglo cattle ranchers did not see themselves as changing the rules or changing the odds for the Indians. They only saw their own interest, their own chance. If they did not lease the land, if they did not purchase an allotment that came up for sale, some other person would. That is how it worked. You did not survive in the cattle business by refusing the opportunity of more land—especially more land near yours that you could have for little money.

For those with imagination and nerve, there were dreams still to be realized; one did not have to relinquish what one sought or turn to what one perceived a lesser occupation. "I have done a lot of bad things in my life," cattle rancher Bruce Siberts later recalled, "but I never did stoop to sheep ranching."[12] In the Dakotas, from Siberts's perspective in 1891, the cattle business appeared a good bet.

Everybody you talked to was thinking about doing the same thing. It figures good on paper. Borrow money at ten per cent, buy a few cows, and the herd will double every three years. . . . There was lots of grass in that 11,000,000-acre pasture taken from the Sioux in 1889, and there were very few settlers.[13]

Siberts purchased an ivory-handled Colt 45, traded in an ancient saddle for a Menea made in Cheyenne, and began to see himself as "quite a fellow." "In the 5,000 square mile area, bounded on the south by the Black Hills-Pierre Trail, on the east by the Missouri, and on the north and west by the Cheyenne," he recalled, "were no more than forty whites." One of them was already attempting to claim most of the region. Siberts cheerfully concluded, "Iowa was never like this."[14]

So one could have opportunities not available in Oskaloosa or Ottumwa. Uncle Sam waved them on. In the Dakotas, in Montana, in Oklahoma, in the Southwest, opportunity beckoned. Both on lands vacated by Indians and on lands still occupied by various Native communities, a new start could be achieved. Again, comfortable and convenient myths eased the way. Nonetheless, the historical record reveals how overwhelmingly the foundation of third-, fourth-, or fifth-generation white cattle ranching families today would be built on an Indian base.

South Dakota presents an obvious case in point. As the country west of the Missouri River—the West River area, as South Dakotans call it—had been part of the Great Sioux Reservation, leaders in the twentieth-century cattle business made their start on what had been Indian land. What is more striking is the degree to which remaining reservation acreage proved critical to the establishment of family enterprises. In *Last Grass Frontier*, Bob Lee and Dick Williams pay tribute to the South Dakota stock grower heritage. In a volume sponsored by the South Dakota Stock Growers Association, one somehow anticipates detailed attention to leaders of such an organization. One is not disappointed. Time after time, such men had a stake in what remained of Sioux country.[15]

Although he never served as president of the Western South Dakota Stock Growers Association, Lemmon joined it at the outset and served on the executive committee until 1915. Murdo MacKenzie, whose unusual first name became immortalized when it was taken by a small West River community, managed the Matador Land and Cattle Company with huge leases on different reservations in the state. MacKenzie not only was active in the western South Dakota group but in 1906 assumed the presidency of the American National Livestock Association, formed from the merger of the National Livestock and American Stock Growers associations. H. A. Dawson, a member of the Western South Dakota Stock Growers Association from 1908 to 1912, had another title. His experience as a clerk for the Indian Department and a trader and stockman at Pine Ridge made him a familiar figure on the western South Dakota reservation, where the local residents dubbed him Pasu Hamska (Long Nose). He may not have appreciated his new moniker, but he saw at Pine Ridge an extraordinary chance in the reservation estate. With another non-Indian, Will S. Hughes, who had arrived from Maryland in 1889, Dawson initiated his herd with 400 head of cattle bought in 1892 from a widow in the Interior area. Hughes and Dawson then acquired another 200 head in northern Nebraska and in 1893 obtained 450 two-year-old steers previously owned by Sioux cattlemen.

Hughes later remembered it all. "Free grass, no income tax, no county tax, only a small state tax, no feed bills, small losses, open range from the reservation north to the state line and from the Black Hills to the Missouri River made it possible to build up the cattle numbers under this brand with just a foreman and one or two men, except during round-up time." Dawson guessed all it cost was one or two dollars a head to do business. By the turn of the century, he built his herd up to 4,000 head, and then a drought necessitated a move from Pine Ridge. Where could he find greener pastures? On the neighboring Rosebud reservation, where he remained temporarily, until drought conditions improved and he could move back a bit to the west.

The Brules at Rosebud reluctantly ceded a portion of the reservation in 1902, and that land came open in 1904. Some of the Lower Brule opened up in 1907; more land became available in Rosebud in 1908. Cheyenne River and Standing Rock lost land in 1909, and still more land beckoned from Rosebud and Pine Ridge in 1911. Is it any wonder that the West River population mushroomed from 57,575 in 1905 to 137,687 in 1910? And more would have come, if they had been permitted. More than 81,000 people, for example, registered for the 10,000 parcels offered at Cheyenne River and Standing Rock. Such inroads literally changed the complexion of western South Dakota. They also made it far more difficult for the fledgling Indian cattle business to develop.[16]

Other prominent West River cattle ranchers gained a foothold on Indian land. Tom Jones, president of the South Dakota Stock Growers Association during the 1930s, came to the state in 1891. As an employee of W. I. Walker, he helped provide beef to the Sioux at Standing Rock. Together with Scotty Philip, who married into a Sioux family and later gained lasting fame for his efforts to save the buffalo, Jones for a time leased the entire Lower Brule reservation. Later he leased land on Pine Ridge. To cite just three other examples, the families of association presidents Emmett Morgan, Louis Beckwith, and Merton Glover also took advantage of cattle leases on Sioux lands. Morgan's father, C. J. Morgan, eventually lived in Rapid City but focused his cattle business at Pine Ridge beginning in the 1910s. And John Glover, Merton's father, was the foreman of the Quarter Circle 71 outfit of the Newcastle Land and Livestock Company, which ultimately acquired 500,000 acres of lease land at Pine Ridge. Lee and Williams describe John Glover gaining "trunk loads" of leases from Sioux holding allotments. By 1920, Glover purchased a quarter section on Porcupine Creek. The Glover Ranch has been there in the heart of Pine Ridge ever since.[17]

Other newcomers to Sioux country married Lakota women and in the process gained special opportunities to graze cattle because of their newfound family associations. In her *History of the Range Cattle Industry of Dakota*, Hazel Adele Pulling notes "extensive herds owned by men who had married Indian women and who ran their herds on the Indian Reservation of Cheyenne and the Standing Rock in the northern part of South Dakota." She mentions as the largest of such operators, Narcisse Narcelle, with 4,000 head of cattle; the Dupris family, with 3,000; George, Fred, and Robert LaPlant, with 6,000; and Scotty Philip, with 8,000.[18]

Cheyenne River also became a haven for cattlemen who had to retreat in the face of the growing farmer-homesteader presence in the West River. Late in the first decade of the new century, companies pushed in force onto the reservation. Even if representing a temporary victory, the inroads were impressive. The Matador Land and Cattle Company ran about 17,000 head. The Sword and Dagger grazed 15,000 head. For good measure, E. Holcomb had 10,000 head of cattle on 360,000 acres, and Michael Mullin increased Holcomb's holdings by 1,000 on the same number of acres.

Western South Dakotans, white or Indian, are fond of telling stories. So many hail from long-established families, and there are many memories of days gone by. Individuals cherish the accomplishments of their ancestors. And while the wind may blow a little harder and a little colder and the snow may pile up a little higher with each passing year and each retelling of a tale, there is no doubt about the affection they bear for the people and the lands. One can imagine 100 cowboys and more riding more than 100 horses across Rosebud from May 25 to June 21, 1902, rounding up a good 40,000 head of cattle owned by non-Indians. Peter Claussen never forgot. A raw eighteen-year-old in 1902, he took part in the roundup. Asked forty-six years later about the Rosebud country, he practically shouted (the *Yankton Press and Dakotan* reported in all caps), "IT'S THE BEST CATTLE COUNTRY THAT LAYS OUT OF DOORS."[19]

In her memoir of early statehood life in South Dakota, Gladys Whitehorn Jorgensen remembered "the vast herd of cattle" coming to Indian country, as "the big companies arranged to lease land from the government and grazed their herds until they grew fat on these nutritious grasses." Big cattle drives to border town communities in 1902, 1906, and 1910, she concluded, "kept those towns booming." Ready access to Indian lands clearly contributed to the overall development of the West River country in these crucial years.[20] One can try to picture letting out two-year-old Texas cows on Cheyenne River pasture, animals of such quality that they are labeled "stuff" in the history of Ziebach County, and then trying to find them after they had wandered around unchaperoned for a considerable period. Or the strawberry roan who seemed especially reluctant to allow any cowboy to stay on him for long. Or the Lemmons's lease of 865,000 acres on Standing Rock, enclosed with a three-wire fence. Raymond S. Griffiths, probably correctly, called it "the largest fenced pasture in the world." But who was lucky enough to help construct the fence? And who got to ride to check on the fence after it had been erected?[21] George B. German flew over the territory, took a deep journalistic breath, and exhaled in one heroic sentence,

From the glamour of the old covered wagon, rough hard-riding cowpunchers, and the dust kicked up by some 40,000 moving, rumbling footsore longhorns and whitefaces, we stepped up into the cabin of the flying station wagon, flapped our wings and flew out over those millions of acres of rangeland—some of it rangeland that will never change; an empire still loved and cherished by those who rode its dusty trails and slept out beneath the stars and a bright smiling moon that still lights the way for the weary coyote and the wild horse that shies from the giant modern bird that streaks the skies.[22]

Other Native lands provided new opportunities for newcomers. Oklahoma, of course, symbolizes that rush for real estate. In the popular imagination we remember the great run of 1889—that onrushing mass of humanity of boomers and sooners that permeated and dashed the dream of an Indian state. There is inherent drama in that scene, people on horseback, on foot, and even on bicycle scrambling over the line and dashing off for a place of one's own. However, as Indians of Oklahoma remember full well, the run of '89 was only one chapter in a seemingly never-ending saga of land rushes and reductions. Outsiders sought access to Indian land as soon as the Civil War concluded. The Cherokee Outlet is but one example.

The Cherokee Outlet encompassed lands to the west of the Cherokee country in the northeastern part of what became Oklahoma. This tract of approximately six and one-half million acres had been reduced to just over six million acres by the end of the 1860s, but it obviously represented extraordinary possibilities for the non-Indian cattlemen who sought to use it. The combination of water and grass quickly captivated the cattlemen from Texas and elsewhere. The Arkansas, Cimarron, North Canadian, and Salt Fork offered water and rainfall that were usually generous enough to nurture native grasses, from bluestem to buffalo grass as one moved east to west.[23]

The Cherokees were physically separated from the Outlet and thus were not in a position to graze cattle themselves on this rectangular stretch of country. For most of the 1870s, they could not impose taxes on the growing number of cattlemen who used the pastures. Under the leadership of Cherokees Dennis Bushyhead and D. W. Lipe, the tribe began to move more aggressively to collect taxes. In the best American tradition, the cattlemen resisted. Employed to offer counsel, old-time cattleman Joseph McCoy did not try to deny reality. In the absence of federal troops, the non-Indian ranchers would pretty much do as they pleased.

However, the cattlemen soon faced problems of their own. Even those individuals who dutifully paid their taxes confronted intruders who sought their animals, their timber, and their water. These occupants of what had become known as the Cherokee Strip began to organize. In short order they turned from organization to the best way they knew to protect their interests. They began to fence the land. The minor detail that others owned the land did not discourage them. Perhaps they thought the pendulum of events would swing inevitably in their direction.

In the end the Cherokees and the cattlemen both lost. The greater losers were the Indians, for congressional action would open the Strip and the lands would pass out of their control. For a time in the 1880s, the cattlemen had secured a lease through the tribe and had momentarily gained the approval of the federal government for essentially exclusive rights to the land. But there were too many people, and the land was too good. Monopoly could not be maintained, if it meant excluding too many others who also sought land.

Although the cattlemen were not happy to have to deal with the Cherokees and the Cherokees were divided over how to deal with the cattlemen, it would have been fascinating to see how long the fragile accommodation could have been nurtured. In some ways, the conflict over the Strip represented a kind of precursor to the battles of the twentieth century in which both cattlemen and Indians would be surrounded by others who had different priorities for their land and would be faced with a federal government whose officials had little sense of the distant rural people with whom they were dealing.[24]

Elsewhere in Oklahoma the cattlemen also sought Indian acreage. Members of Native communities divided over how or whether to lease part or all of their lands to these people. The grim inevitability of allotment and heirship and the pronouncements of commissioners of Indian affairs often extracted a toll in a sort of piecemeal leasing that in a perverse domino effect, once begun, could not be stopped. Historians have not been kind to those intruders. Donald Berthrong refers to "land thieves" at the Cheyenne-Arapaho agency. Berthrong singles out Texan Cato Sells for particular censure for the commissioner's acceleration of Indian land alienation; it is difficult to disagree with that judgment. And as Berthrong reminds us, the Cheyennes and Arapahos shared a common fate. Nearby the Kiowas, Comanches, and Kiowa-Apaches lost their "surplus" lands through the Jerome Agreement of 1900. Before the agreement opened the doors of the Big Pasture to others, cattlemen had enjoyed the prosperity guaranteed to them. They encouraged resistance and delay. They bought a little time. In the end, the result looked familiar. The Indians lost. So, eventually, did the cattlemen. Kiowas, Comanches, and Kiowa-Apaches remained in southern Oklahoma, as did some cattle ranchers. The reservations as such came to an end, however, and the power of the cattle industry once more had been overridden.[25]

Expansion of the cattle industry intermingles Indian and white fates elsewhere as well. As any reader of *Lonesome Dove* or *The Log of a Cowboy* can testify, Texas cattle interests looked as far north as Montana. Those who made that extraordinary journey almost all the way to the forty-ninth parallel initially did face occasional ambush and possible loss of life. In the longer run, after the Blackfeet, Crows, Cheyennes, Gros Ventres, Assiniboines, and other Indian tribes had been confined to reservations, the same pattern witnessed in Oklahoma and the Dakotas asserted itself once again. Land allotment splintered tribal communities, dooming some people in another generation to become what Northern Cheyenne president John Wooden Legs in 1960 termed "landless gypsies." In remarks that can be applied to more than the Cheyennes, Wooden Legs said,

> Our Cheyenne land is cattle country. Sensible people knew it would be wrong to take cattle land like ours and divide it up into little pieces—big enough for grazing rabbits, but not cattle. . . . My people did not know what allotment was. . . . Nobody worried . . . except white ranchers and speculators. They were waiting to defeat my hungry people with dollars the way soldiers defeated them with bullets.[26]

This is not to suggest that all Montana non-Indian cowboys and ranchers had nothing good to say about Indians. Indeed, as E. C. ("Teddy Blue") Abbott phrased it in his characteristic way, "There was plenty of cowpunchers in that early day who were not ashamed to marry an Indian girl."[27] Granville Stuart, discoverer of gold and later big-time rancher, married a woman Abbott says was Shoshone, and Abbott married one of the Stuart daughters. Other cowboys, like the inimitable Charlie Russell, had a healthy respect for the old Indian way of life and regretted its passing, even if they helped expedite the process. As Russell once said to Teddy Blue, "They've been living in heaven for a thousand years, and we took it away from 'em for forty dollars a month."[28]

To be sure, the working assumption of the late nineteenth century did not center around division of Indian land but the elimination of Native landholdings altogether. The existence of Indian reservations initially may have been useful to beginning white ranchers, for it offered a ready and convenient market for their beef. But as the land began to get more crowded, the reservation quickly represented land to be acquired one way or another. In discussing the need for access to Blackfeet land, the *Helena Herald* in the early 1880s summarized popular sentiment: "These ranges are needed for our cattle and they are of no use in the world to the Indians."[29] Allotments and leasing permits appeared to be stopgap, transitional mileposts on the way to the disappearance of land, no more to be locked up than other lands in national forests or other federal preserves foolishly restricted by federal bureaucrats who wanted to deny settlers the right to cut down trees and mine for gold.

Later in the decade, federal negotiators huddled with Blackfeet leaders in the miserable cold of February. White Calf, Three Seasons, and other Blackfeet men were arm twisted into capitulation. For forsaking the Sweet Grass Hills, for relinquishing the eastern chunk of the reserve, the tribe gained a pittance: $150,000 per year for ten years for the cattle and homes they desperately needed and wanted and which a penny-pinching government seemed unwilling to provide. And even so, the problems would not dissipate in the thin northern air.

The Blackfeet land base may have shriveled, but it remained an attractive target for neighboring cattle ranchers who perceived a continuing chance at cheap grass. As the Blackfeet attempted to inaugurate their own cattle industry, thousands of trespassing cattle, owned by the Flowerree Cattle Company or William G. Conrad, threatened to trample the local enterprise. The Indians resorted to a time-honored non-Indian practice: they built a fence—and financed it—and encircled the entire reservation.

A good idea. But it did not work. Outsiders knew how to continue another time-honored practice and did not hesitate to do so. They cut the fence, over and over again. Drought the year the fence was completed, in 1904, and again in the following year turned up the column of the white serenade to Washington: more land. We still need more land. And as the chorus somehow knew, Washington caved in once again. In 1907, the reservation was allotted and a permit system ushered in to allow outsiders' cattle still more access to Blackfeet pastures.[30]

The same pattern repeated itself across Montana. At Fort Belknap, for example, the federal government opened up almost the entire reservation for lease by the Matador Land and Cattle Company. The same land base noteworthy as the site of the famous Winters' Doctrine decision, symbolic of Indian water rights in the twentieth century, mirrored an alternate reality. The government in fact had not pursued the case against Henry Winter, Mose Anderson, and other upstream farmers and ranchers who drained off the water from the Milk River just because it wanted to promote Indian self-sufficiency. The virtuous agent, William Logan, did not seek simply to bolster Gros Ventre and Assiniboine economic development. Actually, Logan and associates sought to protect white interests within the reservation. Henry Winter hurt them as much as he injured the Indians.[31]

On the Crow reservation, cattle interests threatened the reservation on several different fronts. Local cattlemen were outraged when outside interests from Colorado tried to lease Crow lands. They howled in protest because this distant concern had achieved a version of what they had attempted to gain. Ultimately the 1884 agreement did not win federal approval; the aptly named Commissioner of Indian Affairs Hiram Price must have been convinced by a petition from the Committee of Citizens of Yellowstone County.

> When this reservation is thrown open it should be for the benefit and use of such citizens . . . as desire to secure homes for themselves, and not for the exclusive use of a grasping monopoly. . . . Such a lease . . . would result in endless conflict between Indians and cattlemen, with all the horror of savage warfare.[32]

Even though Granville Stuart was married to an Indian, he decried the "sentimental bosh and religious rascality" that permitted reservations to endure. He called for Crow and other Native lands to be allotted without delay and the rest of the reserves thrown open to whites; such an arrangement, Stuart suggested, "breaks up their tribal organizations and sandwiches them in among the whites where they must learn by force of example." Segregating the Indians did not serve them well. At present, Stuart contended, they made no other use of large reservations "than as breeding grounds for a race of permanent and prolific paupers."[33]

Not all the cattlemen lived happily ever after in the wake of their success in reducing the Indian estate. Stuart, for one, lost most of his 40,000 head of cattle in the drought of the summer and the infamous winter of 1886. His first wife died. His second wife was thoroughly disliked by his children, who thought her a bigot. Stuart's family walked out of the new household or went to the St. Ignatius mission school on the Flathead reservation. Soon Stuart had lost his family and his land. The rest of his life was littered with unfulfilled dreams. He died at eighty-four, in town, the author of a rambling Montana history that no one wanted to publish.[34]

In Arizona, tensions and conflicts between cattlemen and Indians also figured prominently in the evolution of territorial life. Until the final surrender of Geronimo at Skeleton Canyon in 1886, he and the Apaches were blamed for misfortunes they caused and did not cause all over the thinly populated Arizona frontier. As reported by contemporary journalists and faithfully rehashed by antiquarian historians ever since, the Apaches appeared to go on vengeful raids 365 days a year or 366 days a year quadrennially. If there is one noun one grows weary of by its numbing repetition in these chronicles, it is "depredation." Apache depredation may have been like those glasses one can see out of but through which your eyes cannot be seen; Native transgressions are perceived, but newcomers' trespasses are invisible in such accounts.

Other than miners, few Anglo-Americans seemed much interested in Arizona until the advent of air-conditioning. Prior to the federal investment in irrigation at the beginning of the new century, the ranchers saw land more suited to their needs than to the farmers'. Although not assisted comparably as were their brethren to the north by the divide and conquer effects of allotment, cattle ranching spread quickly in the 1870s, 1880s, 1890s. As elsewhere, the political clout of the industry either limited the size of the original reserve or expedited access to the reservation after its creation. Often it did both.

On the remaining Apache enclaves in central Arizona, the White Mountain or Fort Apache and San Carlos reservations, agents had their hands full. In the 1880s, cattle companies began leasing reservation land and in many instances occupied it by trespass. Only a stalwart agent, such as Cornelius Washington (C. W., as he understandably preferred) Crouse at White Mountain or somewhat later, James Barbour Kitch at San Carlos, had enough nerve and resolve to take on the powerful cattle interests. Other federal employees took the path of less resistance, and it did not take long for officials of outfits such as the Chiricahua Cattle Company to take advantage of acquiescence.

The Chiricahua company obtained a permit in the early 1890s to run 2,000 head of cattle in the Ash Flat area of San Carlos. By 1899, the Apaches began to complain publicly about the company's abuse of the permit. It turned out that 12,000 rather than 2,000 head of cattle were on hand. Did the company forfeit its lease for such abuse? No. It simply signed a new one, acknowledging the larger number of cattle and paying a small fee per head.[35]

Unfenced and partially fenced land made it more difficult to keep track of cattle and to regulate business at San Carlos. Time after time, cattle company employees exploited the situation. One suspects they somehow knew there were more cattle than there should have been. Little contrition survives in the historical record. Much more resentment surfaces when such increasingly established interests are challenged or even reined in somewhat.

In the meantime, a similar scenario took place to the south. Tohono O'odham cattle ranchers had difficulty competing with non-Indians. Both Anglo and Mexican cattlemen let their animals graze on Indian land. As the Tohono O'odham people did not have a formal reserve, they were particularly vulnerable to such trespass. Non-Indian cattlemen denied the legitimacy of a Native land base. They had the gall to complain when their trespassing animals occasionally were appropriated and eaten by the Indians. White ranchers sank wells, built fences, and did all they could to make usurpation a permanent condition.

The creation of the Tohono O'odham reservation in 1917 partially denied their efforts. However, the reservation would have been still larger without the lobbying of cattle interests, and establishment of the reserve in the Sonoran desert country in southern Arizona hardly ended disputes over animals and property lines. The Tucson Chamber of Commerce and other organizations continued to whine about reserving any land at all for the Tohono O'odham, but once established, the reservation would not disappear without considerable struggle. Non-Indian cattlemen reluctantly shifted most of their attention elsewhere, to land that after all might offer more than the sparse Sonoran terrain.[36]

This discussion has presented a sense of the pattern one witnessed in the late-nineteenth-century and early-twentieth-century West. One could reinforce the impression already established by other examples from other locales. Elsewhere in Arizona and elsewhere in the region, the same kind of competition took place over control and use of the land. Again and again, non-Indian cattlemen benefited from restriction of Native holdings and access to the dwindling acreage Indians still possessed. Even when Indians made the effort to become farmers or ranchers, even when they went to Christian church services, even when they sent their children to local or more distant schools, they shared common ground with the Cherokees and other Native peoples of Andrew Jackson's day. In the end, it did not matter. If they became farmers or ranchers, they were not good enough farmers or ranchers. There was no way they could become good enough. Their very persistence and adaptation threatened to deny future prosperity for others. They were, after all, seen as Indians, not cowboys.

CHAPTER FOUR
_____

Indian Cattle Ranching in the Northern Plains

IN THE PLAINS COUNTRY, CONFINEMENT TO RESER-
vations posed myriad problems. The transition presented unprecedented challenges to the social and economic order of
tribal life. How could this new imposed environment become
home? How could families provide for themselves? How could
individual men and women earn respect for themselves and
within their society?

Because the northern reservations have been in place for more
than a century—regardless of the challenges to the land bases
that have continued to emerge through the years—it is easy to
forget how major a change they indeed imposed. Today people
may refer to themselves, as does Vine Deloria, Jr., for example, as
Standing Rock Sioux. This identity had to be forged through
time and through the creation of a new society. It could not

52

occur quickly or easily. It is impressive that it occurred at all. It is a commentary on the seemingly endless ability of American Indians to adapt, to change, to incorporate.

Fowler reminds us that most studies of Plains Indians that consider the relationship between the past and the present "focus on explicating gradual cultural loss, documenting 'persistence,' or demonstrating the effects of increasing 'powerlessness.'" As she notes, there are major problems with such approaches. Culture loss echoes the tendency of many social scientists to emphasize acculturation or assimilation. Such students usually see acculturation as a kind of terminal illness, dooming the affected tribe to cultural death. This perspective denies innovation and fails to recognize that Indians are always reinterpreting and revising their cultures. The persistence model is also static and narrow. It encompasses an important truth. Values and ideals can continue. However, new values can also reinforce identity. Again, one must allow for change. Well-meaning students of Indian life can also emphasize Indians as victims in an effort to show sympathy for the Native American "plight." "Plight" competes with "depredation" as a word one would like to eradicate from discussions about Indian communities. Without being romantic or naive, we can argue that studies of reservation life that see only poverty and despair do not see the whole picture.[1]

In the new day that the reservation obviously provided, we should anticipate new strategies and thus, in time, new symbols. The raising of cattle became at this time an appropriate economic strategy, given the kind of land the Indians possessed and the kind of world in which they had lived. The love of the outdoors, of horses, and of movement all contributed to the positive chord struck by the new industry. But cattle ranching must be understood in a social as well as an economic context. By becoming an owner of a considerable number of cattle, a person could achieve status within the community. Moreover, this individual could use the animals themselves to obtain the kind of reputation generally sought. By giving cattle or beef to one's relatives, by feeding people at a celebration, and in other comparable ways, a person would be seen as generous, thoughtful, and properly mindful of the well-being of others. By becoming or continuing to be a skilled rider, one demonstrated a skill appreciated and noted. By raising cattle of good quality, one showed that Indians could participate on an equal or competitive basis in a pastime that dominated the surrounding non-Indian society.

The final note may be greeted with some skepticism. Somehow, a country that recognized, albeit begrudgingly, the spirit, pride, and determination inherent in Native resistance in the nineteenth century denied that such qualities continued into the twentieth century. Reservation residents became pictured as sullen, withdrawn, passive. They hardly appeared to wish to compete in any way with the dominant society—to employ another label that should give one pause. The twentieth century has exemplified what people have wanted to see rather than what has transpired. Surely a lack of competitive zeal among Indians would have been a surprise to Jim Thorpe, a Sac and Fox who is considered the greatest American athlete of the first half of the century. It would have amused those football teams and track teams unfortunate enough to be matched against Carlisle or Haskell when those Indian schools reached the zenith of their prowess. It would not have been believed by rodeo cowboys who saw Jackson Sundown and other first-rate Indian rodeo participants early in the 1900s. And in our own time it would have been dismissed by the literally hundreds of Navajo fans who have driven hundreds of miles over the past two years to see one of their own, Ryneldi Becenti, star on the women's basketball team at Arizona State University. Arizona state legislator and long-time rodeo participant Jack Jackson puts it straightforwardly: "In the history of Navajo culture, there has always been competition." Well before the days of Navajo rodeo, the Diné raced their horses against each other, with people traveling long distances to watch, to wager, and to compete.[2]

If competitiveness has in fact marked the character of Indian athletics during the past one hundred years, then that quality

FIG. 1. Horse races enlivened fairs at Plains Indian communities. Crow Creek reservation (South Dakota) superintendent Leo Crane captured this scene in the early 1920s. Cline Library, Special Collections and Archives, Northern Arizona University, Leo Crane Collection (Photo #658.859).

FIG. 2. Blackfeet cowboys Lomie Goss and John Mountain Chief participate in a horse-pulling contest, 1907. Photo by J. L. Sherburne, Sherburne Collection. University of Montana Library.

can hardly be expected to have been confined to or expressed only in one arena. Some of the other forums have been more internally focused and witnessed. The powwow circuit of the post-World War II era is a case in point. Doing certain things well—whether it is riding a horse, telling a story, or weaving a rug—remains a central value in Native communities. The lack of interest in the accumulation of material wealth, the denial of conspicuous consumption, has been misinterpreted into an indictment of a culture incompletely perceived.

Fowler's analysis of turn-of-the-century Gros Ventre society is not fully applicable to all Plains societies—nor does she assume that it is—but her discussion is telling and is a good place to begin a more general consideration of the adoption of cattle raising by Indian tribes of the region. Gros Ventre men before the reservation period had acquired horses to sell for trade goods and food, to give away to demonstrate generosity, and to "become somebody" within the group. With the days of raiding drawn permanently to a close, younger men had to turn to other avenues to gain status. The government in the late nineteenth century seemed anxious to encourage the raising of livestock. Ambitious younger men thus beseeched the agent or the missionary or a white in-law for help in acquiring livestock.[3]

Sometimes they succeeded. As elsewhere, sometimes they did not. The agents came and went, often not staying long enough to help or staying long enough to do some damage. Five different agents, or superintendents as they were also called, served at Fort Belknap during the 1910s. The somewhat celebrated William Logan not only looked out for non-Indian cattlemen already ensconced at Fort Belknap. He also looked out for himself. Logan was the agent from 1902 to 1910, a time during which Gros Ventre cattle holdings declined because, the people said, he had appropriated tribal cattle for his own herd.

Despite the promising start of the cattle industry in the early years of the reservation, several related developments doomed it to decline by the end of the second decade of the new century. Federal policy and its interpretation at the local level vacillated from one commissioner and one agent to the next. If ranching were seen as good, then farming might be seen—and generally was seen—as better. Indian economic advancement was good, but if forced to choose, neighboring white economic advancement was better. At times they were not even neighbors; the Matador Land and Cattle Company of Texas leased most of Fort Belknap from 1913 to 1927. The government made "reimbursable loans" so that more cattle could be purchased. The primary benefactor proved to be white men married to Gros Ventre women who needed some help in the industry.[4] So despite protestations the government would have issued to the contrary, there can be no escaping one conclusion: Washington did more to hinder than to help the evolution of Indian cattle ranching.

To the west on the Blackfeet reservation, a comparable drama was played out. Although the government introduced cattle by the early 1880s, the overall pattern mirrored a preference for farming over ranching. As it would on many reservations during the era, federal officials persisted with the dream of irrigated farming. Veteran agent James H. Monteath knew futility when he saw it, labeling irrigation projects at Blackfeet in 1900 "monuments of misdirected energy, being utterly impracticable." Either planning was inadequate, or the Indians did not want the irrigation, or if they did, so did intruding whites.[5]

Not all Blackfeet had an equal chance at getting a start in the cattle business. Washington preferred that cattle be given to "deserving Indians," and not all, apparently, fell into that category. Those who obtained the federally bestowed animals, which bore the "ID" (Indian Department) brand, had other offers. Non-Indians waved cash, marriage proposals, and other enticements to lure Blackfeet into providing pasturage. As of 1903, of the 20,000 head of cattle, only 5,000 had "full-blood" owners.[6]

Moreover, while advocating Indian farming and ranching, government officials did not back away from a continuing program of land allotment. Even though by 1917 it had been a demonstrable disaster on reservations all over the western United States, such overwhelming evidence did not stop the onrushing engine of allotment. Allotment by definition mitigated against successful cattle ranching. How could a rancher survive in western Montana on 160 acres? Bureau employees dutifully bought 1,880 head of cattle for the Blackfeet in 1915, and that number had grown to 4,300 two years later. But allotment followed by drought and bitter winters from 1917 to 1920 made for a mean combination that decimated tribal ranching. Efforts to revive the industry in the 1920s and 1930s would face long odds.[7]

The Northern Cheyennes had realized a long-held but tenuous dream in 1884 when President Chester Arthur issued an executive order creating a small reservation in southeastern Montana. The participation by Northern Cheyenne men as scouts for the U.S. Army helped convince the federal government of Cheyenne worth.[8] The pine ridge country appeared perfect for cattle. The acting Indian agent at the Tongue River Agency (the contemporary name for the Northern Cheyenne reservation), Thomas Sharp, informed Commissioner of Indian Affairs Daniel M. Browning in 1893 that, in fact, it was perfect. Nonetheless, Sharp did not want the Cheyennes to take advantage of it, for "herding leads to a nomadic life" and "a nomadic life tends to barbarism, and the more horses the Indian has, the greater savage he is."[9]

Too little or too much snow, unfailingly hot summers, and the tendency of grasshoppers to hold major conventions in southeastern Montana eventually discouraged the early rosy prognostications for agricultural success. James McLaughlin, who seems to show up on every reservation north of Mescalero during these years, visited the Cheyenne reserve in 1898. He told his superiors that the government ought to increase the reservation in size and "buy out" white intruders who had squatted on the Indian acreage. A veteran of the Dakota country, McLaughlin also knew cattle country when he saw it. Fence the north and south ends of Tongue River, he advised. And buy cattle.[10]

One thousand heifers and forty bulls arrived in the late spring of 1903. They came with private property strings attached.

Wringing their hands over incipient tribalism, federal officials desired to avoid such menacing tendencies on the part of Indians. These must be private, not tribal, cattle. With at least 430 heads of households and 1,000 head of cattle, the arithmetic added up easily but unproductively. Two or three cows per family hardly represented a recipe for the onward march of progress and private property. Each animal received the ID brand and a number for its entrepreneurial owner. A barbed wire fence stretching ultimately to 135 miles in length did its duty: it kept Indian cattle in and white cattle out. The Crow reservation fence to the west and the Tongue River to the east completed the rectangle.[11]

Superintendent James Clifford lobbied Commissioner of Indian Affairs Francis E. Leupp to increase the Cheyenne herd by 1,000 head. By 1906, the tribe had obtained the additional cattle. Clifford's successor, John R. Eddy, served in the post from 1906 to 1914. Eddy had big dreams. One of those "lifers" who peopled the reservation agent or superintendent position at this time, Eddy brought a decade and a half of experience to Lame Deer. Buoyed by such extensive service, he took immediate and firm control. If anything, his imagination exceeded the bounds of the short-term potential of the Cheyenne range. If the Cheyennes held a little over 2,000 head in 1906, the superintendent wanted to increase that sum tenfold. Knowing somehow that the federal officials would not spring instantly for the kind of investment needed to bolster the herd by that amount, Eddy leased surplus lands to other cattle ranchers. At first glance such a scheme sounds like the typical ruse of the time, concocted solely to benefit outsiders. Eddy actually had genuinely surplus land under his control, and he truly wanted the leasing to be a temporary, if expedient, arrangement.[12]

Although the Cheyenne cattle proved their quality during the first years of Eddy's tenure, ultimately the superintendent failed to receive sufficient backing from a new commissioner of Indian Affairs. Cheyenne beef had proven itself in the marketplace, and the men clearly loved the pastime. But Leupp's successor, R. G.

FIG. 3. Cheyenne cowboys take part in a roundup on the Northern Cheyenne reservation, 1911. Photo by Fannie Stohr. Montana Historical Society, Helena (Photo #955-648).

FIG. 4. Cheyenne cowboys with a variety of hats, Lame Deer, Montana, July 18, 1914. Thomas Old Bull is first from left; Charlie Crazy Mule is third from left. Montana Historical Society, Helena (Photo #955-649).

Valentine, did not support Indian cattle ranching and let Eddy and the Cheyennes know it in the most direct and effective bureaucratic fashion. He denied all requests for help and assistance. Eddy could not find adequate capital from private sources, and harder times in the 1910s signaled a downturn in the cattle business.

By 1914, Eddy had left and the large Cheyenne stock owners resisted the notion imposed by the bureau that year that individually owned herds be merged into a tribal herd. Such a dictate, of course, discouraged those who had worked hard to build up their own herds and marked a radical departure from past federal policy. The brutal summers and winters, rustlers, and wolves all took their toll on Cheyenne cattle by the end of the decade.[13] As with the Blackfeet, even during the decline of the industry, individual tribal members retained their affection for the work itself. They had taken pride in their ability to work the cattle. The government stockmen working with them had not made them cut their braids but had taught them well. They could be cowboys and Cheyennes, too.

As did the Crows, they loved horses. And working on horseback in the cattle business gave them pleasure. By 1912, if anything, they had too many horses—perhaps 15,000—competing with the cattle for grass. The Cheyenne elders would call this era the "Time of the Horse," for the horses figured centrally in everyday life and in special occasions. People used horses to demonstrate generosity at giveaways. They raced them. Once in a while, they held horse races against their neighbors and old rivals, the Crows.[14] One imagines the excitement, the pleasure, the teasing, and the gambling that might accompany such an occasion. Or the spirit of community evident at gatherings on Christmas or the Fourth of July. The use of those particular days speaks to accommodation and change and the ability to employ symbolically significant national days to heighten community cohesion. Horses and cattle are an integral part of this time, too much ignored and too often misread by historians who only see loss, if they see anything at all.

FIG. 5. A Crow man ready for the community celebration of the Crow Fair, ca. 1910. Photo by N. A. Forsyth. Montana Historical Society, Helena.

Crow cattle ranching also emerged during this period, although land cession and related problems plagued the nascent industry. The Crows loved horses, and cattle ranching afforded a wonderful opportunity to employ that affection. Widespread leasing of Crow land, however, encouraged tribal factionalism and reduced the chances for rapid development of the enterprise.[15] One important exception to the generally prevailing condition may be found in the person of a remarkable Crow man, whose life and career spanned so much of modern tribal history. Robert Yellowtail became a major figure in Crow life while still a very young man by Native standards. By the 1910s, he had become a cattle rancher, an orator, a man who knew the law, and a person who cared passionately about the survival of the Crow community.

Yellowtail was one of those young Indians who had made the long journey to boarding school and been able to come home again. He had gone all the way to the Riverside School in California, where he learned English and to play the clarinet. This knowledge of the larger world made him valuable to the elders, whom he accompanied to Washington, D.C., in 1917. There the Crow leadership made a last-ditch effort to block the threatened land cession that, if implemented, would have splintered the reserve, with eternal consequences.[16]

The old men and one young man checked into their hotel in the nation's capital. They built a fire in a hotel room with coals liberated from the hotel kitchen. They chanted and prayed through the night. They no doubt caused other hotel guests to wonder what in the hell was going on. And then, fortified and strong, they proceeded to the Senate committee hearings.

Yellowtail spoke for the group, a young man using his knowledge of the new language to articulate the elders' concerns. As the old man liked to retell the event in later years, he carried the day. Speaking for hours, providing a kind of Crow filibuster for the increasingly exhausted senators, Yellowtail triumphed. The people survive. Admittedly, this is his version, and there are others among the tribe, such as historian Karen Watembach, who tell a somewhat different story. In any event, the young cattle rancher clearly offered an impassioned voice, speaking for the land, the people, and the animals—speaking for a Crow future at a time when it was very much in doubt.[17]

Across the state line in the Dakotas, the Native communities confronted similar challenges to their lives and lands. Again cattle ranching appeared as a natural outlet for socialization and economic development. Again the people faced one attempt after another to reduce or eliminate their landholdings. Again we must understand that the Indians did not win all of these modern wars. But it is startling that they won at all.

Hoxie's analysis of the changing scene at Cheyenne River illustrates a larger pattern within the region before World War I. The people were not able to prevent the opening of the reservation to white homesteading in 1908, but they did protest vehemently against the imposed incision on the land that potentially had reduced Cheyenne landholdings in half. And they united against Sen. Robert Gamble's bid to make available all unallotted land. Ed Swan from Cherry Creek, Oliver Black Eagle from Thunder Butte, Bazille Claymore from the Agency District, Straight Head, probably from White Horse, and Charles Jewett made the trek to Washington and hurled six counterproposals at the commissioner of Indian affairs. The Gamble bill languished and died. Another battle had been won. The people would continue.[18] How would they use their land?

The Cheyenne River reservation had not been established officially until 1889 in the wake of the agreement that fractured the great Sioux reservation and threw open to white settlement millions of acres in the West River country. Over a decade before, the people living near the government agency obtained their first cattle. The four bands—Two Kettle, Blackfeet, Sans Arc, and Minneconjou—that were to comprise the reservation population each received their share of the 450 heifers and 4 bulls. Using a ratio of one cow to about every 17 people, the Two Kettles obtained 186 cows for their 122 families, the Blackfeet received 57 cows for 42 families, the Sans Arc received 85 cows for their 55 families, and the Minneconjou families received 122 cows for their 87 families. From this initial bequest in 1877, supplemented by natural increase and two more purchases, the herd had grown to almost 2,000 head by the middle of 1879.[19]

The inauguration of the Cheyenne River cattle industry followed the advice of agents stationed at the agency who cautioned Washington that the land was much better for ranching than farming. Some limited farming did take place, basically because federal employees kept receiving directives from the Potomac insisting that it be encouraged. No rain in the summer, grasshoppers, and disinterest killed most of the crops. Once in the proverbial blue moon, Native farmers enjoyed a banner year. In 1885, Cheyenne River farms raised 750 bushels of wheat, 8,000 bushels of corn, 6,000 bushels of potatoes, 7,000 bushels of that old favorite, turnips, 800 bushels of onions, 200 bushels of beans and other vegetables, 180,000 melons, and 180,000 pumpkins. However, that bounty surfaced in an extraordinary year, one whose conditions should have prompted even more of a harvest. The degree to which Agent Charles McChesney had been impressed may be surmised by his recommendation in his report for 1887. He advised the government to focus its effort completely on cattle ranching. A little subsistence farming would be fine. He cited the traditional laundry list: the hot winds of July and August dried and burned up the crops, too little rain, irrigation too costly, and frequent wind- and hailstorms.[20]

For a time the government heeded McChesney's counsel. It imported purebred cattle. The agency itself provided an immediate market for Cheyenne River beef. Of the two million pounds consumed at the reservation in 1980, one-fourth of the total came from Sioux cattle. Herds continued to grow, and Indian cowboys gained more valuable experience in the industry. Some took part in the great roundup of 1902. Others, often "mixed-blood" ranchers, had become important operators on their own. Pete Dupris's Circle D, Narcisse Narcelle's NSS, and Felix Benoit's LB ranch numbered among the most successful.[21]

Unfortunately, federal wisdom intervened at the expense of native ranching. The Interior Department agreed to lease reservation land to non-Indian companies. By 1904, the Matador Land and Cattle Company of Texas had arrived, and its brand, the Drag V, soon spotted the northeast section of the reserve. The company paid just three and a half cents an acre. They also drove 16,000 head of cattle onto Cheyenne River just as quickly as possible.[22]

The Turkey Track leased the southeast section, almost 500,000 acres, at the same basement price. By 1907, even with this deal, the Diamond A Cattle Company purchased the Turkey Track and eventually doubled the herd to 20,000 head. Combined with the Sword and Dagger, the HO, and the 73, little land remained for Native cattlemen. At the outbreak of World War I, the wave of homesteading farmers had swept into western South Dakota, and coupled with bad weather and falling prices, all cattlemen were in trouble.[23] Cap Mossman, who ran the Diamond A cattle, still wanted his lease renewed in 1920. Naturally, given poor market conditions, he did not want his leasing rate raised. Sells, the commissioner of Indian affairs, took Mossman's side. Perhaps more than any other commissioner, Sells expedited the separation of Indians from their land base.[24] Writing to Cheyenne River Superintendent James M. McGregor in 1920, Sells contended,

> Many reservations in the Northwest are disposing of their surplus lands at this time, either by allotment or otherwise. It is presumed that Cheyenne River, being similarly situated, will, in all probability, follow the same course within the next two or three years. In view of this and the extremely demoralized condition of the cattle business at the present time, it was decided to grant without delay the application of Messrs. Mossman and Zimmerman for the extension of their permits at the same rate per head as paid now.[25]

Sells made his decision despite good advice to the contrary. McGregor responded four days later that the Mossman and Zimmerman leases made up "a very large part of the reservation and naturally cause more or less agitation and unrest among the Indians who are really interested in the stock industry, but it especially gives the political element of the Indian population an opportunity to agitate."[26]

Federal employees at Cheyenne River indeed had been getting an earful about the abuses and problems of the leasing program. At a meeting held on September 20, 1920, at the agency, about twenty-five Cheyenne River Sioux let themselves be heard. Red

Eagle said the benefits from leasing were "very small, not enough to bother with." He wanted the leases stopped. Red Eagle and others blamed loss of their own stock on the lessees, while government men believed that Sioux desires for greater control of their own lands were simply illusions. The remaining tribal lands undoubtedly would soon be thrown open to white settlement. A memorandum on grazing at Cheyenne River dated December 4, 1920, put it bluntly, speaking of "the final disposition of the tribal property of the tribe." "It is believed," the memorandum stated in its finest bureaucratese, "that the final disposition of the remaining tribal lands and the opening of the reservation should not be delayed longer than two years from the present time—in fact, the period of two years is mentioned only because that is probably the shortest period in which the necessary steps can be taken to accomplish that end." It concluded, "If it could be accomplished sooner it should be done."[27]

Although giving the lessees credit for keeping fences repaired, conserving water, prosecuting cattle thieves, and destroying coyotes and wolves, the memorandum also acknowledged the impact of the leasing program on the attempts by Cheyenne River Sioux to further their own cattle business. "Some complaints have been made that the running of the steers on these ranges is detrimental to their success in the cattle business because" Indian cattle are "more apt to stray from their home locations than would otherwise be the case. This is undoubtedly true in some instances." The memorandum then suggested that better attention and cooperation would remedy the situation in the future.[28] This acknowledgment by McGregor and the anonymous author of the memorandum, however, speaks to the kind of problem that leasing clearly posed for the development of a Native cattle business.

Given federal commitments to leasing as a national policy, the Cheyenne River pattern would be replicated elsewhere in the Dakotas. On Pine Ridge, the Oglala Sioux had moved on from the trauma of Wounded Knee. In the 1890s, Agent Charles G. Penney argued for maintenance of a tribally owned land base and pushed specifically for cattle ranching as the best use of that acreage. Interest in this enterprise appeared to grow annually. By 1901, Pine Ridge Sioux cattle holdings had reached 19,000; the following year they could count 31,000 head.[29]

After a decade of general growth, prosperity, and optimism, the 1910s marked a downturn in the Pine Ridge cattle industry. Leasing began to envelop the reservation; discouraged Sioux ranchers sold their cattle for good prices and got out of the business. As of 1917, the large outside cattle companies had taken control, as they had elsewhere. So much for the promising start.[30]

John Glover, who served as range manager of the 7L at Porcupine and who eventually obtained his own land at Pine Ridge, remembered that the government had supervised the Sioux cattle business. "The Indians run a round-up wagon of their own to brand the calves," he recalled, "and sell old cows and steers like any other ranch operation." Glover suggested that "winter loss" and "various things that beset big herds of early day open range operations" caused Sioux cattle to dwindle in numbers until they were almost gone by the time of the First World War. Glover's interpretation is convenient: the war made federal officials worry about having food, and with the land idle the decision was made to lease the land "to produce more beef."[31]

You can hear his voice rising on the page: "I want to say right here the Indian Department OK'd these leases and practically all the Indian land owners were satisfied with the leasing because they needed the money the leases would bring them." Practically all. "These lease contracts," he insisted, "were very tough on the cowman." Leases had to be paid a year ahead of time, one had to be bonded for the full five-year term, and one had to fence the land, drill wells, build dams, develop springs for stock water, and not run too many animals. Glover does not mention the amount of the lease and does not address the obvious: such improvements were in the interest of the cattle companies. He does admit that "a number of Indians made good cowboys and worked with the wagon as long as the 7L operated there."[32]

Many Pine Ridge Lakotas became cowboys. Working for the 7L outfit of the Newcastle Land and Cattle Company were Walter Ten Fingers, Thomas Black Wolf, Alex Pablo (who also translated for John Glover), George Mesteth, George Two Two, Sam Rabbit, Albert Pourier, Jim Bring Plenty, Bob Council, Charlie Rock, Charlie Twiss, and a good many more. Glover lists them with non-Indian cowboys without distinguishing between them. He also contends that the older Indians and the older non-Indian cowboys had "a certain affinity" between them, "from the mere fact that they were both outdoor people, both loved a horse, and loved to get on that horse and chase something, preferably a cow or buffalo." There is that commonality straight-forwardly expressed. Like many of the old-time cattlemen, Glover also admired the patriotism of Indians. He especially respected the many volunteers for World War I, when Indians were not eligible for the draft. George White Bull of the Porcupine area volunteered for the war, and Glover gave him a job with the 7L outfit as soon as he returned; White Bull, just for good measure, served in the Second World War as well.[33]

At the neighboring reservation of Rosebud, the Brule Lakota also turned to cattle ranching in the late nineteenth century. Although the people had some animals prior to the Ghost Dance movement, the real beginnings of ranching occurred after 1890. Agent Wright promoted the evolution. He established farming districts at Rosebud, employing a farmer and an Indian assistant to oversee farming and ranching. The two activities could reinforce each other; if one had grown sufficient alfalfa to produce an adequate supply of hay to get cattle through the winter, then one could receive cattle purchased for the tribe. The summer of 1892 brought more rain than usual, encouraging the grass and the hay. The people obtained more than 2,000 head of cattle that year, with each animal getting two brands—a number for the Lakota owner and the ID brand.[34]

The first years appeared encouraging. The Rosebud Sioux lost just 4 percent of their cattle the first winter. Federal officials continued to buy beef, and the Rosebud cattle offered a ready supply. Even with the initial enthusiasm for the industry, familiar problems surfaced. Without a fence on the reservation's southern boundary, Indian cattle wandered right into Nebraska. Nebraska cattlemen requested a ransom before returning the strays. Some Lakotas killed their cattle to have beef for feasts. Wright particularly frowned on veal being provided at such gatherings and threatened punishment for the slaughter of calves. Rustling also presented a recurring dilemma.[35]

Trespass increased as a scourge as the decade progressed. The former Pine Ridge agent, Charles McChesney, succeeded Wright in the summer of 1896 and immediately faced hundreds, if not thousands, of illegal cattle. The spring roundup of the following year gave McChesney the chance to make his presence known; he nabbed almost 500 head of cattle that should have been somewhere else. He even employed a fellow from the Missouri River Livestock Association who knew a thing or two about brands to keep an eye of things. And the Rosebud people showed their displeasure over trespassing by denying their approval of a cattle trail in the western part of the reserve.[36]

Despite such precautions and protests, the situation worsened. The 1899 roundup turned up more than 5,000 transpassing cattle. Furious, the Rosebud Sioux balked at additional leasing. McChesney thought there was enough land to permit more leasing and no doubt felt pressure from Washington and local and regional cattle interests to overturn popular Indian sentiment. By February 1904, the dogged McChesney had convinced a majority of the Rosebud Sioux to change their minds. Simultaneously, Major McLaughlin made Rosebud a stop on his victory tour of Indian country. He used the *Lone Wolf* decision as a battering ram against Native resistance. Cessions carved out of Rosebud in 1904 and again in 1907, together with the ravages of allotment, contributed mightily to the avalanche of Rosebud land loss. The reservation shrank by two-thirds over forty years. From 3,228,161 acres in 1889, Rosebud shriveled to 1,093,000 acres by the New Deal.[37]

Rosebud cattle ranchers did the best they could under the

circumstances. They built fences and corrals. Brule cowboys worked on leases. A number of them participated in the famous roundup of cattle in 1902. Some of the most successful Rosebud ranchers were of mixed descent, with a working knowledge of English and Lakota and of the cultural practices of each world. One such individual, William W. Jordan, was the son of Charles P. Jordan, a native of Ohio, and Julia Walks First, an Oglala. Charles Jordan came west to Fort Robinson in 1874, where his brother served as an officer at the post. Charles gained an appointment as chief clerk for the quartermaster department and later moved to the Red Cloud Agency in Nebraska to work as head clerk. Eventually, he became a rancher south of Wood on his second wife's land in Mellette County. His first wife, also an Oglala, died in childbirth; his second wife, Julia, and he had nine children. One of them, Edwin, drowned in the dam near the family ranch in 1905, when in the process of helping with a roundup, he tried to swim his horse across it. William Jordan homesteaded near his father's land and prospered for a time by purchasing cattle issued to Indians in the White Thunder Creek area. The Rosebud superintendent charged him with monopolizing the ID cattle by buying them under market value and denied him a permit. Jordan charged the government with forcing Indian cattle owners out of the business.[38]

Other Rosebud men worked as cowboys. Sam Yellow Robe, born on June 26, 1890, in the Lower Cut Meat community near Parmelee, South Dakota, left school in 1906 to work for the 6L Cattle Company in the Interior area. Returning home, in the following year he became a cowboy for the H E Cattle Company. Yellow Robe worked for years for the H E, riding fence, and on at least one occasion, in 1911, he went over to Pine Ridge as the company's representative to check out the roundup there. Sam White Horse also was a cowboy during this era. Born in Mellette County on March 17, 1897, he went to school in Rapid City and Pierre, before leaving in 1912 to work on the spring roundup. At this time the county had been divided into six districts, and each had a wagon roundup for Spring Creek or Rosebud, Parmelee,

Norris, White Thunder or Ponca, Wood or Butte Creek, and White River. White Horse remembered not only an ID brand but also a TID brand, for Trust Indian Department.[39] Perhaps, although it reminds one of the BIA brand used in the 1930s, which one Indian solemnly insisted stood for "Bosses Indians Around."

Here, too, the races, parades, and rodeos became cherished in the collective memory. Some of the Lakota cowboys gained considerable renown. Perhaps the most famous of his day, George Defender, born in 1891, learned his skills as a cowboy on the Standing Rock reservation, working for the DZ, L7, and ZT companies. By 1914, he won first place as a bronc rider at the Miles City Roundup. His career eventually took him to all the big rodeos, from the plains country all the way to Madison Square Garden. He rode some amazing horses, blessed with wonderful names: Tipperary, Sky Rocket, Black Diamond, Spinning Boy, Heart River Croppy, Leave Me with a Smile, Grand River Blue, Z Horse, and Golden Rule. David Blue Thunder, born on November 15, 1891, the son of John Blue Thunder and White Buffalo Woman, shared his brothers' and sister's interest in horses and cattle. He took particular pleasure in raising horses to compete in the relay races at the Frontier Days in White River. In addition to winning first place money in that event, he was an accomplished bronc rider and entered other races in Murdo, Winner, and Parmelee, South Dakota, as well as Cody and Valentine, Nebraska.[40]

Rodeos and celebrations took place both off and on the reservation. One flyer in 1897 proclaimed, "The greatest celebration that ever occurred on an Indian Reservation will be held on the Rosebud Reservation one mile from the Agency beginning July 1st and continuing until the 6th during which time all kinds of Indian sports, dances, sham battles, games and races will be given by the Indians." Several events catch one's eye. All of July 3 was devoted to the Corn and White Buffalo dances. The program makes note of contemporary BIA policy discouraging tribal ceremonies: "These Dances having been prohibited, special

FIG. 6. The Rosebud Reservation Rodeo drew a full house in the 1930s. Illustration by Andrew Standing Soldier in *The Grass Mountain Mouse*, reprint edition, 1954, p. 56.

permission has been granted to have these occur on this day for the last time." July 5 began with a parade, with music by the Rosebud Cornet Band and a reading of the Declaration of Independence.

The six-day event concluded with "bronco" and wild steer riding and five races: a one-mile footrace, half- and quarter-mile horse races, a 200-yard footrace, and a "slow horse race." The one-mile race offered the top prize of $15. And on the sixth day, following a drill by the Indian police, a sham battle imitating the Custer fight was reenacted, with the "Indian police" and "Mixed Bloods against Full Bloods." Six thousand Indians attended the festivities, organized by Reuben Quick Bear and photographed by John Anderson.[41]

Despite such events and the interest so many displayed in cattle ranching at Rosebud, the same reversal occurred on this reservation as on other northern plains reservations. The increase in leasing, bad winters, and unfavorable market conditions combined to discourage even the hardiest Native rancher. Under the administration of Commissioner Valentine, the situation worsened considerably. World War I ushered in high prices for beef. Most Rosebud residents sold their cattle. More than 25,000 head of cattle disappeared, and by the end of the decade the tribal cattle business had died. Leasing offered some money, but it was a pale substitute for the dream of a self-sufficient Native enterprise.[42]

The small Lower Brule reservation in central South Dakota imitated the story of larger Sioux communities in the state. Henry Livingstone, an agent appointed in the early 1870s who had been a physician at the bordering Crow Creek reservation, knew the country and knew the odds on transforming the residents of Lower Brule into successful farmers. He wrote to Washington, recommending an emphasis on cattle ranching. As he put it in his annual report, "If they can be induced to care for cows as faithfully as they do their ponies, they would in a very short time become successful stock growers."[43] Washington, however, demurred.

By the time William Dougherty had replaced Livingstone in 1878, the Lower Brules had more horses but not more cows. There were plenty of cattle in the neighborhood. Unfortunately, they belonged to outsiders. Equally unfortunate, said outsiders proved determined to graze on reservation grass without paying fees. If they were delivering cattle for beef rations, it made it difficult to argue with them, and they did not always turn out to be the most cordial lot in any event. Dougherty was not much more sanguine than his predecessor about the Brule Sioux as future farmers of America, and the meager yields at harvest time bore out his somber commentary, even if he believed farming a good idea.[44]

Crow Creek and Lower Brule sometimes had one agent and sometimes two. When there was but one, he tended to pay more attention to Crow Creek. Despite such benign neglect under Agent W. W. Anderson in the mid-1880s, residents of Lower Brule made a modest beginning in the cattle industry. They did not eat all of their ration cattle but put aside a few and inaugurated two tiny herds, at times using the Medicine Creek and Little Bend areas for pasturage. Without any prompting, let alone assistance, from Washington, the people began to try to make a go of it.

Their quiet determination ran into prevailing federal policy. The late 1880s, of course, witnessed the Allotment Act and general pressure on plains reservations to allot or cede their lands. New towns along transportation routes, such as Hayes, Kennebec, Midland, and Presho, sprang up. Never destined to be major metropolises, they nonetheless signaled the advance of white settlement and the expectation that the entire reserve soon would be a thing of the past.[45]

Relentless winters in 1896 and 1897 killed off most of the Lower Brule cattle. Lacking help from the Bureau of Indian Affairs, the people were sufficiently desperate that, at least according to the latest agent, in 1900 they were willing to give up 50,000 acres to gain the necessary money to fence the reservation and buy more cattle. The alert reader will have already guessed it: James McLaughlin had been here, too. April 1906 marked final passage of the act opening over 55,000 acres to homesteaders. The deal resembled Wind River and other cessions of the time; land was set aside, and the Indians were to receive from $1.25 to $2.50 per acre, depending on the judged quality.

However, by this point toward the closing of that proverbial frontier, homesteading often resembled more a trickle than a flood. Proceeds dribbled into the tribal coffers, and purchases of cattle proceeded with deliberate speed. R. H. Somers, now the agent, reported in 1907 the acquisition of 474 heifers and 24 bulls. Almost 5,000 other head of cattle were also now on Lower Brule courtesy of permits approved by Somers. Such an arrangement raked in a paltry sum of $6 per capita, but naturally it did not expedite growth of the Native cattle industry.[46]

Nonetheless, the Lower Brules held 825 cattle and over 1,000 horses in 1909; at that time, 2,050 cows and 68 bulls were brought in to the reservation. Somers preferred that cattle be distributed among the people on a per capita division, regardless of family size or quality of agricultural or grazing land. Such arbitrary planning made for simple arithmetic but did not reflect good judgment, let alone knowledge of ranching. Each family seemed limited to small herds, if they wished to participate in the business at all.

Events and priorities of the 1910s exacted the same toll at Lower Brule that they did elsewhere in the Dakotas. Ernest Schusky concludes, "the reasons the Indians failed to become cattle ranchers are far from clear" but then proceeds to suggest why they could not reach this goal in this instance. White competition did not allow the Native industry to develop, agents did not know much about the business, and immediate cultural demands for sharing and generosity cut against long-term planning and growth of individual herds.[47]

The government made sporadic attempts to bolster Native ranching. The report of a special investigator, C. M. Knight, in 1917 revealed the purchase of 55 two-year-old heifers in 1913, with 500 heifers and 55 bulls bought in 1914. In 1917, 75 additional bulls augmented the Lower Brule holdings. The government and the tribe had invested $64,221 during this five-year period. So far, so good. But, Knight said, "the herd should have totaled twice as much; moreover the excess numbers of bulls indicated poor management. In addition, heifers often were bred at the wrong time of year; feed was inadequate; the manager was inexperienced; shelters were poorly constructed; cows were not culled; and Indians probably stole calves for their individual herds."[48]

Like Pine Ridge, high cattle prices following World War I, together with the internal problems depicted above, inspired most Lower Brule cattle ranchers to sell and get out of the business. Three agents in three years did little to slow down the process. E. M. Garber in 1918 said the tribal herd ought to be sold. C. H. Gensler arrived in 1920, replacing F. Campbell, and seized on the losses incurred in the 1919–20 winter as reason enough to abandon cattle ranching. Gensler preferred farming to ranching. He also did not mind leasing. All in all, it spelled doom for most of the Lower Brules who, despite everything and everyone who had conspired against them, had hoped to persist in the business.[49]

A final example, although not the last that could be cited, comes from Fort Berthold in North Dakota. As described in the remarkable volume presenting the memoirs of a Hidatsa family, *The Way to Independence*, the Hidatsas told a story about the origins of cattle.

Only Man and First Creator, the first two beings on earth, split up the job of creation. They made the river and the plains and the creation. To populate them, First Creator made the buffalo. But Only Man picked up a dead wolf and created a white man and the spotted cows the white man raised. When First Creator saw what Only Man had done he said, "You are foolish to make these things." The white men were a queer kind of men, — they will always be greedy! And the spotted cows all had short hair, too short to protect them from the winter. "That is so," said Only Man; and so he opened

FIG. 7. Cattle helped feed the people. On the Fort Berthold reservation in North Dakota and on other reservations in the plains, family members helped dry meat. Photo by Gilbert Livingston Wilson. Gilbert Livingston Wilson Photography Collection, Minnesota Historical Society (Photo #IV-52-1910).

a hole in the earth and sent all the spotted cattle down underground. "But," he said, "when the buffalo are all gone they will come again and cover this earth as buffaloes did."[50]

As with the Navajo story about their acquisition of sheep, the addition of cattle is linked culturally to cultural heroes rather than to Euro-American intruders. It provides a bridge from dim past to demanding present. It approves this transition and offers optimism when that commodity is much needed.

In this Missouri River country of west central North Dakota,

FIG. 8. Hidatsa cowboys at Fort Berthold branding cattle, 1915. Photo by Gilbert Livingston Wilson. Gilbert Livingston Wilson Photography Collection, Minnesota Historical Society (Photo #VIII-4-15).

Fort Berthold included three Native communities: Hidatsa, Arikara, and Mandan. By the late nineteenth century, the first two had become larger than the third, so decimated by the smallpox epidemic in the late 1830s. Their remaining lands were better for ranching than farming, even if the peoples historically had been skilled farmers in the short growing seasons of this northern region. The government officials had pushed agriculture; the people liked horses and after a while, cattle, too.

The Hidatsas did not want to make big profits from their herds. They liked being able to kill a cow and share the meat with their friends. They liked the social dimensions of the roundup. Families would camp and wait for the younger men to ride out, find the cattle, and drive them back to the corrals where they would be branded. The old men eagerly awaited the arrival of the young men and the animals, no doubt remembering the buffalo hunts of old and the good feeling of riding fast against the sun and wind.[51]

The sale of cattle offered opportunities for some money and some adventure. Within a decade of the introduction of cattle by federal officials, some of the people of Fort Berthold were disdaining the offers of local non-Indian ranchers and checking out greener pastures in the urban Midwest. Men such as Wolf Chief and Water Chief and Henry Bad Gun and Louis Baker drove cattle to Hebron's railroad stockyard, "where the stock commissioner counted the cattle onto the train. The men rode in the caboose, sleeping on bare board shelves that served for bunks. A German livestock dealer from Hebron named Charlie Weigel went along to translate for them."[52]

The group rode to St. Paul, anticipating the end of the journey and a satisfactory price. Maybe the price was not quite what they had hoped for, or just maybe they were having a good time. Maybe they heard prices were better in Chicago. Maybe they heard other stories about Chicago and just were not sure when they would have another chance to go there. Weigel later insisted that they went to Chicago because he had discovered higher prices there. Maybe.

They reboarded *ma'ti aku tidia*, the boat that runs. Weigel later recalled, "There was a bad hill there and our train got stuck. . . . We stopped a little while till another engine pushed us up. Then he went awful fast, . . . kind of dangerous and pretty near we went off our seats." They did make it to Chicago and visited the stockyard and facilities of Swift & Company, where they witnessed firsthand the kind of scenes that Upton Sinclair immortalized. They went to Lake Michigan, by far the biggest body of water any of them had ever seen.[53]

FIG. 9. Hidatsa cowboys displaying varying degrees of enthusiasm, 1916. Photo by Gilbert Livingston Wilson. Gilbert Livingston Wilson Photography Collection, Minnesota Historical Society (Photo #IV-25-1916).

And they observed another dimension of the white world, largely shielded from them up to now. They saw poverty and, moreover, a lack of the kind of generosity and reciprocity they valued so much among themselves.

Back of a hotel in Chicago they threw old foods that they did not want any more on their tables. I saw some poor women, dirty and in rags, take off the covers of the cans, and they took out the food to eat. I said to myself, "These poor white women must be hungry," and I did not understand how this could be in Chicago where there was so much food. If an Indian man is hungry, no matter what he has done or how foolish he has acted, we will always give him food. That is our custom. There are many white customs which I do not understand and which puzzle me very much.[54]

On the way home after getting checks for their cattle, they stayed in St. Paul for three more days. They lobbied for treaty money that was overdue. But they also had more chances to see the women and men of the city and to eat beefsteak and eggs with just about every meal. Wolf Chief came home, distributed the money, and promptly gave a feast. He was happy. And yes, he went back to Chicago. In 1915, before the hard times came, the Hidatsas had 2,596 cattle and 3,274 horses. And more stories to tell.[55]

On reservation after reservation in this era, cattle ranching obviously represented the best chance for native communities to build a local economy and rebuild a society. The photographs, oral histories, and other documents from the time all testify to the appeal of the new pastime. Even with the discouragements and disappointments of the era, the hope remained that cattle ranching would persist in the years to come. The involvement in ranching had helped to bridge the transition from treaties and agreements and the early reservation days to the final years of an assimilationist era. They could be like white men and not be white men. They were finding new ways to remain Indians.

FIG. 10. A young Hidatsa cowboy with angora goatskin chaps and, perhaps, a patient relative, 1916. Photo by Gilbert Livingston Wilson. Gilbert Livingston Wilson Photography Collection, Minnesota Historical Society (Photo #VIII-22-1916).

CHAPTER FIVE

Indian Cattle Ranching in Oklahoma and the Southwest

BESIDES THE NORTHERN PLAINS, THE OTHER REGION of major significance for its development of Indian cattle ranching was the area extending from Arizona to Oklahoma. There are those individuals who cavalierly refer to this portion of the United States as the Southwest, but Arizonans know better. When James Gregory refers to Oklahomans as southwesterners in his *American Exodus*, an otherwise fine book, it is enough to cause true southwesterners genuine discomfort. Thus in speaking of Oklahoma and the Southwest here, it should be clear that one does not really belong to the other. Initially, then, we need to consider the experience of Oklahoma and then turn to the true Southwest, which includes Arizona and New Mexico and one adds hesitantly, perhaps on probationary status, the immediate area around El Paso, Texas.

As noted in chapter 3, the Five Tribes in Indian Territory held considerable expectations for the development of a Native cattle industry. With the onrush of non-Indians into the territory in the late 1800s, that dream ran headlong into the harsh reality of competing dreams possessed by the newcomers. Leasing of tribal lands to those outsiders temporarily provided a fair amount of income to tribal members. In time, resentment against large cattle company interests combined with the unfettered anticipations of incipient farmers and ranchers to make large-scale cattle leasing more untenable. In addition, leasing represented a kind of easy way out. It worked against individual and group ambitions by yielding money without efforts; it denied land to those within Indian communities who wanted to farm or ranch.[1] Leasing also promoted factionalism. "Full-bloods" particularly distrusted the practice, sensing its potential for trespass, corruption, and the infiltration of unwanted and unneeded influences and practices.

A glance at the map of Indian country in Oklahoma soon after statehood or today confirms the kind of avalanche that buried it. Without the protection afforded by reservation status, Indian landholders were largely victimized by land allotment and sale. Within a generation the Native estate had been drastically reduced. In the period prior to statehood, nonetheless, there are examples of individual Indian ranchers who enjoyed fleeting success and prosperity.

Wilson Nathaniel Jones may have not been "the Indian cattle king of the territory," as William Savage remarks in his brief overview of Native ranching in Oklahoma during this time. However, he certainly is an interesting sort of Indian capitalist who saw in cattle ranching one of several ways to exercise his entrepreneurial talents. Born in Mississippi in 1827, Jones came west as did so many of the tribe, forced out of their home country in the removal era. First a farmer, then the operator of a general store, his initial entrance into the cattle business proved disastrous. His supposed partner, James Myers, sold the 1,000 head of cattle the two men had purchased and vanished with the proceeds. Wiser but undeterred, Jones eventually prospered after the Civil War. In the final decade of the century, he could boast of 5,000 head of cattle among his many holdings. Serving as principal chief of the Choctaws from 1890 to 1894, he demonstrated that success in business often translated into political success as well.[2]

Other prominent men among the Five Nations parlayed cattle business profits into active careers that brought them renown. Among the Creek Nation, William Fisher at one time owned 2,000 head of cattle; Judge David Carr, 1,200 head; Samuel W. Brown, 800 head; and Judge Elijah Permigine Lerblance, not only a wonderful name but 2,500 head. James Dandridge Willison may be included among those Creeks who owned considerable pasturage and rented it out to others. Cherokee Principal Chief Joel Mayes, Cherokee Treasurer DeWitt Clinton Lipe, Chickasaw Governor William L. Byrd, Creek Principal Chief L. C. Perryman and his brothers, Thomas Ward Perryman and George B. Perryman, all were involved in the cattle industry during this period. However, their considerable acumen and achievements could not withstand the tide of buyers and ranchers who poured into Indian Territory and ultimately overcame Native resistance.[3] They gained access and generally title to most of the land that members of the Five Tribes had wanted to keep perpetually as tribal estate.

Plains Indians to the west in what became Oklahoma may have come from a different cultural tradition, but they would confront a common dilemma. The lands of the Cheyenne-Arapaho reservation and the acreage within the Kiowa, Comanche, and Kiowa-Apache reservation offered grass as attractive as that to be found in the other major target, the Cherokee Outlet. Nonetheless, for a short period of time, government personnel attempted to foster the cattle industry among the Cheyennes and Arapahos on their reservation in the southwestern portion of Indian Territory. They did so for the reasons the attempt was made to the north: the land was better suited for ranching than for farming, and the men were far more interested in cattle than corn. Agent John D. Miles concluded that a white man would "starve to death if placed on 160 acres or even a section of the lands in this country." Already Arapaho leaders such as Powder Face, Left Hand, Yellow Bear, and Curley had taken the cattle given them by federal funds and bred them to bulls provided by A. E. Reynolds, the local trader at Fort Supply. By 1880, the Arapahos had 3,000 head of cattle, almost ten times the total of the initial purchase of 325 in 1877.[4]

Such headway and Miles's good judgment ran counter to the prevailing wisdom in Washington that preached corn rather than cattle; the agent and the Indians received precious little help in the promotion of ranching. Washington's attitude irked John H. Seger, too. Seger, who ran the Cheyenne-Arapaho Manual Training and Labor School, had chosen to stress the raising of cattle and hogs, to be owned in common by the boys at the institution. Seger's success demonstrated the practicality of livestock and the interest the young Cheyennes and Arapahos had in the enterprise. However, after the government invested in the school herd and had been advised of the good use of its investment, it promptly demanded that the so-called mission herd be divided up and given to the reservation populace.[5]

As Miles and Seger predicted ruefully, such a dispersal undermined the base of the school herd, was quickly dissipated by the immediate needs of the people, and defied common sense. Cheyennes and Arapahos received only a few head per family. They ate or sold the cattle. If, as Miles had argued, the herd could have been allowed to expand to 15,000 head, young people could have been given eventually 30 or so head when they had finished their schooling. Wanting to generate income and demonstrate the viability of cattle ranching, Miles turned to leasing reservation land to outside cattle interests. By the middle of the 1880s, non-Indian cattlemen must have assumed that out of sight of the Potomac they must have been also out of mind. Emboldened by large leases and relatively lax enforcement, they succumbed to an understandable temptation to graze more cattle on their lease than they should have and to graze additional cattle on unleased land whenever they could. For a few years, they must have grown more smug by the month. Lack of people to back up paper proclamations or faint federal edicts called up images of distant, effete bureaucrats. Finally the federal government got tough; in 1885, President Grover Cleveland stepped in and said, "Out. All cattle, all horses, all property on the reservations must go. All leases are void. Out. You have forty days."[6]

Fine. There remained one small detail. By this time more than 200,000 head of cattle were ensconced on the Cheyenne-Arapaho reserve, and thousands more were grazing on the Kiowa, Comanche, and Kiowa-Apache lands. The government succeeded in removing the animals, but the cattlemen, not too surprisingly, had insufficient time to relocate their animals and brace for what turned out to be a horrendous winter. With the floodgates opening in the run of 1889 and subsequent land rushes, Carl Tyson concludes that "the day of the cattleman in the Indian territory was gone forever."[7]

Quanah Parker would not have agreed with that assertion. The same scenario had been played out on the Kiowa and Comanche reservations during the early years of the 1880s. Quanah, as he has become more properly known, numbered among those who used changing times to propel himself to a position of leadership. The son of a captive white woman, he gained an understanding of both worlds. Quanah understood in time that the cattle interests could not be denied entirely and came to advocate leasing tribal lands. More Comanches than Kiowas favored leasing, and Quanah had to endure a variety of taunts from those who opposed leasing and who disliked him. He persisted, however, and in addition to trying to make room for other people's cattle, he started to find room for some of his own.[8]

Using stock provided by the government and other cattle offered to him by the Texas ranchers who sought access to reservation land, by 1884, Quanah had started his own modest herd. By 1886, he claimed 425 head of cattle, 200 hogs, and 60 horses; as with so many other Indian communities, the horses symbolized wealth and offered pleasure more than utility. As his life and career progressed, Quanah exemplified the kind of amalgam that

FIG. 11. Quanah Parker, Comanche cattle rancher, and his wife To-nar-cy, 1901. Archives and Manuscript Division of the Oklahoma Historical Society (Photo #6471).

the new day encouraged. He remained proud of being Comanche and being an Indian; he served as a tribal leader and an influential advocate of the Native American Church. At once both conservative and progressive, Quanah like other Indian cattlemen reminds us by his actions and words that such labels were relatively meaningless in the context of the era.[9]

Although by far the most publicized of the Comanches who became involved in the cattle business, Quanah was hardly alone in his interest in it. Given the tradition of Comanche pastoralism, as with other Plains Indian groups, the transition from bison to cattle made cultural as well as economic sense.[10] Other Comanches and a smaller number of Kiowas worked as cowboys or held relatively small herds of cattle. The government represented an immediate market for local Indian beef, and again as elsewhere, having access to beef cattle allowed for demonstration of generosity and reciprocity. Yet the same scythe cut across potential ambition and dreams; the Jerome Agreement, negotiated in 1892 and finally ratified in 1900, opened most of the reservation. The occasion of Lone Wolf's protests, made famous through the *Lone Wolf v. Hitchcock* decision of 1903, the Jerome Agreement not only reduced the Native land base but paved the way for subsequent congressional action that splintered and reduced remaining tribal acreage. The paltry allotments with which the people were left hardly permitted the evolution of a significant cattle ranching industry among the Indians.[11]

Within the true Southwest, the picture appeared brighter for the evolution of Native cattle ranching. Although other Indian communities raised livestock in the late nineteenth century, three particularly significant examples of Indian cattle ranching may be analyzed for this area during this time. The Tohono O'odham community along the Mexican border, the San Carlos Apaches, and the Apaches of the White Mountain or Fort Apache reservation present important case studies of the promise of the industry. Unlike Oklahoma, Arizona remained relatively lightly populated by non-Indians until after the turn of the century. Thus, tribes in the territory—Arizona did not receive statehood until Valentine's Day, 1912—had a better chance of avoiding land allotment, let alone the complete dismantling of their reserves. Even as late as the 1910s, Indian reservations were being established in Arizona; in fact, the largest of the three Tohono O'odham tracts would be formally created in 1917. All three of the reservations to be discussed were large, with the Apaches possessing especially good grazing land. As we have already noted, Indian lands in the territory surely faced challenge. Nonetheless, time and circumstances proved kinder to the Indians of Arizona than the Indians of Oklahoma.

Unlike the Apaches, the Tohono O'odham had considerable experience in working with cattle by the time of the American era. However, as Rolf Bauer and other students of the subject have observed, long acquaintance did not mean that cattle ranching as the term is normally understood was universal among the people. Some of the cattle brought in originally through the Spanish padres had become wild, more prey to be hunted than animals to be domesticated. Yet by the years after the Civil War, the Tohono O'odham clearly were making a transition toward modern cattle ranching. New cattle, tied to the Anglo rather than the Hispanic cattle industry, provided a foundation for a different stage of Native cattle raising. By 1871, the Arizona superintendent of Indian affairs contended the Tohono O'odham were specialists in this field.[12]

Despite all the problems caused by conflict over the range in southern Arizona, the Tohono O'odham persisted in the live-stock business. They did so because the pastime had become important socially and culturally as well as economically. Families raised cattle primarily for subsistence rather than for commercial purposes. Chosen by the older man who reigned as patriarch of the particular Tohono O'odham family, younger men served as cowboys with special responsibility for the family's animals. Most families owned just a small number of cattle.

When the Tohono O'odham lands gained reservation status, presence of federal administration began to alter some cultural patterns. In particular, the stockman employed by the government started to supervise the individuals chosen by different Tohono O'odham villages to be in charge of local roundups and cattle sales. Also a few families in the southern reaches of their country became increasingly interested in the potential of cattle raising as a commercially profitable undertaking. Given the sizable acreage available to such families, by the 1930s, seven or eight family groups had moved vigorously to improve the quality and the quantity of their cattle herds. Such families also seized the opportunity to take advantage of enhanced economic status to hire relatives and to occupy heightened social and cultural positions within the immediate community. This pattern, of course, is reminiscent of the development already described among other native groups.[13]

In her study of cattle raising among the Tohono O'odham published in the mid-1930s, Gwyneth Harrington Xavier discerned that in some portions of the tribe a more individualistic approach had begun to at least partially supersede the old emphasis on family. Those with particular aptitude or greater concern for the industry naturally assumed greater risks and exercised more chances for the accumulation of more cattle and therefore more wealth. Xavier also noted the place of children in the larger distribution of the animals. Boys and girls received heifers, cows, or calves either through inheritance or gifts from family members. They learned responsibility through caring for the cattle as they also gained wealth with the gradual increase in these small herds. At a time when a young woman or man married, she or he might also receive cattle as a gift.[14]

As one might anticipate, such social and cultural forces encouraged not only a growth of interest in the raising of cattle but a natural stake in the growth of the industry. With more cattle, an individual or a family could be more generous or make more money. In turn, despite the size of the Tohono O'odham range, the problem of erosion caused by overgrazing became more apparent by the 1920s. One estimate had 30,000 to 50,000 head of cattle and 8,000 to 10,000 horses on tribal lands by 1914. Any person who has been to this Sonoran country recognizes that if these figures are even close to correct, one has a problem. Consider Bernard Fontana's sparse prose, mirroring the land he describes and loves.

> The Papago country is a stark land. It is desert. . . . There are few trees. There is little underbrush. Giant saguaro cactuses spring skyward from precarious platforms on the sides of chocolate-brown rock hills. Paloverde and mesquite spread their thin shade over arroyos; creosote bushes and bursage provide the only greenery for miles of intermontane valleys.[15]

We are not talking about the flint hills of Kansas or the tall grass country cherished by the Osages near Pawhuska in Oklahoma. This is not country immediately appealing to people just arrived from Grand Rapids or Kalamazoo. It is home to the Tohono O'odham and taken on its own terms, stunningly beautiful. It is also fragile and unforgiving—land easily scarred, land that remembers. Long before contemporary debates about the impact of cattle grazing on public and private lands, people such as the Papagos were being confronted by soil conservationists about the matter. They would be told: you have too many cows; the land has a different carrying capacity; you must reduce the size of your herds. As we shall see, to the Tohono O'odham such an edict would pose a major dilemma. For as the preceding discussion should have illustrated, livestock reduction also meant a reduction in generosity, in status; it threatened the social and cultural order in a fundamental way.[16]

Rations and reservations went together in the late nineteenth century, and the newly created Fort Apache or White Mountain (to use its current name) reserve linked the two from the outset. Established in 1871 by executive order, White Mountain obtained its first cattle from Gen. Oliver Otis Howard but two years later; the provision of beef for the Indians even preceded the executive order. The contractor providing the beef wanted to continue to do it. When Apaches began saving ration tickets in order to purchase cows, he offered only steers. The Indians complained. For once, the government did something about it, issuing about 1,100 head of cattle in 1879 to the jointly administered San Carlos/Fort Apache enclave. Additional cattle were purchased in 1884, primarily being delivered to the San Carlos area. One hundred fifty-five head were diverted to White Mountain. They may have not been of the best quality. A visitor, Robert Frazier, studying reservation conditions for the Board of Indian Commissioners, wryly noted,

> The cattle supply . . . is still a source of considerable merriment to the Indians, who have a keen sense of humor. Any question about it

was sure to provoke their laughter. . . . Alchise [Alchesay] said that "the Great Father sent him up a lot; some were yearlings, others were older than this world, and had not a tooth in their heads. . . . Those that did not die of cold, died of foot disease or of hunger because they had no teeth to eat with."[17]

Apparently of Alchesay's fifteen head of cattle, three died the morning after they had been turned out to pasture, and nine more had succumbed within three days. The remaining three proved wild enough to escape across the reservation boundary to be acquired, Alchesay duly reported, by the local Mormon ranchers.[18] Despite such rather inauspicious beginnings, the cattle business at White Mountain did not vanish. It did not prosper immediately, either, for in the first years of the reservation the Apaches still could hunt. As game decreased, so in due course did the cattle, for the people seemed to get hungrier by the year, with limited rations and a growing population. Washington perhaps heard the pleas of the agent to buy more cattle, but little happened until the arrival in 1901 of C. W. Crouse.[19]

Crouse once described himself in less than glowing terms: "an insignificant, unprepossessingly and ugly old fellow, but under the tough old hide . . . a man who wants to treat you right." Blue-eyes, somewhat balding, and boasting a vintage Victorian mustache, Crouse was not a bad looking fellow.[20] More important, he was one of those relatively rare agents who surmounted his early prejudices against Indians, thought about their best interests, and went to bat for them. Like his counterpart, James Kitch at San Carlos, Crouse made a vital difference in the evolution of a Native cattle industry.

In the twelve years he served as agent at Fort Apache, Crouse faced one challenge after another. There must have been days when he wondered why he had left the low-key delights of being president of the Phoenix Title, Guaranty and Abstract Company. It did not take him long to realize that nearly all of the reservation was good grazing land. It took him even less time to realize that only by freeing the Apaches from dependency on the six-month-a-year ration system could they take the first step toward greater self-sufficiency. Bureau officials in Washington, ever-watchful for opportunities to pare spending, promptly seconded the motion. After an abortive attempt to impose the raising of sheep—a brilliant bit of advice imposed from the District of Columbia—Crouse returned to his idea of cattle. The Indian Office had characteristically observed that it had no money to buy cattle and told Crouse to use the resources available. Trespassers on the White Mountain range had already demonstrated the attractiveness of Apache grass. Crouse moved swiftly to establish a permit system to bring in money and discourage illegal grazing on the reservation.[21]

A variety of permittees flocked in to take advantage of Crouse's initiative. Some, such as Henry Stephen Boice's Chiricahua Cattle Company, wanted large pieces of the reserve to call their own. Others turned out to be more transient, such as the sons of William Flake, the man whose name together with that of fellow Mormon pioneer Erastus Snow had created the nearby town of Snowflake. Crouse initially had been optimistic about the permit system, but he had underestimated the demand the permittees would place on him and the land itself, and problems of trespass continued to plague the administration of the reservation. Cattlemen Henry Barrett and Prime Coleman clashed over grazing sites; Barrett allowed many of his cattle to wander off his lease to a point where Crouse ordered the stray Barrett cattle rounded up. A furious Barrett accosted Coleman instead of Crouse. In the confrontation the two men made local dentist Zane Grey proud. They shot at each other with rifles at pistol length range. Coleman fell first, and Barrett, though seriously wounded, summoned sufficient resolve to beat his rival again and again over the head with his rifle. Coleman somehow survived. Barrett did not.[22]

This kind of excitement only accelerated Crouse's desire to promote cattle raising by the Apaches. With the sale of grazing permits and the reduction of money devoted to rations, he justified the purchase of 150 heifers and 8 bulls. In November

FIG. 12. Rather independent-looking cattle near Oraibi, Hopi reservation, ca. 1918. Photo by Leo Crane, who had a controversial tenure as superintendent. Cline Library, Special Collections and Archives, Northern Arizona University, Leo Crane Collection (Photo #658.242).

1902, the animals arrived, shipped from the herd of Lawrence V. McCourt of Willcox, Arizona. They were Herefords — the breed destined to be the trademark of Apache cattle ranching. From these modest beginnings and with the inevitable difficulties of a new enterprise — theft, loss, an occasional barbecue — a start had been made. Fire, drought, and other dilemmas also plagued these efforts. But the cattle, branded "ID" as they were elsewhere, were here to stay. [23]

Here to stay, but for whom? Crouse and the BIA favored giving cattle to school graduates, whom they reasoned would take better care of their investments. For some reason, Apaches who were not the products of this kind of schooling protested but for the time being, to little avail. Crouse also took the lead in choosing a reservation brand to be applied in addition to the ID. The agent knew something about symbolism. He chose the broken arrow brand to highlight the transition the Apaches had made from war to peace. [24] By the time he gave up his administrative chores in 1911, Crouse had every reason to believe that he had played a vital role in these crucial years.

He also had witnessed the emergence of a number of prominent Apache cattle ranchers. The three children of Corydon E. and Mollie Cooley had a kind of head start and took advantage of it. A veteran of General Crook's army as chief of scouts, Colonel Cooley had married the daughter of an Apache leader and had prospered as a rancher on 600,000 acres just off the reservation in the area of present-day Show Low (a card game this time), Arizona. Cooley did not use White Mountain land, but his children did. His daughter, Cora Agnes, married a white man, Charles H. Pettis; the Pettises used her access to Apache land to develop several small areas of the reserve. His sons Charles P. and Con had several hundred head of cattle, and another son, Albert, worked as a cowboy. After their father's death, however, they gave up interest in the business. [25]

Belle Crook Cooley, the oldest daughter of Corydon and Molly Cooley, married Abraham Lincoln Amos. This branch of the family persisted for a longer period in the cattle business and

FIG. 13. Crane and other superintendents hoped that new Hereford bulls would improve the quality of Indian cattle. These newly arrived bulls are listed in the Crane Collection as "Billy Pete and Hosteen Nez," suggesting Navajo ownership. Photo by Leo Crane. Cline Library, Special Collections and Archives, Northern Arizona University, Leo Crane Collection (Photo #658.243).

relinquished its land at White Mountain only with considerable reluctance. Abe and Belle Cooley had six children: Roy, Paul, Byde, Thomas, Elsie, and Jack. Several became involved in cattle ranching as adults, including Elsie, who had married a Mormon from the nearby community of Lakeside.

That marriage, when Elsie was seventeen and Earl West was twenty-one, had been against her father's wishes. He had kidnapped her, Abe Amos charged, and the young bridegroom was marooned in a Phoenix jail, until Elsie West came forward and told the court she had kidnapped her husband. Regardless of who kidnapped whom, Abe Amos had more than the usual reasons to distrust his new son-in-law. Earl West and his dad had been arrested at White Mountain not too long before for sleepering, which in the 1920s involved putting your brand on other people's cattle. The Wests forfeited any grazing privileges they might have gained at White Mountain.

Earl and Elsie West returned to the reservation and over the years developed a thriving ranch, the Dry Valley, not far from the old ranch home of Elsie's father. Superintendent Charles L. Davis's departure in 1927 opened the door for the Wests to get a foothold at White Mountain and gain access to the range they needed. They became one of a small group of "mixed-blood" ranchers who posed an interesting problem for the government. Were they entitled to the same obligations or opportunities as the "full-bloods"? These "individual Indian rights" ranchers, as they became called in federal reports, ran against the grain of contemporary bureau sentiment calling for all Apache ranchers to join livestock associations and to ranch cooperatively rather than individually.

Over a generation this small number of mixed-blood operators waged a losing battle. The tribe and the federal government really held the cards, for White Mountain had not been allotted, and the land was subdivided by permission rather than by private property. As the tribal government became more established and politically powerful on the reservation, individual ranchers' hold on their acreage became more shaky. Earl and Elsie West held out for over a generation before being forced off the land in the 1950s.[26]

Wallace Altaha is deservedly the most famous of the White Mountain Apache cattlemen. Born in 1866, he became interested in cattle prior to Crouse's arrival. A born entrepreneur, he observed how his father had begun with one cow and built up a small herd. Altaha obtained a beef contract with the military at Fort Apache when he was a young man. He then acquired land near Cedar Creek near the fort so that he did not have to drive his cattle too far, with them losing weight in the process. He soon became known by his individual brand, R-14.

R-14 already had 500 head of cattle at the time Crouse arrived. He worked with other family members, happily known to history as R-15 (a brother), R-31 (a sister), L-3 (a brother-in-law), and L-6 (a brother-in-law), to build a substantial herd. Butchers in Globe started buying from him in 1904; in 1906 and 1907, other butchers in Winslow, Taylor, and Springerville, Arizona, joined in. Although things did not always go smoothly, on balance R-14 and his family prospered. Those who are familiar with the location of Cedar Creek and Globe know they had to work at it; driving cattle through Salt River Canyon is a challenging undertaking.

Wallace Altaha lived until 1937. He may have been, as Donald Kristoffersen suggests, the wealthiest individual Indian cattleman in the United States. He certainly is the most famous of the Southwest. His Spear R cattle herd grew as large as 10,000 head; in 1918, he sold $45,000 worth of beef, bought $25,000 worth of liberty bonds, and just for good measure soon thereafter purchased $5,000 worth of victory bonds. He personified generosity, and he demonstrated that "traditional" Indians could succeed without benefit of extended schooling or wealthy or influential parentage.[27]

As is sometimes true of the president of a university or a nation, Crouse's term may have been too long. In the waning days of his administration, he not only clashed with the commissioner of Indian Affairs but also battled local government stockman Thomas Little Bison, who seemed to cause problems wherever he went, and others. Crouse was frustrated that R-14 had

FIG. 14. Indian cowboys and a declaration of independence with the outcome in doubt, ca. 1918. The Crane Collection lists the site as the corrals of Hubbell's Trading Post. Lorenzo Hubbell owned trading posts on the Hopi and Navajo reservations. His name is especially associated with Ganado in Navajo country, but he also operated posts at Keams Canyon and Oraibi on the Hopi reservation. Photo by Leo Crane. Cline Library, Special Collections and Archives, Northern Arizona University, Leo Crane Collection (Photo #658.249).

not been awarded the agency beef contract, being barely under-
bid by other suppliers. Nonetheless, at the time of his departure,
R-14 and other Apaches grazed 8,000 to 9,000 head of cattle;
21,000 head of cattle and 55,000 sheep of permittees brought in
in excess of $45,000 a year. Before too long, under the assertive
leadership of the agency Superintendent Davis, a bureau veteran, Apache ownership would soar by the mid-1920s to 20,000.
Leasing remained a problem; Apache cattlemen continued to
need more land, and Davis ultimately would have no other
choice than to evict permittees—a nice dilemma and a true
commentary on the evolution of Native cattle ranching at White
Mountain.[28]

Today San Carlos overshadows White Mountain in the fame of
its cattle industry, but cattle ranching at the southern reserve
took longer to develop. The outside companies had spied San
Carlos grass and were well established there prior to the twentieth century. Some of the same interests as one would expect
used the range of both reservations. For example, Boice had the
largest permit in San Carlos in 1913, with a range capacity of
20,200 head and an annual rental of $28,280. Fifteen other per-
mits had been issued for that year with a total range capacity of
44,050 acres and a total rental fee of $61,961.50. That amount of
land and money seemed enough to continue to encourage leasing
and to discourage the rapid evolution of Native ranching.[29]

In his survey of the San Carlos cattle industry, Harry Getty
interviewed an elderly Apache man, who said, "Cattle were first
issued in 1884. Five head to each family head. They were a black
cattle. But most Indians slaughtered the cattle right away. My
family didn't." Pressing immediate needs and lack of much
encouragement to save the cattle and develop herds led many
individuals and families to eat beef rather than save cows. In
1910, the superintendent reported that "about 100 Indians are
engaged in cattle raising. The stock consists principally in cattle
and horses although there are a few small mules and burrows.
They have approximately 1,800 ponies, 900 head of cattle, 100
mules, and 200 burros." He added, "One or two Indians own

from 100 to 125 head of cattle apiece, but the average is from 10 to 25 head."[30]

Nine hundred head represented at least a foundation, but the report suggests there were more than a few obstacles standing in the way of building up the herd. The following commentary may be dismissed as the grumbling of a disenchanted employee, but it is worth consideration, nonetheless.

> There is no material increase either in size or quality of the herds, as the Indians keep the young stock killed off, and have no idea as to the proper breeding of their stock. . . . Further efforts will be made to arouse their interest in bettering their herds. 500 heifers and 10 bulls were purchased this summer and issued to 50 Indians, chosen as ones who would take an interest and attempt to get good results.

The report concluded by noting the supervisory efforts of a white stockman "who is willing and able to teach them." Despite such general caution, fair warning was provided. The superintendent noted that cattle on permits did not hinder "the Indians' raising stock, but in the future when more territory is needed for Indian stock, it is the intention to require the permittees to lessen their herds according to the territory remaining them."[31]

In the following year, the superintendent made it clear where the economic future of San Carlos lay. "This is really a cattle grazing reservation," he stated. "More Indians should be engaged in stock raising." The estimate of Indian cattle rose to 1,000 head, but "the Indians expect to be helped with everything." Significantly, he added, "There should be a material increase in the permit fee." If there must be leases, they should be longer in duration. Year to year bidding did not encourage responsible parties to bid or stay put. Trespassing "is too common," in 1911 as well.[32]

The annual reports reflected a slow but steady increase in the size of the Apache herd. By 1914, there were about 1,500 head; by 1921, the herd had grown to 5,000. In fact by the 1920s, the Apaches needed more land for their cattle. "We must have more

FIG. 15. Four Apache cowboys ready for work, ca. 1920s. Francis J. Uplegger Collection. Archives and Manuscripts, University Libraries, Arizona State University (Tempe).

range," the 1921 report noted straightforwardly, "if the tribal herd was to increase." So the superintendent lobbied Washington. Commissioner Cato Sells departed his post on May 6, 1921, to be succeeded by Charles H. Burke, a former South Dakota congressman. Burke did not want to immediately reverse the Sells legacy. After reviewing the matter, he ruled against allowing the tribal herd to increase further. Burke chose not to take range away from the present grazing permittees. Indeed, he cautioned that it would be necessary to reduce the size of the Apache herd.[33] The Apaches, no doubt, disagreed with this analysis, even if they may have acknowledged a simplicity about the reasoning.

The arrival in 1923 at San Carlos of the new superintendent, James Kitch, altered the picture. A graduate of the Georgetown law school, Kitch had served as superintendent at Standing Rock from 1917 to 1921. He liked the work; his wife and son hated the weather. In the best spirit of marital compromise, Kitch capitulated and asked for a transfer. In the best spirit of the Indian Bureau, the government transferred him to the Mediterranean climate of Fork Peck, Montana. San Carlos is not Phoenix, but it looked like Miami to the Kitches after two years in northeast Montana. And Kitch quickly discovered that there was work to be done.[34]

Before the year was out, Kitch had rifled a series of letters to the commissioner of Indian affairs, expressing his intention to revitalize the San Carlos Apache cattle business. He remarked that 285 Apaches owned 2,500 head of cattle, representing at least a half of the families on the reservation. But more people wanted to be involved, and the superintendent said that he wanted to give those who owned no cattle or only a few head priority. The people needed more cattle, and they needed more land. If the government really believed in hard work and all the rest, then, essentially, it was time to put up or shut up.[35]

Kitch had his eye on the Ash Flat range. If he could get the white permittees off and put Native cattle on the 100,000 acres, he and the San Carlos Apaches would be on their way. In 1924, he won.

FIG. 16. Two San Carlos Apache cowboys in town, ca. 1920s. Francis J. Uplegger Collection. Archives and Manuscripts, University Libraries, Arizona State University (Tempe).

Drought that year slowed down the process of transfer, but by the time he wrote his report in 1925, Kitch could barely contain himself. Calf production had practically doubled from the previous year, thanks to the work of stockman Chipman and his assistants and "the proper placing of bulls" on the range. "Proper salting and care of mountain springs and development of water" had also impressively decreased the loss of cattle. Steer sales were termed "excellent in price," in fact "selling higher than any other cattle except the Chiricahua Cattle Company" and thus representing a pinnacle of performance in the regional marketplace.[36]

What Kitch labeled "the only proper home industry" of the San Carlos Apaches had turned the corner. Eleven hundred eighty-six heifers had been added to the tribal herd. With limited culling and sale of some of the heifers, by 1926, the tribal herd would have 2,000 head "of breeding stock between the ages of two and eight years," comprising a uniform "white face"—that is to say, Hereford—herd. Younger and better bulls would be brought in, and already the effort to use purebred bulls had been started. The tribe had enough land for now, but within a year or two they would need still more land. Again, another permit would have to be canceled for the necessary expansion of Apache cattle ranching.[37]

All well and good. But as James Kitch and Charles Davis of White Mountain discovered, not entirely to their surprise, that year, by promoting the growth of the Native cattle industry, they had run headlong into established cattle companies used to having their own way—on Indian reservations, on national forest lands, or anywhere else. At a time in the American West when cattlemen had the ear of congressmen, they did not hesitate to yell. Times had grown increasingly tough for the cattle business by the mid-1920s. The drought that had hit the Apaches had hit them, too. Prices for beef were not great. Fees seemed too high on national forest and Indian lands. And now to be forced off Indian land, even before the permit had expired? Fortunately, a subcommittee of the Senate Committee on Public Lands and Surveys had scheduled hearings in June 1925. It provided a nice opportunity for one and all to be heard. In less than three weeks, participants generated a thousand pages of testimony. Beginning in Douglas on June 4, the committee members trudged on to Tucson, Florence, Globe, Phoenix, Prescott, Flagstaff, the Grand Canyon, Holbrook, St. Johns, and Springerville. Dozens of cattle ranchers lined up to talk. So, too, did Kitch and Davis.

These extended conversations focused on public lands rather than Indian lands. The two categories obviously overlapped in the minds of most westerners. Charles Davis made the distinc-

FIG. 17. Preparing to head out, San Carlos, ca. 1920s. Francis J. Uplegger Collection. Archives and Manuscripts, University Libraries, Arizona State University (Tempe).

tion clear: "The Fort Apache Indian lands are not public lands, as has been spoken of here, or public domain. Many people are confused on that point." Davis then added, "Congress has legislated to the effect that these lands, when duly set apart, as this reservation was, about 1871 or 1872, that they inure to the tribe for which they are set aside very much the same as private ownership."[38] Not only did cattle and sheep ranchers dispute the matter but, significantly, so did Sen. Henry Ashurst of Arizona.

Sheep ranchers had pressed Davis for a right-of-way to drive their sheep—a driveway, they called it—through White Mountain. Davis had dissented. Ashurst apparently could not believe it. The two men went back and forth in the kind of timeless dance one still observes in the Arizona legislature or in the U.S. Congress.

ASHURST: Do you think that they ought to have a driveway through there?

DAVIS: No, sir.

ASHURST: All right, now you think they shouldn't have a driveway?

DAVIS: No, sir.

ASHURST: Notwithstanding the fact they are American citizens and taxpayers who are paying your salary, you think they should not have a driveway?

DAVIS: The Indians are citizens the same as they are.

ASHURST: Isn't it a fact that when you refuse to grant driveways you prevent other citizens from reaching their property?

DAVIS: Not in that case.

ASHURST: They can get there?

DAVIS: They have been doing it all the time.

ASHURST: How do they get there?

DAVIS: Go around.

ASHURST: It is a circuitous route?

DAVIS: Certainly.

ASHURST: If the national forest can give driveways, why can't the Indian reservation?

DAVIS: I am trying to tell you why.

ASHURST: I would like to have you tell us why the driveway was left out.

DAVIS: It would cross the Indian lands over their farms and their homes, and if it had been granted it would virtually have destroyed the homes and the industry of quite a number of the tribe.[39]

Davis did not back down. It became painfully apparent to the senator from Arizona that there was not a whole lot he could do about it, other than heap a little more invective on this contrary soul.

The Indian agents . . . are going to have their own sweet way; I have found that out. You are not different than any other man employed by the government. The Indian superintendents are like the governments in Europe; they are little worlds in themselves. . . . We must not forget that American citizens must not be left at the whim of some Indian agent.[40]

Like the senator from Arizona, the cattle ranchers spoke as people accustomed to having their own way. One remembers that by this time in the West, well before the Wall Street crash, the depression was settling in the West; every other farm in Montana was lost in the first half of the 1920s. Now, new and increasing problems emerged. The golden age of cattle ranching was long gone. The cattlemen needed more land, and there seemed to be little, if any, for the taking. So much of the land in Arizona and elsewhere is federal land of one kind or another, and access to it is crucially important. Not just access, to be sure, but cheap access.

Congress met them partway, remitting fees for national forest grazing for part of 1925 and knocking the fee of a dollar per head per year down to fifty-eight cents. That remained too much, claimed Fred Bennett of Tombstone: "Everybody in the cattle business here is broke and anything you charge them at all is excessive, because they are broke." Bennett wanted fees canceled for the next two years. Now that Senator Ashurst had brought the matter up, a permanent reduction would offer a chance to recoup. No doubt about it.[41]

Davis and Kitch were charging more than a dollar a head for

leases on the reservation. The going rate in 1925 was $1.75. The non-Indian ranchers expressed their displeasure; Henry Boice, who had a lot of cattle on Indian lands, called the rates "uniformly high and out of line with other grazing in the State." Boice and company were angry as well about the drought and about the market. They worried about soil erosion. J. M. Ronstadt of Tucson, a relative of the singer Linda Ronstadt, admitted the public domain had been overgrazed and the range was deteriorating.[42]

And so as Davis and Kitch pushed for more cattle for the Apaches, more of the Apache land for the tribes, and correspondingly less Indian land for outsiders, the outsiders were threatened not only by loss of cheap land but by competition from the Indians themselves. In America, one cannot really complain about competition. Complaining about unfair competition, however, may be permitted.

In Boice's words, "Another thing which the cattlemen of this state object to is the policy of the Indian Department in maintaining tribal herds. They felt at the time these herds were established it was an improper move and they feel much more strongly now. They feel that the Government is producing cattle with great advantage in competition with them." A. T. Crocker of Clifton, manager of the Double Circle Cattle Company with leases on both White Mountain and San Carlos, joined the chorus. It is, Crocker concluded, "a matter of right and wrong. . . . They don't have to meet the taxes, grazing fees, or interest, which I don't think is right."[43]

The loss of the land also rankled, for the leases were not only not being renewed but in some cases they were not being allowed to run to their full term. The evicted ranchers had nowhere to go. T. S. Kimball of Thatcher called the situation "awful" and added dramatically, "It is a good thing these Arizonians have tamed down, by golly, or they never would stand what they have stood." Ashurst quickly chimed in about sharp injustices and oppressions being borne "rather patiently, too patiently."[44]

Oppression being borne rather patiently, too patiently? By

golly, for a moment one might have thought he was talking about Indians rather than cowboys. The testimony of Kitch and Davis and, later, the chief of the industrial section of the Indian Office, H. W. Shipe, allows us to understand that the actions being taken on the Apache reservations were less precipitous than pictured. The leases, it turns out, said that the permittee may be evicted at any time. Only as the land was needed could it be reclaimed. The permittees generally had not had to bid competitively for the land but had enjoyed renewals. Some had not paid their fees.

Shipe's remarks near the end of the congressional committee's foray provide a fitting coda to the discussion and attest to the fact that the pendulum was starting to swing away from the pattern of the past half-century. Here a federal employee from Washington actually spoke for, not against, the Indians. He reminded the members of the committee of Indians "who are good farmers" and "who are splendid cattlemen and splendid sheepmen." Were the Indian herds well managed? "Some of them are well managed and some of them are poorly managed, just as is the case with the white men." White permittees could be excluded from the reservation, for it "is their property and we want them to develop their property to their own best advantage."[45]

Let us listen to one last, telling exchange. Mr. Bowden grilled Shipe for the committee.

> BOWDEN: Do you think that in these times of depression you should try to increase the Indian herds at the expense of the white livestock men using the Indian reservation?
> SHIPE: In answering that we must assume that the property belongs to the Indians. Now, then, it is just as essential during the hard times that you speak of that the Indians keep on using their property as much as they can as it would be if times were good.
> BOWDEN: Of course, in hard times the Government ought not to put anyone out?
> SHIPE: Not if it were public land, but it is not. Do you know of anybody who is keeping from increasing his business just now because he might be hurting his neighbor? We are all trying to increase our business.

BOWDEN: And your treatment then of Indian lands is analogous to the manner in which a private owner would treat his land?
SHIPE: Yes, sir.[46]

Yes, sir. It is their land. Despite the Allotment Act, despite Maj. James McLaughlin, despite *Lone Wolf v. Hitchcock*, despite Sen. Henry Ashurst, there is still Native land. Yes, sir.

CHAPTER SIX

The New Deal Years and Indian Cattle Ranching

WHEN YOU WANT TO KILL SOMETHING, AN OLD proverb cherished in all nations says, form a committee to study it. If you want to reform some element of government, for heaven's sake do not ask an institute for government research to offer you suggestions. If the institute staff pulls off a miracle and offers substantive criticism, by all means do not assume the government will actually do something in response. All that, you know, white tape.

The same month the Senate subcommittee on the public lands received testimony in Arizona, the secretary of the interior, Hubert Work, bowed to the inevitable. Heeding a growing storm of protest about the state of Indian affairs, he concluded that a study of the contemporary situation would not hurt. Perhaps the findings might deflect all the harpoons being tossed in his direction by that arrogant, self-righteous troublemaker. What was his name? Collier, John Collier. Anyone who had associated with the likes of John Reed, Max Eastman, Isadora Duncan, Bill Haywood, Emma Goldman, and Mabel Dodge Luhan, . . . well.

There was no getting around it, even if one did not happen to share Work's worldview. Collier was an odd duck. Born in Georgia, he migrated north and eventually became a social worker in New York City. From 1907 to 1919, he had had ample opportunity to witness the ravages of industrialism and the crushing uniformity expected of European immigrants. Such obliteration of distinctive cultures seemed all wrong to Collier. He assisted in putting on the Pageant and Festival of Nations to celebrate and preserve linguistic and cultural diversity. While in New York, he met Mabel Dodge, a wealthy Fifth Avenue salon keeper who recruited a potpourri of intellectuals and activists to her weekly soirées.[1]

Collier finally tired of New York, where his efforts at reform seemed to be thwarted by one fiscal problem after another. Somehow, he landed a job that appeared to hold great promise, and he moved to California in the autumn of 1919 to become director of adult educational programs. Collier lasted barely a year, before right-wing zealots who had heard about his interest in the Bolshevik triumph persuaded the state legislature that his services were no longer needed. Intending to rally his spirits, if not his finances, on an extended outing to Mexico, Collier impulsively accepted an invitation from his old friend, Mabel Dodge, to come for a visit to Taos, New Mexico.

You can almost hear Collier practicing his pronunciation. Taos. Tahowus. Mabel Dodge had changed her name as well as her residence. Married to Antonio Luhan of Taos Pueblo, she would lure all sorts of people to discover her new world. D. H. Lawrence and John Collier numbered among those who made the journey. Lawrence never fully converted to the mystic appeal of this picturesque northern New Mexico area, but it likely took all of five seconds to mesmerize Collier. From the time he sighted the ancient Indian pueblo at Christmas 1920, he was hooked.

As luck and fate would have it, Collier happened in to New Mexico at a critical juncture in Pueblo Indian history. The peoples of the different villages soon confronted a threat of impressive dimensions that threatened to dislodge them from their communities. Work's predecessor, the unsavory Albert Bacon Fall had enlisted the help of a New Mexico senator to craft a bill ostensibly to untangle complex land questions in the state. With a name like Holm Olaf Bursum, the senator should have represented Minnesota rather than New Mexico. He drew up legislation that if passed almost assuredly would have uprooted Pueblo residents. Collier joined and soon helped lead the crusade against the Bursum bill. His prominence increased as the decade wore on, and by the time Work ordered his study, Collier had surfaced as a nationally known critic of the way in which the government had administered its trust responsibilities. In the spring of 1933, this diminutive, absent-minded man would be chosen commissioner of Indian affairs.[2]

That unlikely selection lay nearly seven years in the future as Lewis Meriam of the Brookings Institution (or the Institute for Government Research) began to assemble his staff to undertake a daunting assignment. The research team's findings, published in 1928 as *The Problem of Indian Administration*, sprawled over eight hundred pages. Meriam and his cohorts divided the indictment into eight sections: a general policy for Indian affairs, health, education, general economic conditions, family and community life, the activities of women, Indian migration, the legal aspects of the Indian "problem," and missionary activities among the Indians. The massive volume roundly condemned the federal government's actions in fulfillment of its trust responsibilities. Although the Collier commissionership inaugurated the so-called Indian New Deal, the reformer-turned-bureaucrat had the benefit of not only detailed, careful research but a call to action in Meriam's report.[3]

Together with health, education, and women, family, and community, the Native economy represented one of four subjects receiving extended attention in the study. The issuance of rations, land allotment, and the leasing of Indian land were labeled policies "of a type which, if long continued, would tend to pauperize any race." "It almost seems," the report sneered, "as if the government assumed some magic in individual ownership of property" would have worked to create a functional Native economy. Instead, allotment and leasing had spawned quite the opposite. Rather remarkably, some Indian land remained. In a steadily deepening recession, what should be done with it?[4]

In considering the alternatives, staff members realized the character of the Native estate: "much of the Indian's property consists of land that is often arid, semi-arid, or mountainous, valuable chiefly for grazing, unsalable except in very large tracts, and often capable of little development for other agricultural purposes." To take as much advantage as possible of tribal lands, allotment had to be ended and widespread leasing halted. Leasing had conveniently presented to some reservation superintendents "the easiest way out of a difficult task." Indians should be encouraged to become more self-sufficient, and the "chief economic possibility for the great majority of Indians" lay "in some form of agriculture."[5]

A survey of students enrolled in Indian schools revealed 84 percent of the children's fathers who had worked were either farmers or ranchers. Farmers made up nearly two-thirds of the work force at 65.2 percent; ranchers added another 15.8 percent. The government must provide much more thorough and effective agricultural education to children, women, and men to build for a better Indian future.

> In that future, "stock raising" should occupy a central place: Ample evidence demonstrates that stock raising is the most promising form of agriculture and, in fact, the most promising of all pursuits for a large number of Indians. Not only does the average Indian show considerable aptitude for this work, but enormous areas of Indian land, tribal and individual, are of little value except for grazing.[6]

In order for livestock raising to progress, all lands leased by whites or not fully used by Indians ought over time to be put to

Native employment. The Meriam report argued for the value of both tribal herds and individually owned herds of animals. Tribal herds, it observed, had apparently "fallen into disrepute" for two main reasons. The cattle industry nationally had been in depression, so it was "not surprising that the tribal herds operated by government officers were unprofitable." Also many of the stockmen responsible for these herds did not have the kind of technical knowledge necessary for the job.

Rather like the New Deal it anticipated, the report ultimately sought traditional ends through temporary, more progressive and cooperative means. In the long run, tribal herds should make way for individual ownership. However, even if transitional, the tribal approach "should never be broken up because of temporary losses or depressed market conditions, but only when it has achieved its object and has made it possible for the entire pasturage of the reservation to be consumed by livestock owned by individual Indians." This process would take years, staff members acknowledged.[7]

Perhaps mindful of the recent lively discussion about the subject in Arizona and elsewhere in the West, they urged white lessees be given adequate notice about their leases, if they were to be canceled. But, they added, if land were needed for Indian livestock, they "should on no account be permitted to retain reservation land." As we have just seen, they did not describe a hypothetical situation.

> The government should in such cases refuse to be influenced by the appeals of wealthy or other ranchmen to be permitted to continue to lease land that the Indians need. Such appeals are often difficult to withstand, since some of these men have come to regard a privilege long exercised almost as a vested right and doubtless in some cases would not only seek to discredit any enterprise on behalf of the Indians which would deprive them of their leases but would use political influence in order to retain their leases.[8]

Call it the Ashurst Principle.

In addition to the obligatory, rueful note that "many reservations are now overrun with worthless horses," the writers of the report suggested a limit on how many livestock an individual Indian could graze on tribal land free of charge and encouraged more stockmen to consider raising sheep instead of cattle. They argued that the cattle business "is always somewhat speculative and often highly so" but that sheep required "more attention and care than cattle." The first contention is surely easier to buy than the second, and the judgment that "sheep should as a rule be given preference over cattle on most reservations" is open to considerable question.[9] Indians such as the Apaches who had adopted cattle ranching would be no more likely to switch to sheep than the Navajos would turn primarily to cattle. The Navajos already ran a few cattle, and sheep would not be completely unknown on some of the reservations devoted almost exclusively to cattle. In the final analysis, the recommendation is couched narrowly—and not necessarily correctly—on economic terms. By this time the social ramifications ranked as important as the economic consequences. Traditions and social patterns had been established. Native cattle ranchers, if confronted with the choice, would have echoed such sentiments.

As noted, they soon did confront the odd specter of a reformer in charge of the Indian bureau. Many Indians were as mystified by Collier as the regulars in a rural café frequented on one autumn afternoon by the traveling Collier family. The following story, told years later with great relish by one of John Collier's sons, is too good not to be true. The locals were mired in hushed conversations while the radio blared out across the room as the family entered. As the Colliers found an empty table, without inquiry or invitation, Collier climbed on a chair and turned off the offending radio. Silence. Glares. "Oh, you weren't listening to that, to that babble, were you?" It was the World Series. The final game. The ninth inning. Tie score. They were listening.[10]

Collier came into office determined to transform how the bureau did business. In the context of the New Deal, he operated, especially at first, in a supportive environment. The Roosevelt administration shared a commitment to revive community. The depression had taken the wind out of the balloon of rugged individualism, and citizens of all cultures in the West and elsewhere needed help.

However, even desperate times do not usually encourage radical actions or solutions. Recall that Republicans in Congress balked at that weird innovation, social security. Congressional representatives and other traditionalists clung to old ideals, even as they hesitantly backed emergency relief measures. Communalism should only go so far. Moreover, vested interests rebelled at significant alteration of a playing field in which they had not been terribly constrained. Christian missionaries did not rise up as one and give a standing ovation to Collier's endorsement of freedom of religion for traditional Native ceremonies; after a half century of railing against sun dances or snake dances they were not about to be converted to cultural pluralism. Anglo-American farmers and ranchers did not applaud wildly as Collier tried to end land allotment, consolidate Indian landholdings, and even add to the tribal estate; times were difficult, and this guy who probably could not park his bicycle straight was out to get them, depriving them of the land to which they had had access. Veteran Bureau employees, whether schoolteachers or superintendents, had usually bought in to the assimilationist goal. Even James Kitch wanted the San Carlos Apaches to use cattle ranching as a means toward absorption rather than separation from American society. And more than a few Indians suspected that Collier had to be up to no good. What was he trying to do, turn back the clock? Pull a fast one?

Based on his experience in working with the village communities of New Mexico, Collier tended to see Indians nationally as variations on a Pueblo theme. Such a lens did not necessarily serve him well. He ascribed greater cultural cohesion and more group orientation than often existed. Land allotment, Christian churches, boarding schools had all divided many reservations. In addition, the very size of the largest reserves mitigated against the kind of esprit de corps most easily fostered within a smaller-scale world. Over the past half century on the biggest Indian nations, small towns, settlements, or communities had developed. In many instances, loyalty first came to that unit. However, threats from outside economic interests did tend to encourage a greater tribal nationalism, a sense that it was necessary to pull together.

Into this varied, double-edged scenario, Collier's programs cut in more than one direction. The commissioner succeeded and failed. He won a cessation of land allotment, continued the development of tribal economies while stopping much of the leasing that had strangled that evolution, and in some instances added land to reservations. Collier's defense of the Native American Church and traditional ceremonies, his support of bilingual, bicultural programs in the schools, his encouragement of Native arts and crafts, and his general conviction that Indians would not disappear marked a dramatic change of Bureau policy.

But Collier resembled other reformers in other ages. He knew best. He wanted to move too quickly and impose too much. The Indians needed tribal governments. Hard to deny it. Yet the form of democratic self-government promoted through the Indian Reorganization Act ran against the grain of theocracy in the Hopi reservation or the unquestioned status of elders on other reservations. The doors of power had been opened to new people, often younger and often with different ideas. Many Native communities divided over whether to vote affirmatively on the act and if they voted in favor of it, divided again on its implementation. Such division obviously affected local responses to other Bureau programs. Even if the program might otherwise be received very positively, it could be tarred by the brush of association. A written form of our language? A community day school? More cows for the tribal herd? Let's think about it.

Of course, Collier did not make administrative decisions in isolation from the priorities in other federal agencies. The dust bowl era inspired considerable concern over soil erosion and conservation. As did other lands in the West, some of the Native lands bore the scars of erosion. Why had the problem worsened? The conventional wisdom in Washington held that overgrazing caused erosion. If the Navajos had too many sheep, if the Tohono O'odham had too many cows, then the obvious solution loomed. Reduce the numbers of sheep and cattle and the land will be on its way to recovery. Again, Collier would try to impose what seemed like a good idea. Again, there would be hell to pay.[11]

The pattern of Indian cattle ranching in the Collier years, a period that lasted almost as long as the Roosevelt administration, must be understood within this broader framework. Although the furor over tribal government or soil conservation in some cases worked against the development of Native livestock industries, the prevailing support for local self-sufficiency and productivity and the commitment to the preservation of Indian communities more often than not furthered the pastime. The headway achieved in the 1930s and early 1940s should not be discounted, for shifting political tides in the years following World War II would have been even more corrosive had it not been the pluralist interlude afforded by the Indian New Deal.

Using the Southwest and the northern plains region as examples, we can review the record of this time in regard to Indian cattle ranching. Our concluding points of discussion in the previous chapter, San Carlos and White Mountain, offer an appropriate place to begin. At San Carlos, James Kitch remained as superintendent until 1937. His tenure on the reservation ended unhappily because of disagreements revolving around the new system of government and the conflict he had with Wallace Chinn, an aspiring Apache leader.[12] However, his record of success in fostering the cattle industry—arguably the most successful of any Indian cattle ranching—remains remarkable. San Carlos had emerged by the middle of the 1930s as a model to emulate.

In that decade the San Carlos range completed a transition. The Chiricahua Cattle Company ended its permittee status by 1930. Four years later, the San Pasqual Cattle Company, John Osborne, and G. A. Bryce finished their years on the reservation. And by 1938, the broom had swept clean; Mrs. Blake Hayes, the Hayes Livestock Company, and the Double Circle

FIG. 18. Apache cowboys on a roundup in Gila County, Arizona, 1941. Photo by Gilbert Campbell. Gilbert and Myrtle Campbell Collection, Archives and Manuscripts, University Libraries, Arizona State University (Tempe).

had all departed. Their farewell naturally opened progressively more and more grazing land for the Apaches themselves. Who would be able to graze whose cattle on which acreage?[13]

Although in his many reports and letters Kitch may well have exaggerated the degree to which he succeeded, he made a noteworthy effort "to establish the Indian cattle industry on the basis of native socio-political units." Harry Getty's careful examination of the documents available appears to be on target. What Kitch did was to use the Apache sense of family and extended relationships and combine that with already existing attachments to particular areas of the reservation. Thus while an association of men working a particular range might not all be related to one another, many of them were. They were comfortable with each other, had social obligations to each other, could work productively with each other. The cattle associations formed during the 1930s formalized this arrangement. These groups worked a particular range, rounded up the cattle on it, and shared in the proceeds from the cattle sales. Social and economic benefits obviously overlapped and reinforced each other. Individuals could transfer from one association to another, for one reason or another. Few did.

The San Carlos Apache tribal herd, as distinct from the cattle run by the different associations, became a focal point for quality. Getty notes that by 1933 the tribal business committee recommended that the tribal herd should become one of registered Herefords. In time this herd could yield heifers and bulls to continue to upgrade the numbers and quality of the different association herds. This commitment to the registered stock definitely impressed other cattle ranchers from the region and in due course added to the reputation and therefore the sales of San Carlos cattle.[14]

With the land at San Carlos held in trust rather than divided into allotments, the tribe also felt keenly its responsibility to share the benefits of ranching. On December 6, 1938, the tribal council voted to create a second herd. The IDT or "Social Security herd" would help those without cattle to obtain "surplus heifers," and the profits from the operation would be used for the support of elders, widows, and orphans. This exercise in responsibility ensured that as many tribal members as possible would gain from the enterprise.[15] It is not to suggest that all profited equally or that all were involved but that the social dimensions appear as important as the economic ones.

Contemporary accounts shower praise on the San Carlos cattle industry. A field report for the National Association on Indian Affairs in 1936 observed, "During the roundup we were interested to see how active the Indians were in the cattle work and how rapidly they are learning the various phases of the industry." The report lauds Kitch for his "development of small cattle outfits based on the clan system of the tribe."[16] Civilian Conservation Corps–Indian Department Camp Assistant Harry Stevens, an Apache, would be expected to wax enthusiastic. Nonetheless, his article for the Bureau's *Indians at Work*, published in July 1939, makes some important points. The San Carlos Apaches ranked first among Indian communities in the number of cattle sold and gross revenue derived in 1937. In that year they sold almost 12,000 head of cattle for an average of $32 per head. The registered herd of Herefords, Stevens claimed, is "now what is generally recognized as the largest . . . in the Southwest" with 1,200 total cattle, of which 400 were to be kept registered and the remainder to be used as a breeding herd for reimbursable heifers. With the tribal council annual selecting young men to receive 20 head of good yearling heifers, new people continued to be brought into the industry. Stevens noted 25,000 head of cattle additionally distributed among 600 brands. Overall, of the 700 families on the reservation, about 400 owned cattle.

An article in the December 1940 *Indians at Work* corroborated Stevens's assessment. The tribe had progressed from using 4 percent of its range in 1923, with most of the rest leased, to using all the land. San Carlos Apaches owned almost 28,000 head of cattle — a 1,000 percent increase from 1923. Of the 581 individuals named as livestock owners, roughly one-fourth were women.

The way in which the herd had been built up is a tribute to the resolve of the people. The tribe used its own funds to increase the size of the herd and borrowed money from the Bureau to buy purebred cattle. By the end of 1940, the San Carlos Apaches had repaid a third of the amount and planned to repay the balance over the next two years. Not exactly the usual image of Indians in the West, then or now.[17]

The pride taken by the community in its success in the business must have been reinforced by yet another article in *Indians at Work*. As had been true for the last few years, their cattle were bringing "higher prices than that of their white neighbors." Buyers traveled to San Carlos from all over the country, California to Indiana. Probably as gratifying, members of the Tohono O'odham tribe came to this particular sale to observe range management, roundups, and sales. If one takes the piece at face value, the Tohono O'odham were going to "follow along the same lines adopted by the Apaches" in their future management of their cattle. All in all, the era reflected the maturation of the industry at San Carlos. Even with Kitch's departure, the people were in a position to continue to move forward with an enterprise that had proved its value.[18]

Grenville Goodwin, an anthropologist who had spent nearly two years off and on at San Carlos from 1930 to 1936, documented the transition in a report he submitted to the Bureau of Indian Affairs in 1937. Focusing his remarks on the Bylas district of the reservation, Goodwin observed that the cattle industry had generated "absorbing interest" and often served as "the current topic of Apache conversation." Particularly at roundup time, the people "talk of little else but preparing to ride out, how the work is coming and when the herds will be in, the sales of the cattle, what the prices are and all the other details."[19]

In Goodwin's judgment, Washington still controlled too much of the organization and function of the industry. It is evident from his commentary, nonetheless, that the industry was making rapid progress in its absorption into the life of San Carlos. It could be perceived "in the clothes sported by the young men,

FIG. 19. A competitor in the Indian Powwow Rodeo, Flagstaff, Arizona, 1940. Photo by Gilbert Campbell. Gilbert and Myrtle Campbell Collection, Archives and Manuscripts, University Libraries, Arizona State University (Tempe).

after the White cowboys; boots, spurs, bright-colored shirt and all, and the pride taken in their mounts and saddles." Goodwin added,

> At Fourth of July celebrations as well as other summer gatherings, the younger men organize roping contests and some of them enter outside Rodeo competitions. Even young boys play cowboy and rope dogs, goats, anything they can from their burro mounts. To ignore the effect of the cattle industry upon these people would be impossible. The cattle industry is undoubtedly a fortunate choice for the Reservation, and Indians I have known like the idea of cattle work, for they feel it is something worth a man's effort. They like an occupation which supplies action and at present when the cowboy is so idolized in the West, the idea of being one is attractive to young men.[20]

There it is in a nutshell. The cattle industry had started to influence attire and the play of children, it offered action, it provided a kind of role model not only that one would want to aspire to but one that could be achieved. The economics mattered. Cattle sales and income from cowboying paid the bills. However, it had already emerged as considerably more than an economic venture. It had permeated the social fabric of the community.

During the 1930s, the administration of White Mountain finally confronted several unpleasant realities about the Apache range. One dilemma involved wild horses. Thomas McGuire described the problem concisely and colorfully: "Scruffy wild ponies, too small to break as saddle horses, scoured the Fort Apache range in the 1930s. Called broomtails and buzzard heads, these unneeded horses were voracious eaters, and reservation officials became alarmed that the ranges would be destroyed." They feared that perhaps as many as ten thousand horses roamed White Mountain; two consumed as much as three yearling steers. Even this figure proved inflated; it took twenty years to take care of the unwanted animals. Perhaps the outcry against killing Navajo stock limited their choices, and the effort had to take place in piecemeal fashion. In any event, it would not be until 1950 that most of the horses had been eradicated.[21]

FIG. 20. The Indian Powwow Rodeo in Flagstaff, Arizona, attracted entrants from many Indian communities. Photo by Gilbert Campbell, 1940. Gilbert and Myrtle Campbell Collection, Archives and Manuscripts, University Libraries, Arizona State University (Tempe).

In 1930, fourteen white permittees still used 687,970 acres of Apache pasture. That number had to be reduced not only to increase tribal participation in cattle ranching but to save the range, for the intensive grazing of outside animals had taken a visible toll. Drought in the decade accelerated the need to evict whites as well as wild horses. Again, it took time. Nonetheless, by 1950, the whites were mostly departed, too. Only six permittees remained; their holdings had shrunk markedly, allowing for concomitant expansion of Native ranching. Apache grazing districts thus ballooned from about 823,000 acres in 1931 to 1,418,683 acres twenty years later. Such growth was important

FIG. 21. Horses on the San Carlos Apache reservation, Arizona, ca. 1920s. Francis J. Uplegger Collection, Archives and Manuscripts, University Libraries, Arizona State University (Tempe).

not only in terms of available land but also in terms of increasing the ecological diversity for ranchers. More able to move their cattle seasonally, Apache ranchers gradually could improve conservation of White Mountain rangeland.[22]

The quality of White Mountain Apache cattle also improved significantly. Superintendent William Donner tirelessly promoted the quality of the Herefords to be sold at auction. "These hardy, mountain-raised cattle give a good account of themselves," he trumpeted, "when moved to lower ranges and to feedlots. Our browse crops and great variety of grasses develop a rib-spread, and our rough range a stamina that is seldom found in cattle from lower altitudes." The caliber of the stock combined with Donner's salesmanship. A "big buyer" from the Texas Panhandle, a bank president, made the scenic drive northwest out of greater Amarillo and bought nearly $10,000 worth of steers. Other buyers made equally scenic drives across the Mohave to come from California to White Mountain. Sales in 1939 generated over $111,000, and a report in late 1940 suggested at least a comparable revenue for that year.[23]

At the conclusion of the 1930s, White Mountain boasted 25,000 head of cattle owned by thirty-five women and seven hundred men who belonged to the twelve livestock associations. The people had borrowed roughly 600 head from the revolving cattle pool of the Bureau in 1934–35. A loan of purebred cattle already had been paid back by December 1939. As at San Carlos, the White Mountain Apaches had reason to be optimistic about the future of their industry.[24]

The Tohono O'odham present a more mixed picture for the New Deal period. Here stockmen managed to expand their operations, increase the size of their herds, and generally improve the quality of their cattle. But as late as the mid-1930s, Xavier could argue that "range control, organized selling, a proper inspection system, cattle associations, government stock supervision, etc., were practically not existent when the Agency's new stockman arrived." Although some headway would be achieved during the latter part of the decade, the general state of the industry clearly had not reached the level of San Carlos or White Mountain. Complicating efforts for improvement were the federal attempts to impose livestock reduction.

The new stockman, a Mr. Nation, had his work cut out for him. Tohono O'odham death loss for cattle figured at about 10 percent, or at least twice the percentage for good range in the state. Ranchers on the reservation did not have enough bulls, and so the annual calf crop consistently fell short of expectations. Some of the breeding cows stayed on the range past their most productive years, also reducing the number of calves produced.[25]

Culture and climate both figure into this intricate picture. Tribal ranchers may have been brought up to Apache country to observe how to do things, but Xavier's study suggests that many returned home not entirely convinced. Traditionally, cattle had served as a kind of bank for members of the community. When one needed cash, one sold a cow. One could not always know when that need would arise, and one had to act quickly in some instances. The government wanted to encourage regularly scheduled, large-volume, well-advertised sales. That sounded fine, but it assumed a degree of control over one's life that one did not always have.

Who would buy the cattle under this kind of arrangement? Would it be the big guy from greater Amarillo? As a matter of fact, no. Rather, the little fellow from Ajo or Casa Grande would swoop in after hearing that a particular rancher had some cattle to sell. The little fellow wouldn't want many cattle, for he couldn't handle many. He would naturally try to pick out the best cattle he could and pay the least he could, cheerfully assuring the seller that he was getting market price. Right. To make matters worse, the buyers advanced money to Tohono O'odham ranchers, with the sum payable in cows rather than cash at a later point. It was a sweet deal, and it built up obligations. It could become a habit. The superintendent noted in his report for 1935–36 that the average price per head was only $20.85. Even in a depressed economy, this figure hardly represented top dollar. By 1939, the average price had risen to $22.85, and through most of 1940 it had escalated to $25.44 per head. Stockman Nation, Superintendent Hall, and Tohono O'odham ranchers had made progress.[26]

It had not been easy. Tribal Chairman Pete Blaine spoke for more than his own people when he described the confusion of directed change. "The white man tried to direct us without knowing the full facts or being asked," he said. "An Indian is not like the white man. A white man hears one thing and okays it right away. Indians, they don't. They wait and wait and wait. They consider everything." The white man's ideas often were acceptable, but the Tohono O'odham opposed them because they believed they lacked information. The whites, Blaine asserted, "never made an effort to go and see the people." They waited for the people "to come to them," but the people "were afraid to come."[27]

As did the Navajos, the Tohono O'odham argued that the problem was not overgrazing. If the tribe had the land that it deserved and if the rains returned, then all would be well. Not too long ago, Blaine remembered, there had been plenty of cattle, plenty of grass, and plenty of rain. In 1922, "cattle were all over and the grass was high" — blue grama and common grama grass and "cotton grass" four or five feet high. Drought, not overgrazing, not mesquite trees, not rodents, was the culprit. If it did not rain, some cattle would die. "If cattle are going to die, let them die," Blaine argued. "But they will die here on their reservation. Right here in their home country." Their reservation. Their home country. The cattle and the Tohono O'odham shared it. It belonged to both.[28]

Despite such obstacles, the 1930s were marked by significant efforts to improve the quality of Tohono O'odham livestock and range management. "Reimbursable cattle," "New Mexico rehabilitation cattle," and "drought relief cattle" all added to the tribal herds. The people purchased the reimbursable cattle from the government and had to pay it back at cost and a 5 percent carrying charge. In addition, in 1936, the tribe gained 320 head of stock to be grazed and 400 head targeted for the dinner table. The former had to be paid back via a yearling per head; the latter only required a minor handling charge. The Tohono O'odham kept all the cattle, rather than consuming some of them. Finally, in the previous year, the community had obtained 845 head of registered Herefords, with a yearling to be paid back for each cow received.[29]

Xavier acknowledged that it was premature to judge the overall impact of this infusion but noted that some members of the tribe preferred the New Mexico rehabilitation cattle to the registered Herefords. The latter were deemed fine cattle but "pasture cattle," not well equipped to handle the demands of the severe Sonoran climate and terrain. The New Mexico cattle reminded one of the old folk saying about the rigors of New Mexican life — so far from God, so near to Texas. These cattle, in other words, were used to adversity. They were lighter, more willing to "rustle for themselves," and capable of covering more miles for water and food.[30]

Not all members of the Tohono O'odham echoed these sentiments. Some, if not most, of the cattle from New Mexico had been culled from herds or taken from bankrupt ranchers in the state. When the government shipped some of the animals down to Sonora, José Ignacio, Pete Blaine, and Richard Hendricks, the superintendent, traveled south of Nogales to pick them up. "They were just skin and bones," Blaine recalled. "Some of these relief cattle were bad; in fact, some of them died on the way to the ranch in San Vicente." Perhaps 20 percent of the shipment did not make it alive.[31]

Stockman Nation also lobbied for improving water sources, employing salt-feeding and salt grounds, feeding more hay and cake, and selling more animals by means of scheduled sales. Salt had not been part of the raising of livestock, and it quickly proved its utility through a demonstration in the tribal ID herd. More water sources constructed through the Emergency Conservation Work Program began to await the cattle, but more remained to be done in this area. As students of both the Navajos and the Tohono O'odham would recognize, this matter was crucial in reducing soil erosion. The 1930s generally were unusually dry years, and in any event, rain never falls in large quantities in this country. To the uninitiated, it is hard to imagine just how dry a dry year can be in southern Arizona. Consider the amount of precipitation received in the western portion of the Chuk-ut-kuk district in the winter of 1937–38: 0.56 inch.[32]

Without adequate wells and springs, ranching families had to take extreme measures. They brought water in barrels; they drew water from a deep well. They drove their cattle long distances. Naturally such problems limited weight gain. The native charcos, built to store water in the foothills of the Baboquivari, helped but were still not sufficient. Fencing of Tohono O'odham land reduced land erosion but also kept some ranchers from reaching range or water they had used in the past. When one throws livestock reduction into this mix, it is only surprising that there was not more overt ill will toward John Collier or the fledgling tribal government. There was some, that is for sure.

In fact, as Bauer concludes, drought and disease more than government intervention reduced Tohono O'odham livestock. The tribe owned perhaps as many as 27,000 head of cattle at the end of the 1930s, although other estimates from contemporary observers did not put the figure quite that high. In any event, by 1950, the number had dropped to 13,000. The horse poulation had also declined drastically during the same period, from 18,000 to 7,000. This drop had been caused primarily by the outbreak of a dourine infection in the 1940s. As Indians elsewhere, the Tohono O'odham loved their horses. They did not care if these horses were no immediate threat to win at Churchill or Ruidoso Downs. Soil conservationists may have cheered their departure; the Indians mourned the loss of old friends.[33]

The Tohono O'odham and Navajo situations seem in many ways to be very comparable, even though the latter had hundreds of thousands of sheep and a much smaller number of cattle. For the Navajos, sheep were central to the functioning of the social system. They were used for barter; they were a primary source of meat; they were used to pay religious leaders; they were used to feed people at ceremonies. Losing these animals cut at the heart of tribal life. And many never were convinced that the men from Washington had been right and they had been wrong. And they wept for a world that apparently never would return again. Ernest Nelson remembered many years later,

> Before stock reduction, it rained all the time. There was a lot of livestock everywhere, and it rained and rained. Then, when John Collier put a blockade on livestock, the rain ceased altogether. Before that you could see livestock everywhere, and it rained continuously. You could see the golden blossoms of sunflowers growing for miles and miles around. Much grass grew. Pigweed grass grew thickly everywhere you looked.[34]

Even in difficult times, the Tohono O'odham and other tribes found ways of emphasizing community. It is not surprising that the Tohono O'odham Fair and Rodeo, held in the reservation agency headquarters town of Sells, began at this junction. Inaugurated in 1937, an all-Tohono O'odham board, using tribal funds, had complete responsibility for the three-day celebration. Those who chose to attend had a lot of pleasant alternatives: exhibitions of farm produce and the superb baskets created by the women, two football games, a carnival, a dance orchestra, and, as they said at the time, a motion picture show. But the rodeo ranked as a clear crowd pleaser. It grew from a qualifying round for the upcoming Indian Day at the Tucson rodeo. In November 1939, fifty-nine Indians and nine white cowboys competed in calf roping, bulldogging, steer riding, bronc riding, and horse racing. The photographs are wonderful in the December 1939 *Indians at Work*: cowboys riding and roping and looking properly pleased with themselves.[35]

To the north in the plains country, the government attempted the long task of rebuilding the Native cattle industry, so decimated by the policies and economics of the past generation. Gordon Macgregor did not exaggerate when he called the loss of

FIG. 22. The Tohono O'odham Fair and Rodeo proved to be an immediate success. A crowd has gathered on October 16, 1937, in Sells, Arizona. University of Arizona Library Special Collections Department.

their cattle herds "the greatest disaster that had befallen the Pine Ridge Indians since the vanishing of the buffalo." The "bitter experience" of the severe social and economic depression that had gripped Pine Ridge and other northern reservations had taught a lesson—that the cattle industry represented "the only permanent economy possible." Macgregor knew the locale well. In 1946, he ticked off with immediate familiarity the problems the government had encountered in trying to reestablish the pastime: land inheritance, land sold from inside natural cattle ranges, credit limitations, and the temptations of relief wage work, on the one hand, and war-related employment, on the other.[36] Nonetheless, a start had been made.

In 1936, the Oglalas had owned 3,000 head of cattle. Passage and implementation of the Indian Reorganization Act, regardless of the havoc it may have generated in the tribal government, did make a positive difference. Through the Indian New Deal, the people of Pine Ridge had access to more cattle, more loan funds to improve their operations, and encouragement to form livestock organizations and cooperatives. The Indian division of the Civilian Conservation Corps helped construct fences, dams, and reservoirs. By 1940, the Sioux at Pine Ridge owned 11,479 head of cattle; five years later, that number had nearly doubled to 22,386. Increasing cattle ownership by more than seven times in one decade had to be considered an impressive accomplishment. Macgregor thus could conclude on a note of cautious optimism: "There are traditions of the past and value in both the old culture and the adopted 'cowboy culture' that give promise of successful transition" to a modern economy.[37]

Macgregor's analysis reminds us once again that conditions on the Plains were not identical to those in the Southwest. The ravages of the allotment era had exacted their fiercest toll in the Dakotas and Montana. Even with a federal administration more sympathetic, at least in many respects, to the needs and wants of Native communities, the task ahead in the 1930s and 1940s proved far more complex. With checkerboarded lands as well as a reduced acreage, Indian reservations resembled Humpty Dumpty. They could be put back together again to some extent but not entirely—and surely not as completely as Collier and company had hoped.

Lower Brule in South Dakota is a case in point. In "Salvaging the Wreckage of Indian Land Allotment," contributed to a symposium held by the Institute on the Future of the American Indian in March 1941, Bureau of Indian Affairs administrator Allan G. Harper selected Lower Brule as an average allotted reservation, neither the worst nor the least affected by the process of land division and sale. If Lower Brule was indeed average, Indian country faced major problems. Forty percent of the reservation land as of 1900 had passed into white ownership. The Indian New Deal had halted the continuing sale of heirship lands and had purchased lands from whites to try to consolidate Lakota landholdings. These were essential steps, ones that saved Lower Brule from extinction. The Collier era allowed for survival; it did not create instantaneous prosperity.[38]

At the start of the Indian New Deal, Harper alleged, checkerboarding and leasing had caused "a sort of creeping paralysis over Indian economic activity." Whites used all nineteen range units on Lower Brule. The federal government encouraged taking back the land through the establishment of a livestock association. And that association began the slow process of reclaiming the range, taking over three of the nineteen units during the decade. The Resettlement Administration officials knew submarginal lands when they saw them and thus could under their authority gain title to nearly 14,000 acres of land on the reserve. Section 5 of the Indian Reorganization Act of 1934 allowed for funds to obtain additional acreage; 21,000 acres were put back into Native control through these means. Another component of the act, section 10, provided for a revolving loan fund of $10 million. By the beginning of the 1940s, Lower Brule had garnered $143,000 of the $220,000 allocated to it. Where did the community choose to use most of the money? To buy cattle and to develop the fledgling livestock industry. The Lower Brule cattle herd started with several hundred "drought-stricken" cattle, and by the advent of the Second World War, the herd numbered 1,667. Reaching that pinnacle had not been easy. In 1936, the herd had been reduced to all of 80 head, thanks to problems associated with the drought.[39]

These are shocking statistics, but it must be remembered that if the nation's attention focused on the dust bowl of the southern plains, things had become equally miserable in states such as South Dakota. Pioneering families still tell stories about the heat and the drought and the migration out of and through their country. Whites who had carved out a life in this rough terrain often lost hope, or worse, their lands. Those who had found a way to lease Indian land now found that they could not pay the rent. In a memorandum of August 24, 1933, to Secretary of the Interior Harold Ickes, Commissioner Collier recognized fully the gravity of the situation: "These Sioux, who were long ago allotted, are always poor. This year, the drought and the grasshoppers . . . have about cleaned them out. Their white neighbors have been equally cleaned out; and the whites who lease their allotted lands cannot pay their rent."[40]

Both whites and Indians benefited from the federal programs of the New Deal. Given ties to the land and to local communities, as many farmers and ranchers as possible, more perhaps than one might have imagined, chose to tough it out and stay put. Trust land on Indian reservations could not be foreclosed; whites concluded that if they could not sell their lands, they would wait another year and see what happened. Donald Worster observed in *Dust Bowl* that the banker might say no, but the grocer helped many people get by. Indians understood those values; they had tried to practice them prior to the depression and would try to practice them in the years to come. Neither group wanted to come to terms with the ecological consequences of their use of the land. Nature, not people, had caused the problems. Worster concluded, "The values a people hold, their notion of success and their way of achieving it, are among the first things to be formed, the last to be reformed." Once the dirty thirties were history, the Cimarron farmer "was sure he would soon have the earth back in hand, and he was ready once again to extract from it a long desired, long postponed wealth—to collect a deferred payment on his dreams."[41]

The Plains Indians generally wanted to be ranchers rather than farmers, and the Indian New Deal encouraged them to dream. On the Fort Belknap reservation, government officials sounded off about programs in the livestock industry. A photograph of people from Fort Belknap recorded their presence at the South St. Paul market at some point in 1935. They rode with their twenty-seven-carload shipment of cattle and helped sort and prepare their cattle for sale. According to the trade publication *Cooperative Shipper*, "The cattle sold well"; the Indians are described as "having an instinctive like for cattle."[42]

Fred Varnum, a farm agent, observed familiar problems in his survey published in May 1936. The government had tried "to make irrigation farmers, hay farmers, sugar beet farmers and wheat farmers out of the Indians but with little success." The heritage of allotment could be seen in subdivided and checkerboarded land units, too small in size to be productive and overgrazed. With the efforts over the past few years, things had begun to take a turn for the better.

To be fair to Collier's usually neglected predecessor, Charles J. Rhoads, the movement toward creation of grazing associations began prior to the New Deal in the spring of 1931. Within five years, nearly all livestock owners at Fort Belknap had joined one of six associations, which had come to lease nearly half of the reservation land. These associations tackled prevailing problems: trespassing horses and cattle, hundreds of "semiwild" Native horses, limited fencing (all of it illegal), lack of water for livestock, and scattered grazing areas of small numbers of stock.[43]

The largest of the associations, the Milk River Stock Association, leased sixty thousand acres for summer pasture, with slightly more than half of the land permitting a breeding pasture for cows, calves, and horses; the rest of the land held heifers, steers, and more horses. A separate pasture, with a portion reserved for bulls, consisted of five thousand acres of irrigated land on the south side of the Milk River valley. Both summer and winter ranges had been aided by the addition of four stock water reservoirs in the latter and ten in the former. Barbed wire fences now encircled association lands. Two riders hired by the group kept up the fence and generally kept an eye on things. They located and returned stray cattle, brought out salt for the animals, made sure the bulls were in the proper pasture, and discouraged trespassing of animals as well as people.

Figuring twenty acres per head, the association charged the going rate in the area for leases to white stockmen: $1.60 per head per year. Given the scarcity of good range and the satisfactory methods of the association, more white ranchers wanted to run their cattle on association lands than could be accommodated. Cooperative shipments of cattle, such as the one to South St. Paul described above, inspired better prices. Varnum praised the advantages of the association over the individual operator, singling out better management and higher prices. He closed, perhaps with a smile, "These advantages would apply to many white communities as well as to the reservation, and it is a matter of some satisfaction to those of the Indian Service who have been working on this problem, that measures of a similar nature are now being worked out on a nationwide scale, under the Taylor Grazing Act."[44]

So far, so good. But there were limits to what the Collier administration could do. Drought cattle distributed at Fort Belknap did not represent a bargain; the people got hamburger or baloney cows and had to pay filet mignon installment prices for them. The government made some loans, but they did not make as many or in as large amounts as they could have. Nearly 30,000 acres could be acquired to supplement the tribal land base, but this parcel purchased in 1937 undoubtedly fit the "submarginal" category. H. N. Clark, of Winnebago descent, proved to be a supportive and sympathetic superintendent during his tenure from 1939 to 1947. He did his best to encourage a greater degree of economic development and self-determination. Of course, he could not stay forever, and the gains recorded during the Clark years evaporated almost overnight when he departed.[45] In all, some useful, even promising initiatives were being put into effect. Such initiatives remained fragile, not deeply rooted, easily dislodged if the political and economic winds began to blow from another direction. And one could count on wind in the Plains.

Other examples of the resurgence of the Native cattle industry in the region abound. The Northern Cheyennes used the revolving credit fund to inaugurate a tribal steer enterprise. After two years of operation, in the summer of 1939, the enterprise had made a strong beginning. The second season had witnessed the purchase of better-quality steers and more time for them to mature on the excellent grasses of the Northern Cheyenne range. Slightly more than two thousand steers had been sold in this season for a return of $94,579.52. This sum surpassed the amount paid for the steers by $23,335.52. The people had borrowed $85,000 each of the two years from the government, but the investment appeared to be a solid one.[46]

The steer enterprise had secondary positive economic effects that rippled through the Northern Cheyenne community. It provided a ready market for hay; almost $10,000 had been paid for hay in the first two years. Three to five line riders gained steady employment, and their salaries totaled $4,370. Others earned smaller amounts for working on fences. Some individually held land yielded lease money. And although it could be admitted that those lands could have been leased for comparable returns from outsiders, those parties generally would not have employed Northern Cheyenne cowboys or necessarily purchased tribal hay.

Operations of such a tribal enterprise offered more than economic gain. A Native board of directors could be put in charge. Appointed by the tribal council, the board could make substantive decisions. The board may have been subject to review by the superintendent, but the current official, Charles H. Jennings, appeared willing to allow it considerable autonomy.

Board members helped purchase the steers and traveled with them to market. They undoubtedly grew more confident as their level of experience in the business increased. And the promise of the steer enterprise suggested that more could be done to bolster individual ownership by Cheyenne stockmen. Jennings and the credit agent at large, F. A. Asbury, commented that "the general objective of the economic program . . . is to bring the entire reservation into use by Indians."[47] Indian lands being fully used by the people themselves? What was Indian country coming to?

The Northern Arapahoes on the Wind River reservation in Wyoming also invested in the livestock business. Meeting in general council on November 23, 1940, the tribe voted 124–0 to start a tribal livestock and farming enterprise on the lands of the Padlock Ranch. The ranch included 3,746 acres north of Owl Creek; this land was to be added to the northern border of the reservation. In addition, Padlock owned 9,000 acres of land that had formerly been part of Wind River and had permits for 134,000 acres of rangeland. This new enterprise would be jointly owned by the two tribes who occupy the reserve, the Shoshones and the Arapahoes. As the Shoshones had money in a judgment fund for land purchase, the Arapahoes agreed to pay back its share so that it could be a 50–50 deal, with the actual operation an Arapahoe responsibility. The Arapahoes also had obtained rehabilitation funds of $175,000; $125,000 were earmarked for buying cattle, machinery, and equipment from the ranch.

By the time of the formal agreement to purchase Padlock, an additional $90,000 in rehabilitation funds had found their way to the Arapahoes. This infusion of needed capital allowed the Arapahoes to buy over 3,000 Hereford cows, over 1,150 purebred bulls, and 750 heifers. With the acquisition of the ranch, tribal members hoped to make more effective use of nearby allotted lands lying idle or being leased to non-Indians. Even with a white manager in charge and the reservation superintendent and Commissioner Collier keeping a wary eye on the enterprise, Bruce Grosbeck, the chairman of the Arapahoe tribal council, and his colleagues had to be pleased. Perhaps one of their own would manage the enterprise one day. Perhaps that day would not be too many years in the future.[48]

The first few years of the tribally owned Padlock Ranch surely fueled optimistic future projections. From an initial 3,939 head of cattle, the Arapahoe Ranch, as it quickly became called, had increased its holdings by January 1, 1944, to 7,417. The carrying capacity of the ranch had been reached, and the Arapahoes hoped to keep its herd at about that level through animals born into the herd rather than infusion of other stock. Net profits for this first three-year period came to $160,489.70. A little over half of these profits, $134,900, had been invested in livestock; $28,619.50 had been placed in U.S. securities. Trustees of the ranch had even been able to offer a $5 dividend payment in 1941 and 1942, a $10 dividend in 1933, and a $20 dividend in June 1944. Experience with the Arapahoes already had encouraged individuals within the community to ponder the prospects of beginning their own operations.[49]

Although beyond the scope of our chosen focal points of the plains and the Southwest, other Indian communities had become active in the cattle business during the 1930s. Among those reservations where an annual cattle sale could be anticipated were Fort Hall (Idaho), Western Shoshone (Nevada), Klamath (Oregon), Yakima (Washington), Uintah and Ouray (Utah), and Warm Springs (Oregon). Within the Plains and the Southwest, additional groups that had emphasized cattle ranching included Mescalero Apache (New Mexico), Jicarilla Apache (New Mexico), Hualapai (Arizona), the Pueblo villages of New Mexico, and Fort Berthold (North Dakota). Nearly seventeen thousand Indian cattle owners could be counted in 1939; this figure had almost doubled during the Indian New Deal. Bureau officials took pride in this comparison as well. Native cattle ranchers had earned $263,095 from cattle sales in 1933. In 1939, they had earned $3,126,326. That amounted to an increase of 1,088 percent, the officials crowed. Not bad. Not bad at all.[50]

With the sudden beginnning of the Second World War, the Indian New Deal wound down toward its conclusion. Federal

FIG. 23. Two young Jicarilla Apache cowboys, nineteen-year-old Captain Vicenti (left) and Steven Vicenti, Jicarilla Apache reservation, New Mexico, ca. 1929. Courtesy of the Vicenti family.

resources and national attention lay outside of Indian country. Various bureau initiatives, such as the day school program, declined without adequate funds to support them. John Collier, who served longer as commissioner of Indian affairs than any person had, would, will, or should, had grown weary of the struggle toward the end of his tenure. The country, he knew, had begun a retreat from the experimental collectivism, one might say almost tribalism, of the Roosevelt era. Although the war emphasized a collective patriotism, it also rekindled a belief in the cherished, time-honored values of individualism and capitalism. The assumptions that had supported the thrust of Collier's program were bound to come under scrutiny, to say the least, when the war came to an end.

On occasion, which is to say just about every time he spoke or wrote, Collier advertised the triumphs of his administration. As C. L. Sonnichsen remarked in *The Mescalero Apaches*, Collier and his associates publicly had little doubt about the kind of impact they had. In vintage Collierese, the commissioner gushed,

> The Mescaleros abandoned their slum camp and resettled themselves out where farming and cattle-running could supplement each other. Their net income from cattle jumped from $18,000 to $101,000 in three years. They closed out all leases to whites and they now use their entire range and have built up its herbage and soil while using it. . . . Long-range economic planning has become a matter of course with the Mescaleros. Their energies surge. They have their war-way once more, their chance for combat, for leadership, the endless universal war-ways wherein nature is antagonist and collaborator in one.[51]

Whew. An English professor and prolific historian, Sonnichsen enjoyed rhetorical excess as much as the next person. But even he warned his readers that "anyone in close contact with Indians was apt to be skeptical of Collier's lyric flights. "The energies of the Mescaleros," he added, "as their friends very well knew, did not 'surge.'"[52]

Recent judgment of the Collier years and the Collier legacy has been more critical than kind. The tribal governments created through the Indian Reorganization Act have particularly been singled out for censure. Even the renaissance of Indian cattle ranching could be perceived skeptically. For example, Alison Bernstein in her study of Indians and the Second World War suggests that Collier's version of Native economic development "could also be interpreted as encouraging a form of 'corporate assimilation' to the prevailing society." "He pointed with pride," she writes, "to Indian controlled cattle associations and farm cooperatives, not acknowledging that these efforts brought the economy of these tribes squarely into the non-Indian mainstream." Or one might note Richard White's examination of Indian economies in *The Roots of Dependency*, in which he contends that livestock reduction for the Navajos represented a final stage in their absorption into the market.[53] Collier is less pluralist than assimilationist, more well meaning than effective, more exaggeration than reality.

However, in debunking some of the self-serving excesses of the Collier years, some historians have gone too far. D'Arcy McNickle, the Salish and Kutenai writer and scholar, worked for the bureau during Collier's administration. To appreciate Collier, McNickle said, what one had to do was to consider what had happened before him and what happened after he left.[54]

Livestock associations, tribal herds, expansion of the Native estate, and related developments all marked a turning away from the avowedly assimilationist period from after the Civil War until the 1930s. Even if imperfect, even if flawed, the Collier years merit better marks than some of its critics are willing to give them. As McNickle noted, consider what happened next.

CHAPTER SEVEN

Indian Cattle Ranching in the 1950s and 1960s

WRITING DURING THE COLLIER YEARS, BIA DIREC-
tor of Education Willard W. Beatty noted that historically and in
the present day, so-called friends of the Indian gave bad advice.
To become "civilized," they told reservation residents, "you need
to leave the land and get some kind of job in the cities." Non-
Indians had not wanted to accept "the transition from buffalo
hunting to cattle herding as a normal and gradual adjustment for
the Sioux." If Indians heeded the modern advice to go urban
rather than west, Beatty then observed, "it has been interesting
to note that their places on the land have been taken by white
men." Leasing or renting should not be roads taken; Indians
ought to use the land themselves. Beatty concluded, "It should
be self-evident that if land owned by Indians is coveted by whites
for purposes of farming or stock raising, it is probably pretty good

land for Indians to hold and use for the same purposes themselves."[1]

Once Collier left his commissionership, once the Second World War had come to a close, all the old pressures for assimilation and non-Indian use of Native land redoubled. Such tendencies, of course, had not really disappeared during the New Deal. With the New Deal over, with Collier gone, with Harry S. Truman in the White House having other things on his mind and with little, if any, interest in Indian life, it is hardly surprising that pluralist initiatives soon would be in disfavor.[2]

New federal policies emphasizing individualism and Washington's withdrawal from the role of trustee for Indian communities meshed with the national mood. Americans anxious over the Soviet Union and China and the growth of Communist influence looked antipathetically at more communal Indian societies. The crabgrass frontier beckoned a steady flow of people to the suburbs; town and city appeared to offer more of everything: better schools, better jobs, better opportunities. By contrast, rural America loomed as an economic dead end and the increasingly distant home of rubes and hicks. When confronted with statistics about reservation underdevelopment, federal officials were more likely to ask why the government should invest in such remote areas. Few Americans saw Indians other than in the movies or in comic strips, and Natives thus became people of the past and people of the margin, easily susceptible to prejudicial policies. Attorney Felix Cohen, a leading authority in the field of Indian law and special counsel to Collier and Ickes during the New Deal, wrote in despair,

> It is a pity that so many Americans today think of the Indian as a romantic or comic figure in American history without contemporary significance. In fact, the Indian plays much the same role in our American society that the Jews played in Germany. Like the miner's canary, the Indian marks the shifts from fresh air to poison gas in our political atmosphere; and our treatment of Indians, even more than our treatment of other minorities, reflects the rise and fall in our democratic faith.[3]

Ironically, the Native experience during the war also mitigated against tribalism. The Navajo codetalkers' performance in
the Pacific campaign, the presence of Pima Ira Hayes as one of
the flag raisers on Iwo Jima, the individual exploits of Indians in
the armed services, and the contributions made by Indians to
war-related industries all spoke to an ability to survive and
prosper in the new world of postwar America. Sen. Arthur
Watkins (Utah) and Rep. E. Y. Berry (South Dakota) began to
lead the fight in Congress to "liberate" the Indians from the
shackles imposed by the Bureau of Indian Affairs. Echoing the
sentiments of reformers in the late nineteenth century, they
argued Indians should be equal before the law, should be treated
just like everybody else. Watkins lobbied for what he termed
"decontrol." The senator saw the Indian New Deal as an aberra-
tion, a deviation from the "continuing Congressional movement
toward full freedom." But times had changed. The old dream of
equality had come alive again, and to Watkins it embodied a
Lincolnian nobility: "Following in the footsteps of the Emanci-
pation Proclamation of ninety-four years ago, I see the following
words emblazoned in letters of fire above the heads of the
Indians—THESE PEOPLE SHALL BE FREE!"[4]

If Watkins saw himself as an agent for dramatic achievement,
Berry probably felt even more strongly about what needed to be
done. A resident for many years of McLaughlin on the Standing
Rock reservation, he had witnessed firsthand Indian life and the
use of Sioux lands and had drawn his own conclusions about the
proper course of action. Closely allied with the powerful white
cattle ranchers in the Dakotas, Berry argued for the full exercise
of capitalism on the open range. Leasing of Indian land, he
asserted, should not be discouraged. Rather, the lessor-lessee
bond was a warm, personal arrangement through which "the
Indian was happy." The Indian "generally got more out of the
lease than the lease called for," Berry believed. For example,
"when the snow was deep and the Indian was out of work and out
of funds, he would go to the rancher who was leasing his land and
get some flour and a few chickens to tide him over." When the

Indian's family got sick, "he called on the rancher lessee who always took his car and took the sick person to the hospital." As Berry saw it, the rancher wisely knew that "if he didn't provide these services, the Indian allottee would not lease his land to him the following year." Why, Berry clucked, leasing led truly to one benefit after another. "The Indian was learning to handle his own affairs, take care of his own land, send his children to school, and teach them the value of individual enterprise."[5]

Berry ranked as a charter member of the Operation Bootstrap approach to Indian economic development. He actually preferred the term "Operation Moccasin."[6] In the more conservative era following the Second World War, such sentiments became the conventional wisdom. As one would imagine, the effects on Indian cattle ranching of the return to assimilationism were immediate and far-reaching. And as is always the case in Indian country, the results were not always predictable. This period, called the termination era by observers because of the federal attempt to terminate federal obligations and responsibilities in the guise of offering freedom and opportunity, did create inroads in tribal approaches to Native land use. However, the effects of the Collier years could not easily be erased, and the threat of benign neglect or state and local interference also inspired a new level of Indian activism. Depending on local conditions and leadership, the results varied considerably from one reservation and one region to the next.[7]

The Pueblo communities of New Mexico offer an interesting case in point. In the 1930s, the Bureau of Indian Affairs had made a vigorous effort to prosecute trespassers on Pueblo village lands as well as to support the establishment of small cattle trusts. Given the limited acreage held by such communities and the landholdings of Hispanic and Anglo farmers and ranchers which adjoined Native terrain, frequent controversies had erupted. Local non-Indian ranchers had often developed a rather cavalier attitude about their animals just happening to stray onto Indian land and took umbrage at the local superinten-

dent nagging them about the matter. When Superintendent
Sophie D. Aberle warned Malcolm S. Major of New Laguna to
confine his cattle to his assigned land, Major suggested she was
"trying to make an issue out of a very small matter." He reminded
Aberle that he had lived in the country for twenty years and had
"put the best years of my life here building up this ranch and
making a home for myself and family which includes seven
children." "Perhaps you can understand," he added, "how I feel
to have my leases bought from under me and my home and range
you might say destroyed for me. . . . I feel like I have been
jammed around quite enough."[8]

Major would be happier in the 1950s. With the election of
Dwight D. Eisenhower in 1952, Glenn Emmons became commissioner of Indian Affairs. Like John Collier, Emmons had
gained his perspective on Indians through time in New Mexico.
However, whereas Collier had been swept away by the beauty
and power of Taos Pueblo and had been in the vanguard of the
fight for Pueblo land rights in the 1920s, Emmons had been a
banker in Gallup, New Mexico, the self-proclaimed "Indian
Capital of the World" and the toughest of the border towns
rimming the Navajo Nation. No one ever accused Glenn Emmons of being a mystic. And he was unlikely to jam around
Anglo cattle ranchers.[9]

Smaller tribal herds and operations naturally were more vulnerable to neglect or attack in this new era. The Isleta Cattle
Trust, begun in 1934, had 864 cows, 247 calves, and 65 bulls in
the tribal herd the following year. A decade later, those numbers
had declined to 516 cows, 30 heifers, 13 steers, 50 calves, and 67
bulls, or a total of 676 compared to 1,176 in 1935. Individually
owned cattle at Isleta in the same period had increased from 819
to 1,306. By 1953, only 404 head of trust cattle remained, in
contrast to 1,814 head of individually owned cattle. Three years
later, bureau officials proposed the termination of the program.
Acting director of the Gallup Area Office, T. B. Hall, listed five
main reasons for ending the tribal herd:

(1) The range is overgrazed, even though cattle numbers held by the Trust have been substantially reduced through the years; (2) livestock numbers owned by individual members of the pueblo have not been limited to subsistence herds as provided for in the Trust Agreement. The Trust cattle are being crowded off the best range and thereby the Trust is required to operate in high cost areas; (3) the management by the Trust, both with respect to the range resource and the cash assets, has not been up to expectations; (4) with the charging of grazing fees and issuance of grazing permits, the pueblo might expect to receive more income than is being realized under the Trust arrangements; (5) individual ownership and operation of livestock with economic units has many advantages over community ownership and operation and is in line with the objective of developing individual responsibility and initiative.[10]

Bureau officials had cause to be concerned about fiscal management of the Isleta trust, as its secretary-treasurer had been accused of embezzling funds, "investing" some of the money in the Pelikan Bar in Albuquerque. However, the discrepancy had been discovered by trustees who knew that monthly bills and salaries of the cowboys were due and the secretary-treasurer had disappeared. Located promptly in Albuquerque, the wayward tribal official admitted his deeds and said he could repay the money right away. Such behavior in and of itself would not be enough to dissolve the trust. Hall and other federal employees no doubt had greater concern for "developing individual responsibility and initiative," in keeping with the age.[11]

The trustees and the council at Isleta proved reluctant to close down the trust. However, after several years of being prompted by the Bureau, they probably knew a foregone conclusion when they saw one. United Pueblos Agency Credit Officer Woodrow Tiger noted the "indecision" of village officials in autumn 1958. Members of the Isleta community worried over where the money from sale of the tribal herd would go. "It has been rumored to our attention," they wrote to Carlos Jojola, the president of the council, choosing an intriguing turn of the language, "that the money from the sale of the community cattle, instead of being divided among the people as planned, will now be sent to

Washington for a Special Fund." "What for?" they queried. "In case of war?" "In the event of war," they guessed, "the President and the Congressmen will only be concerned with their own survival just like anybody else." In 1959, the doubts came to a halt. Commissioner Emmons dissolved the Isleta Cattle Trust.[12]

In her history of the Gros Ventres at Fort Belknap, Montana, Fowler reports a similar scenario. The Bureau no longer lent money to the Gros Ventres and Assiniboines so they could buy fractionated heirship land for needed grazing pasturage. By 1952, one-third of the Fort Belknap land had multiple heirs. Bad enough, but the feds were just getting warmed up. They turned down tribal bids on allotted lands. They insisted lessees be bonded. They demanded repayment of loans, gouging out money ahead of schedule if they could. Fowler quotes a local rancher: "A loan client came in to pay his bill and figured he would have three to four hundred dollars left. He paid up his loan and then they made him pay for the next year. When they got through with him, he had one dollar and seventy-five cents left. They dug into him until they took all the sap out of him." The tribal cattle herd and bull pool, the hay farm, and just for consistency, the timber operation, all established tribal enterprises, all bit the dust. Discouraged Fort Belknap residents drifted off to town and city to seek work. That result might have been just what the bureau officials had in mind.[13]

The people of the Red Shirt Table community on the Pine Ridge reservation in South Dakota had witnessed a comparable turnaround. Led by future tribal judge and chairman, Moses Two Bulls, the Red Shirt Table Development Association had been organized in 1937. The bureau had not only purchased this land from whites for reservation status but also provided money for irrigation, loaned cattle and needed funds, and helped with management. A cattle raising program, together with chicken and turkey raising and vegetable gardens, appeared to be well received, and most members of the community participated. Although the government had not pledged eternal underwriting, and although the war drew people to work in relatively nearby Rapid City and more distant towns and cities, the lack of any federal support after 1945 seems shortsighted. The people then chose to divide the cattle among themselves, but lacking the cooperative advantage of an association and handicapped by small herds, cattle ranching at Red Table swiftly declined.[14]

This unwillingness to help on Pine Ridge mirrored a common complaint about the bureau in the termination era of 1945 to 1960. Beatty had gone on from his job as director of Indian education to serve as associate program director for Save the Children Federation, a national organization headquartered in Norwalk, Connecticut, which had taken an especially active interest in the well-being of Indian children in particular and Native communities more generally. He grumped to Lawrence K. Lindley, the general secretary of the Indian Rights Association, in August 1959 about a good many developments in the Emmons administration. In fact, Beatty expressed an uncertainty about Emmons's role. "I am not at all sure that Mr. Emmons is more than a spokesman for a policy which he doesn't determine," Beatty ventured. He offered an example:

> It is quite clear that the Bureau deliberately defeated the attempt of the Northern Cheyenne on Tongue River to buy the key tracts of individual land which the Bureau authorized sold. The tribe had money in the U.S. Treasury. Some technicality was advanced by the Bureau for a refusal to release this money to bid on these land parcels. The tribe sold much of its livestock to raise the money, and again the Bureau refused to make available the money thus raised to bid on the land. It also refused to postpoine the bidding until the tribe's money was available. Thus the land went to non-Indians.[15]

Beatty laid the probable blame at the feet of Rex Lee and other old-time assimilationist BIA bureaucrats "who were, and still are, determined to alienate as much Indian land as possible. I don't know who is doing it," he added, "or where these forces get the power they exercise, but the end results speak for themselves."[16]

John Wooden Legs, the president of the Northern Cheyenne

Council, affirmed Beatty's judgment. The council had liquidated the tribal steer enterprise and sought to use $40,000 from
the sale to save tribal land that was being put up for sale in 1955.
But, as Beatty had noted, the money was not released in a timely
fashion by the Bureau. This initial package, known as the Bixby
tracts, contained 1,340 acres of top-quality grazing land with
good water. The man who bought the land, a Mr. Norris, gained
it for $22,458. Norris did not mind adding insult to injury. He
asked the Cheyennes if they wanted the land back. If they did,
they could have it—for $47,736, a tidy $25,278 profit. Wooden
Legs was perhaps too polite a man to tell Norris what he could do
with his offer. In any event, by that time the council members
were too busy scrambling to try to save other parcels of land the
bureau was putting up for sale. The Cheyennes managed in 1959
to borrow $50,000 from the Indian revolving loan fund at 4
percent interest. It was not enough, they knew, but perhaps it
would be enough to buy time.

   Then the council came up with a plan, approved by the people
and blessed by the Keeper of the Sacred Hat, a tribal holy man.
They sought more money, and they asked the bureau not to sell
any more land. The Bureau officials in Billings refused. They put
up an additional thirteen parcels of land, with the usual adver-
tisements. "Certain white men," Wooden Legs remembered,
"were wheeling around like buzzards waiting for the bidding to
start. The Cheyennes could not talk—they were so angry and
sad." Then Interior Department officials, including Secretary
Fred Eaton, called off the sale. The buzzards could not believe it.
Neither, in all likelihood, could the Cheyennes.[17]

   All over the northern plains country one heard echoes of
Beatty's lament. LaVerne Madigan attended a Pine Ridge tribal
council meeting in 1957 as a representative of the American
Indian Fund and the Association of Indian Affairs. Madigan
reported that one councilman after another encouraged the
tribe to start an Oglala Sioux landowners association to "slow
the passage of Indian land into the hands of South Dakota
stockgrowers." Moses Two Bulls, now a judge, said that Oglalas

who could not afford to buy cattle to put on their land and had no jobs "would continue to sell their land in order to eat."[18]

Earlier in the decade Blackfeet Tribal Chairman George Pambrum had charged the Bureau with "doing its best to stir up an old-fashioned cowboy-and-Indian war" on his reservation. Non-Indian cattle and sheep ranchers had been attempting to graze their stock on Blackfeet land, using grazing permits issued by the Bureau, without tribal consent. Seizing on contemporary fears, Pambrum charged, "The Indian Bureau is now using methods of Communist dictatorship against our people." Indian veterans had been trying to run small herds of cattle, but even they were "being liquidated by a one hundred percent increase in rentals imposed by the Bureau." Pambrum concluded his remarks, thoughtfully made available in the *Congressional Record*, with a parting shot: "Stalin could learn a lot about how to run a dictatorship by watching the Indian Bureau."[19]

A year later, the Blackfeet chairman appeared in person in Washington to remind whoever would listen that a generation before, Uncle Sam had stepped in and bought the cattle dying all over Montana because of the drought. The Indians had been the only ones who had not received such cattle free of charge. They had been persuaded to sign a contract to pay back the Bureau for these cattle, head for head. The Blackfeet had paid back the last heifer in 1949; the Bureau, he alleged, had made a big profit. The tribe had understood that when they had made that final repayment, "[they] would have complete charge of the cattle." The Indian Bureau, they had assumed, would then say nothing about how they did things. Of course, it had turned out otherwise, and the Bureau was "still trying to tell us what to do with our tribal cattle."[20]

When one listens to the voices of Wooden Legs and Pambrum, one does not hear notes of resignation. They and others stood up for the right of their people to remain on the reservation, if they so chose. They did not accept the vision of Commissioner of Indian Affairs Dillon Myer, who had preceded Emmons and who believed that all Indians should be glad to have the chance to live and be just like all other Americans and that transformation by definition could only occur off the reservation or when reservations were no more.[21] They did not accept the vision of the Harvard-educated Lakota, Ben Reifel, who as superintendent of the Fort Berthold reservation in North Dakota in 1953 argued that "a reservation is fast becoming just a place where some Indians were born." "The United States is the Indian citizen's 'Reservation' today," he contended. Reifel was born on Rosebud, but he and his four brothers now lived in five different states. They did not go back too often to Rosebud, especially now that their mother had died. He predicted the same would be true for young men and women from Fort Berthold now graduating from eighth grade and high school. A few would stay "to use the land," but most, Reifel asserted, "will have to go out on our 'Big Reservation,' — the place set aside since 1776 as a reserve for free men and women — the United States of America, for their real chance to make a decent living."[22]

Wooden Legs saw his people as back on the war ponies, for he knew they had to fight to save the land and thus salvage the future. He rejected the forced integration of the Cheyennes into the mainstream of American life; he rejected forcing his people "into the slums of some city." This did not mean "trying to keep the Cheyennes in a blanket." It did mean making the reservation "attractive" to the people.[23] The reservation, therefore, as much as possible, had to be kept in one piece, or at least as few pieces as possible. For those who wanted it to remain home, that integrity, that cohesion, was the highest priority. And then the land had to provide. It had to produce more for the people; it had to do so in order to allow the people to remain home. And it had to help create a better society as well as a better economy. The two, to be sure, went together.

In the postwar years, especially as the threat of termination galvanized reservation communities into greater political activity, more and more Indians spoke out. They were emboldened to speak out because the times demanded it. But they also could articulate both grievances and dreams because of where they had been. Some of them had been through the caldron of the war itself. Others had worked off the reservation in war-related industries and had gained more exposure to American society and to a larger sense of the possible. New national Indian organizations, such as the National Congress of American Indians, and traditional older associations, still often led by whites but in which Indians now played a more visible and vocal role, such as the Association on Indian Affairs, offered new forums for expression and new strength in common cause. Tribal newspapers, national newsletters, and other media allowed as well for the expression of ideas and ideals. Improved transportation systems, even intertribal contact through the growing powwow circuit or regional or national Indian basketball tournaments, encouraged individuals from different communities to know each other and learn from each other's travails and triumphs. In sum, we see evolve a situation in which and through which a stiffened resolve is possible about the use of Indian land. And that obviously affected cattle ranching.

Even in the 1950s this transition might mean trouble for white ranchers used to low fees and ready access to Native grazing land. The Oglalas at Pine Ridge announced their plans to impose a modest tax of three cents per acre for the privilege of doing business on the reservation. The tribal council set a rate of $6.25 per head for grazing on the tribal, nonallotted lands over which they had full control. In a rare fit of trust responsibility, the Interior Department actually raised that rate for the allotted lands to $8.75 for the first year, adjustable thereafter in accordance with market conditions. The tribe and the federal government agreed that hay should not be cut on permit lands unless the Sioux landowners and the agency superintendent approved. They also agreed that if a rancher had a permit to graze cattle, he could be required to help develop more water facilities for that acreage.[24]

For ranchers such as Louis Beckwith of Kadoka, South Dakota, just north of the Pine Ridge line, such stipulations appeared outrageous. The future head of the South Dakota Stock Growers

Association then chaired the organization's public lands committee. If anything, the actions of the Interior Department made him even more unhappy than those of the tribal council. Beckwith bleated, "The department is not only running over the tribal council, the Indian and the white man, but it is launching one of Stalin's five-year plans to put all operators out of business."[25] Perhaps he had been reading the *Congressional Record*.

Beckwith urged ranchers not to sign reservation leases now, "unless it is an absolute necessity," for perhaps they could be altered. Notify your congressman, he advised. Congressman E. Y. Berry did his best, but other than making water improvements more voluntary, there was not much he could do this time around. "I appreciate, Louie," he wrote Beckwith, "that this isn't too helpful but we used every argument at our disposal and put it on a political, economic and distress basis." Federal officials would not budge.[26] The flap did not indicate a shocking transition. However, it suggested that tougher times for white ranchers might be just over the horizon. If politics, economics, and distress could not sway Washington, that did not leave much doubt trouble could indeed lie ahead.

Beckwith and company challenged the tribal tax of three cents per acre, and the Interior Department essentially said to the Pine Ridge tribal council, "Well, this was your idea, you take responsibility for collecting it." The white stock growers took the matter to court in 1956. They refused to pay the tax and doubted any court in South Dakota would force them to cough up the fee. Their lawyer argued the Indians were attempting to behave like a "foreign nation" and suggested that resistance by his clients might well be compared to rebels who opposed unjust taxation in the colonies by England. Former Gov. George T. Mickelson, now a U.S. District Court judge, didn't buy it. Permittees had a choice. They could pay the tax or not use Native land. Merton Glover and ten other white ranchers had to pay over $16,000 in back taxes. Judge Mickelson concluded that Indian tribes were "sovereign powers and as sovereign powers can levy taxes."[27]

As Steve Schulte emphasizes in his study of Sioux and white

political leadership in South Dakota, there can be little doubt that such struggles helped the Indians to take on later battles and win them. For example, in March 1963, the state enacted a law giving the state civil and criminal jurisdiction on the reservations. There were no Sioux representatives in the legislature, despite the high Native population in South Dakota, and the Sioux clearly opposed the notion. Local state representatives from Sioux country who supported such a bill, charged Pine Ridge tribal judge John B. Richards, were acting to "represent the wishes of the South Dakota Stock Growers Association." In fact, state Sen. James Ramey had spearheaded the measure in the legislature, and he just happened to be leasing more than 4,000 acres of grazing lands on Pine Ridge.

Angry over the new law, the Lakotas met immediately in Pierre to organize a new association, United Sioux Tribes, and to organize a petition drive to obtain enough signatures to allow state voters to vote on the issue in November 1964. Following an extended campaign in which Indians and sympathetic whites formed a "fair play" committee to urge non-Indian voters to "keep faith with our Indians," South Dakota voters voted 4–1 to repeal the new law. Senator Ramey even lost his bid for reelection. The Pine Ridge tribal council then canceled his leases, and Mr. Ramey moved. Glover, who had lobbied in favor of the law and who leased more than twice as much land on Pine Ridge as had Ramey, stayed.[28]

By the time of the election in South Dakota, it had become clear that Indians had emerged from the worst threats of the termination era. The election of John F. Kennedy ushered in a more pluralist administration, and other than the occasional James Watt, the Interior Department over the past thirty years has generally been less antipathetic toward Native interests than in the 1950s. One can still point to more than a few examples of federal bungling—the issue of Navajo and Hopi landholdings surely is a contender for one of the worst—but as Indians have filled nearly all of the main administrative positions in the Bureau, the problem has more often been bureaucracy than racism. Crucial problems remained for Indian cattle ranchers. Environmental questions stalked the Native range. The specter of land allotment had left northern reservations in a permanently checkerboarded state, defying consolidation or convenient use.[29] Equipment costs continued to soar, while for the first time the American appetite for beef began to ebb. But other than the matter of land allotment, these and other dilemmas also confronted non-Indian cattlemen. Both, in different ways, even shared the pleasure of dealing with the federal government.

Indeed, as the contemporary era began, it seemed more evident not only that Indian and non-Indian cattle ranchers had more in common in the issues they faced but that both were taking an increasingly similar approach to the business of ranching. Land grant universities offered short- and long-term assistance to Indian ranchers, as they did non-Indian ranchers, through a variety of extension programs. Ranching was becoming more technical or scientific. Range management, breeding, record keeping, marketing, and other components of modern ranching demanded much from those in the industry. On some of the most advanced tribal ranches, such as San Carlos, Indians gained growing recognition and respect for their efforts and achievements.[30]

The argument has been made by some observers that one should expect significantly different results from Indian and non-Indian cattle ranching because individual Indians and whites as well as Indians and white communities are likely to hold different values. The white rancher is perceived as more individualistic, more focused on benefits to his or her nuclear family, and more driven by profit motives. The Indian rancher is assumed to be more group oriented, more concerned with ranching as a social or cultural activity, and ultimately less worried about profit. However, Ernest L. Schusky has concluded that for the few successful Sioux ranchers at Lower Brule, it has meant that their profits have had to be reinvested and not shared with other family members; thus those individuals "have either cut or reduced their kin network."[31]

As we will discuss in more detail in the final chapter, one can make too much of these differences. In an intriguing article in the *American Economic Review* brimming over with output factors, input ratios, and other items not easily grasped by some historians, Salish and Kutenai economist Ronald L. Trosper employs profit function tests developed by Lawrence Lau and Pan Yotopolous. Examining Northern Cheyenne and neighboring white ranchers, Trosper argues that both groups "profit maximize to the same degree." The Cheyennes did not reach the same level of output per acre, but this finding must be understood in the context of probably facing more capital market constraints while at the same time demonstrating higher technical efficiency than their white counterparts.[32]

Let me translate. Having different values does not mean automatically that one uses resources differently or less efficiently. Indians had been ranching for a long time; many Indian families had been in the business almost as long as, or as long as, old-time white ranching clans. However, most white ranchers acquired their land base at a time when land was cheap and have managed to hold on to it and absorb neighbors, come hell, December, high or low water, ever since. Vacillating federal Indian policies have not afforded Indian ranchers the same degree of continuity. Indian ranchers tend to produce somewhat less, but they spend less to get what they do produce. Both Indian and white families take relatively full advantage of the "voluntary" labor of each family member. Both are probably more likely to overgraze leased land than land they actually own.

Trosper's study was published in 1978, but his conclusions appear to be just as timely today. Don't assume the Indians don't know what they're doing. Don't assume that "management deficiencies" are like vitamin deficiencies, cured by a dose of expertise only available through properly certified, card-carrying extension specialists. Don't assume they exist at all. And don't assume that all the white ranchers are more flexible, more innovative, and more advanced in their approaches. Trosper does not put it quite this way, but he would no doubt agree that neither rigidity nor imagination is limited to one group.[33] Again, as will be reiterated in the next chapter, what Indian and white ranchers have in common is far greater than what makes them different from each other.

As we have seen, well before 1978, cattle ranching had become ensconced in many western American Indian communities. On nearly all northern plains reservations and in many of the southwestern reservations, it ranked as a major pastime. Within the latter region, in addition to the more publicized herds at San Carlos, White Mountain, and Tohono O'odham, the Hualapais, Mescalero Apaches, and such Pueblo villages as Isleta, Santo Domingo, Taos, and Zia included cattle ranching as a major element of their economy. Other southwestern Indian tribes raised more sheep than cattle, but cattle still represented an important undertaking. Here one would mention the Navajos and the Jicarilla Apaches, as well as the pueblos of Ácoma, Hopi, Laguna, and Zuñi. The Navajos actually had more cattle in 1968 than any other tribe in the Southwest. The size of the Navajo Nation and the fact that the people raised more than ten times as many sheep obscured the existence of a relatively small but still notable industry.[34] The Navajo Cattle Growers Association held its first convention at the Window Rock Civic Center in May 1961, with the future tribal council vice chairman, Wilson Skeet, of Bread Springs, New Mexico, presiding. The association encouraged the same kind of development witnessed on other reservations: purchase of better bulls, better brand inspection, collective sales for cattle, and more communication with the extension program at the local land grant university and the state cattle growers association.[35]

Grazing lands remained by far the most significant type of land on Indian reservations. Effective use of this resource continued to be a central question for future Native development. In both 1950 and 1966, for example, income from grazing lands provided the biggest single source of income for Indian communities. Henry Hough's survey of Indian economic resources, published in 1967, specifically cited Hualapai, Florida Seminole, and White Mountain Apache cattle ranching as examples of successful programs.[36] A more detailed discussion of two major cattle ranching tribes illustrates more fully the evolution of the industry for American Indians by the late 1960s.

Although estimates for the total gross receipts of sales for any community may be open to question, they do give us some idea of the scale and significance of the industry. Tohono O'odham cattle sales in 1955 may have reached $634,000; comparable figures for 1959 and 1967 are $750,000 and $846,000, respectively. Nearly one out of every three dollars of income for the reservation stemmed from this course. Obviously, there is little doubt about the dimensions or the importance of cattle ranching in this community.[37]

Cultural and ecological problems so evident in the 1930s had not disappeared thirty years later. One Bureau of Indian Affairs superintendent after another made crotchety comments about the obstinate folks he tried to advise and, truth to tell, improve. "Their priorities are backwards," said John Artichoker in 1968. However, the people's concern for extended families and obligations to them, as Bernard Fontana noted, "not to mention the cultural constraints imposed on anyone living in small, face-to-face communities, almost always have a leavening influence on individual initiative. This is not to say," he added immediately, "however, that initiative is lacking."[38]

As in all societies, Tohono O'odham tribal members make choices and have choices made for them. One's attitude toward the raising of cattle unsurprisingly varied according to one's position in the social and economic order. More than half of all families had cattle, stated one study completed in 1959. Only a handful owned most of the animals. Two families held more than 1,000 head of cattle; five families held from 500 to 1,000; nine families owned 100 to 500; ten families had 50 to 100; twenty-nine families held 10 to 50; and about four hundred families owned less than 10. Again, to make the natural comparison with the Navajos and sheep, most Tohono O'odham had cattle because they liked having them, not because they were out to make

FIG. 24. Tohono O'odham cowboy, 1965. University of Arizona Library Special Collections Department.

a handsome profit. Such subsistence livestock owners would sell their cattle for extra cash or exchange them for other products and for church holy days or community celebrations.[39] Cattle allowed one to be generous, to feed others, to emphasize one's ties to relatives and friends. The few ranching families that owned hundreds or thousands of head of cattle ran the risk of being labeled by anthropologists, or far worse, members of their own tribe, as "misers" who might wind up "buried with lard cans full of their unspent silver dollars." Their final resting place thus suggested not only a lack of generosity but an absence of status within Tohono O'odham society.[40] How do we measure success, let alone happiness? And, it might be observed, maybe happiness is having silver dollars and not spending them. In any event, in this and other Native communities, one cannot only think in economic terms.

The federal government has encouraged the development of a tribal herd and a ranch reserved for this herd. From its scrawny beginnings, previously described, the herd matured into a carefully managed operation with use of three rotated pasture areas. Rotation permitted land blessed with modest rainfall, about fifteen inches annually on average, to sustain two to three hundred head. The tribal herd included high-quality bulls that could be loaned to tribal ranchers. On one hand, the tribal herd could be seen as successful, for it demonstrated the potential of the land. On the other hand, the small scale of the project on the sizable Tohono O'odham estate may well have limited its impact. In addition, close supervision by Bureau personnel of the tribal ranch throughout much of its history may also have estranged Tohono O'odham individuals from active participation in it. The agency officials had relinquished control of the herd activities in 1956, then reentered the picture six years later at the request of the tribal chairman for more technical support and supervision, then more or less gracefully bowed back out of the scene in 1966 when it seemed to be taking control once again. Such an on-again, off-again history could hardly have encouraged one and all to see the tribal ranch as truly theirs.[41]

In 1935, the government had created grazing districts and, subsequently, district cattle associations. Given tribal animosity to livestock reduction and uncertainty about such an imposed innovation, the grazing associations were predictably slow to take hold. Then the late 1940s brought extreme drought conditions and the kind of desperation that prompts a willingness to try something else. Adoption of a reservationwide land code, sympathetic to the needs of small operators and customary grazing rights and patterns, together with the start of a useful soil conservation program in one district, fostered the kind of sentiment necessary to promote some associations as well as to redistribute and even occasionally reduce the size of herds. The geographically separate San Xavier area established an association in 1953. On the "Big Reservation," Sif Oidak was formed in 1953; Vaya Chin/KaKa/Ventana, in 1957; Gu Achi, in 1962; and Vamori, in 1964.[42]

The Gu Achi Stockmen's Association emerged during the 1960s as the most successful of the Tohono O'odham cattle organizations. The foundation for this success had been erected in the years immediately following the Second World War. The experience of a federal soil conservationist at this time provides a kind of miniature lesson in how to or how not to attempt to implement cultural change. Operating with finite funds and thus, wisely, finite goals, the conservationist tried out his ideas first not at Gu Achi, but at another district, Schuk Toak. Here he came with an idea of what needed to be done, but the people of Schuk Toak had to be sold on it. In the time-honored tradition of white-Indian relations, the agent ran into several interrelated problems that ultimately doomed his well-meaning efforts.

He tried to present the program too quickly; the people had to decide too rapidly; the translations often did not convey fully what the agent proposed; and the people based their judgment in on what had happened before. They saw the new soil conservation initiative as a revival of the old Civilian Conservation Corps days and uttered the Tohono O'odham equivalent of "ah, ha!" The people saw the value of the project in terms of offering work for money rather than achieving an appropriate goal. When told later they would get paid only after a year's work and the project's completion, they uttered, no doubt, other words that need not be translated here. Work did get done, as Henry F. Dobyns records. "A community pasture was built as Queen's Well, a truck trail constructed, a charco at Haivana Nakya was deepened, 15 miles of fence was repaired or built, and five corrals repaired, a new charco was built at Santa Rosa Ranch, brush was cleared from a Johnson grass meadow, and brush dams were put in gullies on the Tribal Herd Ranch." Other than the charco, built by an outside contractor, local people did do all the labor. Yet after the first year, little else was achieved, and other than the limited structures built, the Schuk Toak district had not been fazed by imposed priorities.[43]

The government employee then had a bold thought: I will do something different. And, to be fair, he dealt with a different community, one that had pondered the ravages alternately brought by drought and flooding and actually wanted help. Nonetheless, the conservationist let a local bus driver and a local man working for the extension service make the pitch. The people asked the two questions they would not have asked a strange white man, and, of course, they asked them in their own language. In the end, the people said yes, and they went one step more. They helped come to an agreement over where dikes needed to be built and other work needed to be done, and then the agent "left execution of the project to the people." The project worked. Through it, the Gu Achi residents came to understand more fully what caused erosion and what could be done about it.[44]

This experience helped construct the foundation for the Gu Achi Stockmen's Association. This association achieved greater success in the 1960s because it was established at the request of the people from this district. We are talking about years rather than months in gestation. When the community was ready, it was time. Only then. Members of the association told Rolf Bauer they collected revenue through charging a grazing fee per head of cattle. They placed 7 percent of association cattle sales into a U.S. Treasury account, gave 3 percent from their sales to the tribe, and received 4 percent interest. Gu Achi association revenue was spent on hay for horses and for some cattle during roundups, salt licks, materials for constructing corrals and chutes, well and pump repairs, electricity for pumps and the community building, and gas for the electric generator. Livestock workers from time to time might obtain some groceries or a little cash to tide them over, if they needed it. The members carried out two district roundups a year, conducted cattle sales, and helped plan and construct corrals and chutes.[45]

In part, the association has worked because it accomplishes

FIG. 25. Tohono O'odham ranchers faced many challenges in raising cattle in the Sonoran Desert. This stock tank, water well, and drill rig, photographed in 1965, were essential allies. University of Arizona Library Special Collections Department.

things that need doing and the people recognize that they do need doing. It also has worked because the organization members believe it was their idea, not the government's, to start such an association. Moreover, the actual roundups follow traditional forms of leadership and organization, with the five grazing ranges presided over by a roundup boss chosen by the villages in each range. Even though as of the late 1960s the association had been reluctant to limit grazing, if things got severe enough, it appeared to have gained the kind of status that would allow it to have a better chance of imposing limits than some outside agency.[46]

FIG. 26. Tohono O'odham cattle drink from a portable water trough, 1965. University of Arizona Library Special Collections Department.

And, as it will in the Sonoran desert country, the drought came again. The people in the districts coped as best they could. Arizona congressmen rustled up some extra funds for hay, well, pump, and windmill repairs and improvements to water storage facilities. Sen. Paul Fannin received a telegram, which reads in part,

THE PAPAGO RESERVATION SUBJECTED TO AN ABNOR-MALLY SEVERE DROUGHT STOP RAINFALL SINCE THE BEGINNING OF THE YEAR HAS BEEN LESS THAN 60 PER-CENT OF THE ANNUAL AVERAGE STOP BECAUSE OF THIS THE CONDITION OF THE PAPAGO CATTLE HERD IS DETE-RIORATING RAPIDLY STOP HUNDREDS OF CATTLE HAVE STARVED TO DEATH AND THOUSANDS OF OTHERS WILL BE COMMITTED TO THE SAME IF EMERGENCY RELIEF SUPPLIES ARE NOT RECEIVED SOON[47]

One can hear the desperation in Tribal Council Chairman Thomas Segundo's voice. Elected to a one-year term, the council chairman has little time to take care of business. As one might guess, Segundo did not win every election.

At the close of the period under investigation, the future of Tohono O'odham ranching appeared both problematic and assured. Environmental and economic problems had hardly been resolved. However, the raising of cattle had become too centrally important, socially and economically, to the people for it to be abandoned. The challenge, then, lay in how to make it work. As Tribal Council Chairman Augustine B. Lopez put it in 1972, "We are proud, self-sustaining, desert-dwelling people. Live-stock production is basic to our existence. We must develop water and improve our ecology by our own traditional pro-cedures, using as much of the white man's sophisticated methods as possible."[48]

"Famed Apache Cattle Raisers to Complete Peak Spring Sales," blared the headline in the May 25, 1952, edition of the *Arizona Republic*. Phoenix's morning paper is not generally known for stories promoting a positive image of the state's many

Indian communities. So when W. G. Kneeland began his feature story singing the praises of "the nation's most famous Indian cattle raisers—San Carlos Apaches of Arizona— . . ." and such laudatory sentiments made it through copyediting and into print in this stodgy daily, one could only conclude that the Apache cattlemen had to be really good.[49]

The reputation of the San Carlos Apache ranching industry had become established by the first years following the Second World War. The registered herd continued to offer outstanding bulls for use by the different associations. The years 1945 and 1947 saw a changing of the guard. Painter's Domino C. 366th and two of his offspring had been bought in 1938 at the Painter dispersion sale in Roggen, Colorado. These bulls had been employed for artificial insemination of the thousand or more cows in the registered herd. By 1945 when he retired, Painter's Domino C. 366th had sired over 2,500 calves at San Carlos. Two new bulls, WHR Royalmix and WHR Invader 14th, from the Wyoming Hereford Ranch, arrived in 1945 and 1947, respectively, to replace old 366th. San Carlos families liked the results. The Herefords kept looking better to them and the buyers who kept coming in from progressively larger spheres to bid at auctions. At six separate auctions at San Carlos and Calva in fall 1948, auctioneer Gunter Prude of Portales, New Mexico, sold off several thousand steers, nearly a thousand cows and heifers, about a thousand cows and calves, and between fifty and one hundred purebred bulls and cows from the association herds.[50]

As Richard G. Schaus noted in his article, "Arizona's Apaches Have a Cattle Tradition," for the *Hereford Journal*, to figure out what role the Herefords have at San Carlos one can add up the total sales and deduct the expenses, leaving a "substantial" profit. "The most important thing, however, is more subtle," he added. The cattle associations have encouraged the emergence of leaders. And they have allowed many more people than otherwise could have to remain residents of the reservations. Those who stay or who leave and return, Schaus contended, "make a wise and understandable decision" for it is, indeed,

FIG. 27. The successor of Painter's Domino C. 266th, WHR Roy-almix, had sired over 1,200 calves in the San Carlos Apache purebred herd by the time he posed for this photograph in a sales brochure. Photograph reproduced from the San Carlos Hereford Feeder Sales Brochure, October-November-December 1948. Archives and Manuscripts, University Libraries, Arizona State University (Tempe).

"wonderful country." He dismissed as "nonsense" the conventional BIA wisdom that most Apaches will have to forsake their home to experience the urban delights of Phoenix or Tucson. "The San Carlos is capable of great things, even more than has been accomplished so far," he predicted. Writing in the year Barry Goldwater gained the Republican nomination, Schaus admonished, "All it takes is some private enterprise, vision, and verve."[51]

The artificial insemination program evolved under the direction of John Lasley of the University of Missouri and other technicians. When it concluded in 1955, it may have been the largest beef cattle artificial insemination program in the United States. The general manager for tribal affairs, Thomas S. Shiya,

FIG. 28. Apache cowboys enjoy the view and progress in a roundup, ca. 1950s. University of Arizona Library Special Collections Department.

talked to C. B. Roubicek, head of the U.S. Department of Agriculture Beef Cattle Breeding Research Center at Denver, and Floyd Pahnish, an assistant professor of animal science at the University of Arizona. When Roubicek went to join Pahnish in Tucson, a joint research management project could be inaugurated, one that has benefited the tribe, the university, and the USDA for more than thirty years.[52]

The San Carlos Apaches gained a more efficient and effective operation, including a better percentage of calves (rising from 68% to almost 85%), in less than a decade. To realize that impressive improvement, a series of changes had to be achieved in the day-to-day business. The tribe slimmed the size of breeding pastures from three to four sections to one section (640 acres), with such pastures for one bull and twenty to thirty cows used solely in breeding and calving seasons. In addition, cows that did not have a calf for two years in a row found themselves on the auction block. Breeding and calving seasons were abbreviated. New fencing had to be put in — a massive job on the sizable Apache range.

Of interest to both the Apaches and the researchers: the project developed extremely thorough progeny records. The computer of 1964 would be a joke today, but it surely dazzled contemporary observers who marveled at what could be included on the card punched by this strange newfangled, as perhaps they called it, machine. What the scientists wanted to discern was what they termed the genetic merit of the herd. How much did the calf weigh? When was it born? Who was its sire and dam? What pattern of weight gain did it demonstrate? What can we learn about its liver and blood qualities? Let's count those internal parasites. And, while we're at it, let's check the grass and the general forage available to the cattle. The USDA has some outstanding purebred bulls at its Miles City, Montana, station. Let's take advantage of their presence, and then let's see how they do.

Animal science professors from the University of Arizona had one of the larger large animal research projects in the world. They had what they called a "complete population," with no culls until the animals were over two years of age and no castration. They had a twelve-month-a-year laboratory. The cattle simply were out there all the time, with no barns or separate yards during the winter. What an opportunity for an extended research project.[53]

As Roubicek commented in summarizing the value of the research, it provided information "generally applicable to the industry as well as information primarily useful to the San Carlos herd." His table, Heritability Estimates from Paternal Half-Sib Correlations, is not for the fainthearted, but its contents are actually less complicated than the label. "In the final analysis," said Roubicek, "the feeling of mutual trust and confidence among all active participants forms the keystone of the project."[54]

The growing maturity of the industry also was reflected in a reorganization in 1957 of the original eleven associations into five reconstituted associations. Cassadore, Circle Seven, Hilltop, and Victor became the Anchor Seven; Tin Cup and Tonto formed the Tonto; Clover and Point of Pines combined for Point of Pines; Ash Creek and Mohave took the name of Ash Creek; Slaughter Mountain retained its name. The registered herd, IDT or Social Security herd, and a small unit for the tribal enterprise's feed yard all formed separate additional units. This reorganization, approved by the tribal council, also established the All-Directors Association of board of director members from the five associations. A manager of livestock operations supervised the associations.[55]

Getty's thorough study of the San Carlos cattle industry, published in 1963, concluded, "Much remains to be done in future years in improving the San Carlos Indian cattle industry, but much progress has been made in the last five years." Small owners have often gone out of business and the overall number of livestock has been reduced, with consequent improvement of the Native range. Controlled breeding and earlier weaning of calves are increasingly practiced. Much better records are being kept, and management is being practiced.[56]

The form of the San Carlos Apache cattle business has been influenced significantly by the prevailing forms of the Anglo-American pastime. Getty lists eight parts to the puzzle:

1. The cattle on the ranges.
2. The ranges—forage and sources of water.
3. Owners, range hands, other personnel.
4. Techniques used in handling the cattle—roundups, branding.
5. Association of individual owners—meetings, officers.
6. Sales procedures.
7. Income from sales; use of the income.
8. Range improvements, or lack of them.[57]

Through the 1960s, at least, the San Carlos Apaches used the business of cattle ranching to remain San Carlos Apaches. They gave their own meaning to ranching. They used it to remain on the land. They used it to promote family and extended family ties.[58] They may have been less interested in making a huge profit than their Anglo counterparts. But they wanted to do well. They wanted to be respected and recognized for being good stock raisers. Progressively greater contact with the so-called outside world had increased rather than decreased their identity as San Carlos Apaches. Being cowboys had allowed them to be Indians.

CHAPTER EIGHT

Epilogue: The Indians Are Cowboys, the Cowboys Are Indians

THE INDIANS ARE COWBOYS

"LAK'OTA PTE'OLE HOKSILA HEMAC'A. . . . SUNK'
akanyanka mak'oc'e o'unyanpi ekta omawani," it says in the
primer for Lakota schoolchildren. "I am a Sioux cowboy. . . . I
ride the range." *The Singing Sioux Cowboy Reader*, written by
Ann Clark, with drawings by Andrew Standing Soldier and the
Lakota text by Emil Afraid-of-Hawk, presents the story of a
young boy whose family raises "red and white" cattle and who
enjoys the rodeo. There is little here to mark a separation of this
Lakota family from others. What strikes the reader is the same
enthusiasm for this way of life.[1]

By the 1950s, many Indians had become cowboys. In his field
work in the Piñon, Arizona, community of the Navajo Nation,

SINGING SIOUX COWBOY   Reader

by
Ann Clark

LAK'OTA PTE'OLE HOKŠILA
LOWANSA

Wo'unspe T'okahe

Sioux Text by Emil Afraid-of-Hawk

drawings by Andrew Standing Soldier

UNITED STATES INDIAN SERVICE

FIG. 29. The bilingual *Singing Sioux Cowboy* reader offered Lakota schoolchildren images from home. This illustration by Andrew Standing Soldier is from the 1954 reprint edition. Photo by Keith Jennings, Media Services, Arizona State University (Tempe).

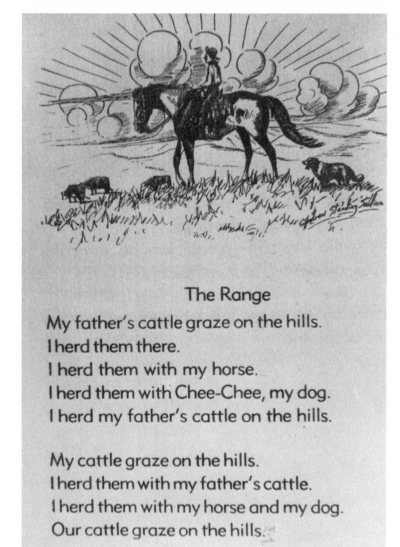

The Range

My father's cattle graze on the hills.
I herd them there.
I herd them with my horse.
I herd them with Chee-Chee, my dog.
I herd my father's cattle on the hills.

My cattle graze on the hills.
I herd them with my father's cattle.
I herd them with my horse and my dog.
Our cattle graze on the hills.

FIG. 30. "The Range," English-language version, in *Singing Sioux Cowboy*, p. 36. Photo by Keith Jennings, Media Services, Arizona State University (Tempe).

James Downs witnessed the emergence of "a new Navajo ideal — the cowboy — and," he added, "the cowboy serves as a platform from which new and non-traditional aspirations can be formed." Downs emphasized, "Although a young man may wish to become a mathematics teacher, a tribal policeman and tractor driver, or leave the reservation entirely to take up a new life in the city, he views himself as basically a cowboy who can rope, ride, and participate in rodeo, a man who knows something of cattle and cattle lore, who dreams of owning cattle and becoming a rancher or cattleman."[2]

Why had Navajos accepted such an ideal? Downs concluded that the acceptance had resulted from "continued exposure to ideas and behavior of an alien culture and society, that of the Anglo-American." Even by the 1950s, even within the part of the United States more devoted to the ranching industry, ranchers were less dominant in the workings of the larger economy and society. But access to movies, border town community rodeos and other gatherings, and the visibility of the cowboy mystique encouraged Piñon Navajos to embrace the cowboy ideal, one "much closer to the life of the Navajo homestead than is any other role in modern American life" for it "requires that a man be a horseman and a roper, have a knowledge of animal ways, and a number of outdoor skills which the Navajo already possesses."[3]

Indian historian Donald L. Fixico echoes Downs in an essay written a generation later. He notes that reservation Indians in the West "habitually wear cowboy hats, leather boots, and other trappings of the American cowboys." Fixico gives some of the credit to practicality and some of it to the power of the cowboy mystique.[4] Written at the time of the urban cowboy phenomenon, which gave us, among other things, a thoroughly forgettable film performance by that old cowpoke, John Travolta, Fixico's essay notes the temporary popularity of the cowboy look. Since that time, country-western music, or variations thereof, has enjoyed somewhat of a resurgence in popularity. Despite the current appeal of such cowboy hat-wearing stars as Garth Brooks,

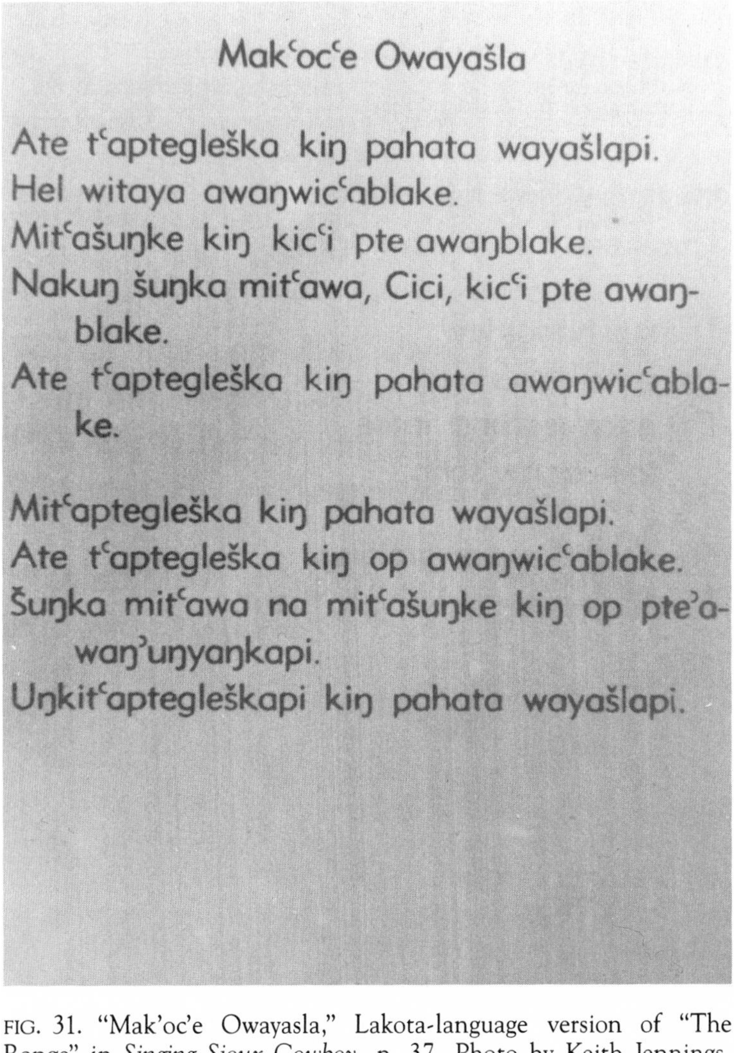

Mak'oc'e Owayašla

Ate t'aptegleška kiŋ pahata wayašlapi.
Hel witaya awaŋwic'ablake.
Mit'ašuŋke kiŋ kic'i pte awaŋblake.
Nakuŋ šuŋka mit'awa, Cici, kic'i pte awaŋ-
    blake.
Ate t'aptegleška kiŋ pahata awaŋwic'abla-
    ke.

Mit'aptegleška kiŋ pahata wayašlapi.
Ate t'aptegleška kiŋ op awaŋwic'ablake.
Šuŋka mit'awa na mit'ašuŋke kiŋ op pte'a-
    waŋ'uŋyaŋkapi.
Uŋkit'aptegleškapi kiŋ pahata wayašlapi.

FIG. 31. "Mak'oc'e Owayasla," Lakota-language version of "The Range" in *Singing Sioux Cowboy*, p. 37. Photo by Keith Jennings, Media Services, Arizona State University (Tempe).

FIG. 32. Navajo cowboy vaccinating a calf, ca. 1960s. Cline Library, Special Collections and Archives, Northern Arizona University (Photo #209.8).

or the recognition afforded a movie such as *Unforgiven*, the dichotomy widens between the rural and urban West. The urban cowboy fad is unlikely to grace the national scene again in the near or more distant future. In contrast to *Unforgiven*, a film set more in the present, *My Heroes Have Always Been Cowboys* sank quickly without a trace. *City Slickers* did better at the box office—but it featured Billy Crystal as an urbanite, completely alien to a cattle drive. Indians of the rural West are just as likely as their non-Indian counterparts to listen to what we might refer to as tunes for the tone deaf, but their willingness to tolerate musical versions of Hallmark cards does not explain why so many Indians mirror cowboys. Quotations from "Cherokee Fiddle"

("Oh, the Indians are dressing up like Cowboys. And the cowboys are puttin' feathers and turquoise on") do not fully answer the question.[5]

Given the economic difficulties plaguing many cattle ranchers in today's West, it is not surprising that on some reservations, a declining percentage of residents rely on the raising of cattle for their entire incomes. At Tohono O'odham, for example, a smaller number of families today may be portrayed as "full-time ranchers." However, this is not inconsistent with larger patterns of contemporary ranching. And on some reservations, such as the Jicarilla Apache reservation in northern New Mexico, cattle ranching is increasing rather than declining.[6] In any event, an impressive number of Native children still spend time with older relatives who herd sheep or round up cattle, and to do so, most still use a horse. The Indian love affair with horses continues unabated. One has only to witness the annual Crow Fair in August or other major tribal fairs to appreciate that affection. Joe Medicine Crow observes that the fair's resumption after the Second World War helped spark a "steady demand" for "race horses, rodeo horses, parade horses, and just kid horses."[7]

It is not accidental that cowboy stories provide two of the five examples of Crow humor in *From the Heart of the Crow Country*. Such inclusion indicates the centrality of cowboys — "those who wear leather leggings" in the Crow language — in Crow culture.[8] One is reminded of the Scandinavian jokes that abound in the upper Midwest, where the ongoing presence of lutefisk is unavoidable, if unfortunate. "The Indian Cowboy's Brain" could really be told — and probably has been — about any cowboy. As Medicine Crow recounts it, medical supply firms sent sales representatives to a seminar where different products were being promoted. One such salesman showed off three containers of brains that could be used for transplants. He said that the brain of a neurosurgeon went for $800 and the brain of a NASA rocket scientist $900. But the asking price for the brain of an Indian cowboy soared to $2,000. When asked why this brain was so expensive, "The salesman quickly replied, 'Why, sir, this brain is

FIG. 33. Beadwork floral designs on the buckskin shirt as well as the hat qualify as traditional attire for Crow historian Joe Medicine Crow in this undated photograph. Montana Historical Society, Helena (Photo #955-745).

like new! It has hardly been used at all! It will be good for many, many years."9 Remember, this is Mr. Medicine Crow's joke.

In the first of a series of short pieces for *Western Horseman*, Barney Nelson found that the Crow and other reservations were "just miniatures of the rest of the American West. They have," she summed up, "personality clashes, public land conflicts, political manipulation, jealousy, and the most beautiful cow country I've ever seen." Using the Yellowtail and Hugs families as examples, Nelson paints a positive portrait of Native ranchers. At the same time, she reports, their achievements have not come easily. Theo Hugs told her, "In the beginning, we struggled against racial prejudices in order to get loans. If you're Indian, those white bankers hesitate to finance you because they feel you're a big risk. We've been real careful in paying our loans, and they finally trust us after 20 years."10

Larry Thompson now lives in Lame Deer on the Northern Cheyenne reservation but grew up as a member of the Lower Brule Sioux community in central South Dakota. When asked about cattle ranching, Thompson is likely to begin with a joke. "Well, you know the reason for the problem of Indian economic development is that when Custer left the Dakotas he said, 'Don't do anything until I get back.'" Or he suggests that for his family, "farming wasn't our bailiwick; you have to get up early and stay late." But then he speaks more seriously of the importance of family for involvement. He rode horses to school and worked on his grandfather's and uncle's ranches. Thompson learned early on that "ranching isn't always that great, especially in bad weather." He recalled without much nostalgia having to bring calves into the house and put them in the tub or at one time keeping thirty-five calves in the basement. When he returned from the army, he wanted to go into ranching. But bankers would not loan him the money. So he bought his first fifty cows from his grandpa.11

Dan Old Elk, Crow, also speaks to the role of family. His grandfather, Sam Bird-in-Ground, obtained permission to leave the reservation and became a world-class bronc rider in Miles City, Montana. As a boy, Old Elk "went to rodeos, broke horses, and did all the things an Indian boy would do." Instead of playing cowboys and Indians, he was an Indian cowboy, but, he adds with a grin, "We did play Indians and Custer." After a proper dramatic pause: "You know, Custer got Siouxed." From 1903 when Sam Bird-in-Ground won that world championship to the present, the Old Elk family has been involved with ranching and with rodeo. And with horses. Dan Old Elk told the apparently true story of one of his relatives reluctantly selling a horse to a white man, protesting all the while that he did not want to do it. "That horse don't look so good," he kept informing the would-be buyer. After the sale, the indignant purchaser soon returned. "The horse is blind! Why didn't you tell me?" Another proper dramatic pause. "Well . . . I told you the horse didn't look so good."[12]

As the story of Sam Bird-in-Ground illustrates, Indians take great pride and pleasure in past and present accomplishments in rodeo. Medicine Crow remembers Indian bronc riders such as Jackson Sundown, Jim Carpenter, and Henry Bruisedhead. Carpenter "was the only one who could ride a horse like Five Minutes to Midnight." And Steamboat—the model for the bucking horse on the Wyoming license plate—why, "Henry Bruisehead could ride him." Thompson recalls with satisfaction his own involvement. At Lower Brule, he got an early start, sneaking his spurs out of the house to ride yearlings. He rode bulls by the age of twelve and in high school captured the state championships in bull riding and steer wrestling. A charter member of the All-American Indian Activities Association and the operator of rodeo schools, he consistently encouraged others to take part in rodeo, including all of his six children and twenty-one foster children. One of David Red Boy Schildt's great-grandfathers was a Texas cattle drover. David Red Boy Schildt, Blackfeet, is now a noted musician, but he acknowledges that "rodeo is still important to me" and sings often about old and young cowboys. Athlete of the year in 1972 at Flandreau Indian School in South Dakota, he won titles in bull riding and later coached rodeo.[13]

These experiences speak to the wide appeal of the sport. The example of respected older relatives frequently generates interest on the part of another generation. Robbie Whitehair of Jamestown, New Mexico, is one of about three hundred Navajos participating in Indian Junior Rodeo Association activities. She gives credit to her late grandfather. "My grandpa Bobby Holyan used to participate in rodeos all the time, and he got my whole family to participate in rodeos. We're just another generation of a rodeo family." The Indian Junior Rodeo Association employs the Larry Thompson principle of an early start. There are divisions for all ages: midget coed (age 3–6), peewee coed (age 7–10), junior coed (age 11–14), and senior girls and senior boys (age 15–18). The cowgirls often earn top honors in all-around in the midget coed, peewee, and junior ranks.[14]

Kim Rhonda Nez is a case in point. A sophomore at Shiprock, New Mexico, High School in 1991, she won the junior coed all-around, with first place finishes in barrel racing, breakaway roping, team roping, and goat tying. She started riding at age three and entered her first rodeo at five. Jennifer Moore, a fifth grader at Red Rock Elementary School in Gallup, New Mexico, took comparable honors in the peewee division. Although she did not begin riding until age five, she quickly emerged as a top competitor on entering rodeo two years later. All smiles, adorned with a belt buckle only slightly smaller than a pie plate, she dedicated her trophy saddle to her grandpa, Henry Moore, Sr.[15]

Another grandfather, Hobert Pourier of Porcupine, South Dakota, was remembered by Avis Little Eagle in a February 1993 tribute published in *Indian Country Today*. Pourier left a legacy as large as his family, which included 75 grandchildren, 128 great-grandchildren, and 24 great-great-grandchildren. One of his grandsons, Larry Pourier, said it well.

> I've learned more about life from my Grandpa than any teacher. He taught me about honor, pride, and the importance of respecting your elders. Not only was he my Grandpa, he was also my friend. He wasn't one to tell you he cared. He showed it by example and by

taking the time to listen, give advice and share the knowledge he gained over the years. I tell you one thing, if there is a horse race in heaven, I'll bet the Lord just made Grandpa the Ranch Foreman.[16]

Born July 27, 1904, on his Grandpa Baptiste "Bat" Pourier's Horsehead Ranch near Manderson, South Dakota, on the Pine Ridge reservation, Hobert Pourier grew up around horses and cattle. Although he attended Rapid City Indian School through the eighth grade, he was more than ready to come home to work on the ranch. He earned his keep driving cattle to Scenic so they could be shipped for sale in Omaha and taking on other imposing chores. Pourier came of age in the difficult times of the 1920s and 1930s. Somehow he managed to provide for his family, including his wife, Isabella, and their eleven children, during an era when in the words of one of his sons, "Grasshoppers were as big as birds."

Pourier held a variety of jobs during his long life, but his leadership in the Pine Ridge ranching community and his veterinary skills are particularly remembered. So, too, is his participation in rodeo at an age when most are likely to forsake the saddle. Pourier proved to be an active competitor in the Old-Timer's Rodeo Association calf roping and breakaway events. At the age of seventy-six, he qualified for the finals of the Old Man's Breakaway in the Sioux Nation Rodeo in Pierre, South Dakota, in 1980. In the final year of his life, he received the Quincentenary Horsemanship Award in Crawford, Nebraska, given to honor the memory of Crazy Horse and the Lakota Great Plains horse culture. In addition, at the Oglala Nation Fair, Pourier was given the Distinguished Service Award. Avis Little Eagle concludes, "Many will remember him as a hard worker, whose strength, fortitude and horseman's skills made him great. Family and friends mourn the loss of this Indian cowboy who journeyed to the spirit world Jan. 19."[17]

Dean C. Jackson did not have the chance to live a long life, for cancer claimed him at the age of fifty-eight. But his death on August 10, 1992, brought forth a comparable outpouring of public sympathy and grief. He, too, was a cowboy, and the rodeo arena in Window Rock, Arizona, now bears his name. In an eventful life, Jackson wore many hats, including president of Navajo Community College and superintendent of schools of the Chinle, Arizona, school district, an area about the size of Connecticut. He belonged to the Native American Church and served on the board of directors for the Native American Church of Navajoland, but he also was a member of the Catholic church and continued throughout his life to know the benefits of Navajo traditional healing and culture.

His many contributions to Navajo education also led him to be a member of the White House Conference on Indian Education and of the American Indian Higher Education Consortium. He worked for many years toward the implementation of an educa-tion system centered in the Diné philosophy of learning and education. Despite these major commitments of time and ener-gy, he never lost his love of horses and rodeo. Jackson founded both the All-Indian Rodeo Cowboy Association and the Indian National Finals Rodeo.[18] Along with his brother, Jack, he labored tirelessly for the betterment of Navajo and Indian rodeo, together with a mutual commitment to Navajo society and its well-being.

One of his greatest pleasures surely came with the involvement of his extended family in rodeo. Among others, his daughters, Carole and Debbie, earned recognition for their accomplish-ments in the sport. In an article mocking the old movie stereo-types, "No Such Thing as Indians and Cowboys," published in the *Navajo Times* in summer 1990, Marley Shebala profiled Debbie Jackson Dennison as an example of those who defied the old dichotomy. Debbie Dennison, "whose maiden name Jackson is synonymous with Navajo cowboys and cowgirls," talked about growing up in rodeo, with early memories of her mother and father and brothers and sisters going to rodeos. She met her husband, a well-known rodeo cowboy in his own right, at a rodeo; they now take their children to rodeos. A high school teacher, she said rodeo kept her "motivated and sane. . . . It's

FIG. 34. Navajo cowgirl Carole Jackson competes in barrel racing at a Holbrook, Arizona, rodeo, n.d. A member of a prominent rodeo family, Jackson has captured many championships. Photo by Monty Roessel. Courtesy of Monty Roessel.

what I use to keep me going." Shebala observed, "Before handing her little girl and boy to her husband and taking her sister's horse through the barrel racing turns, she noted that there are numerous Navajo cowboys and cowgirls who come from a family line of cowboys and cowgirls. For most Navajos, being a cowboy or cowgirl is natural," she said. "Livestock are part of Navajo culture and heritage."[19]

Navajo photojournalist Monty Roessel argued in 1991 that "rodeo is the most popular sport on the Navajo Nation." Looking forward to the Navajo Nation Fair Rodeo, with more than six hundred North American Indian cowboys scheduled to be on hand, Roessel wrote, "On any given weekend across the Navajo Nation at least one rodeo is being held." As the Navajo Nation Fair has been held every September for forty-five years, Roessel's note that the rodeo "has been a fixture at the fair since its beginning" becomes all the more impressive. Such a tradition carries with it the names of outstanding cowboys and their exploits: "Names like Paul Arviso, Felix Gilbert or Sonny Jim have made the history rich and the memories many."[20]

As we have already seen, Indian participation in rodeo goes back to the beginning of the century. By the 1920s, rodeo had evolved in Indian Country, resembling its non-Indian counterpart in some ways yet possessing some distinctive dimensions. Community and family encouraged Indian rodeo more than the prospect of profit. Non-Indian rodeo quickly became professional in its form, offering rules as well as money. Indian rodeo initially was very much of an amateur hour. It also featured old Native games or events, including the chicken pull, races among women, or dances. Parked cars and wagons—probably more of the latter than the former in the twenties—might form a circle to fence in rodeo competition.

The popularity of Indian fairs inspired the growth of Native rodeo. The availability of federal funds in the New Deal era encouraged the construction of more permanent facilities to hold annual tribal fairs and rodeos. Smaller communities, such as the little Navajo town of Lukachukai, Arizona, has began to

FIG. 35. The rodeo clown played an integral role in the proceedings. George Shields prepares for action on the Crow Creek reservation, South Dakota, ca. 1922. Photo by Leo Crane. Cline Library, Special Collections and Archives, Northern Arizona University, Leo Crane Collection (Photo #658.854).

FIG. 36. Navajo cowboys enter for the rodeo at the Navajo Tribal Fair, 1939. Photo by Gilbert Campbell. Gilbert and Myrtle Campbell Collection, Archives and Manuscripts, University Libraries, Arizona State University (Tempe).

sponsor annual rodeos, and the Lukachukai Rodeo, inaugurated in 1932, even gained the same name as the somewhat larger enterprise, the Cheyenne, Wyoming, Frontier Days Rodeo, the granddaddy of them all.

As time went on, the individual rodeos became more sizable affairs, with more entrants and thus more entry fees contributing to progressively larger purses. This development led naturally to a more professional atmosphere and the need to provide fair judges, agreed-upon rules and regulations, and better-quality livestock. Thus in 1958, the Jacksons and other Navajo rodeo cowboys organized the Navajo Rodeo Association, which in due course became the All-Indian Rodeo Cowboys Association, the largest of the Native rodeo groups. Even with added professionalism, the social dimensions of these gatherings continued, with rodeos offering the chance for extended families to gather, compete, and tell stories. The chicken pull and such events as the wild horse race remained staple items at Navajo rodeos well into the 1960s. Bareback riding, steer wrestling, and a revised form of team roping became incorporated along with other roping and riding events.

By the latter part of the 1970s, one could see better-quality livestock contribute to the overall quality of Indian rodeo. Some Native stock contractors joined with longtime non-Indian contractors such as Buster Webb of Farmington, New Mexico, to bring in, for example, Brahma bulls rather than the Hereford bulls that had been used. At the same time, prize money grew as participation increased. Top cowboys could earn thousands of dollars over the course of a rodeo season that might include at least thirty different rodeos. The Indian Junior Rodeo Association, started in 1973, as we have seen, has inspired three- to seventeen-year-olds to compete in the usual riding and roping events, plus pole bending, goat tying, and sheep riding.[21]

In 1979, eleven Indian rodeo associations joined forces to establish the Indian National Finals Rodeo. Buoyed by corporate sponsorship, including Coors, Levi-Strauss, and other major companies, a decade later, the Finals offered $75,000 in prize

money and awards. Indian cowboys also compete at the inter-
collegiate level, with the Navajo Community College rodeo
team enjoying particular success. Each week, major Indian
newspapers include significant coverage of rodeo events, stand-
ings, and prize money.

The September 24, 1992, edition of the *Navajo Times* contains
two columns of "Rodeo Notes." There will be a two-day benefit
roping in Window Rock to help defray medical expenses for
Dean Jackson. The Old-Timers and Open Saddle Roping in
Tohatchi will be this week. The seventh annual Jones Veterans
Memorial Cowboys Association has scheduled its regional finals
for the Navajo County Fairgrounds in Holbrook. The Lazy-J Bull
Riding Classic, in memory of Ray Hosteen, a former Central
Navajo Rodeo Association bull rider, is slated for the Windy
Valley Rodeo Arena south of Many Farms. The Carriso Moun-
tain Bull Bash is coming up in Teec Nos Pos, as is the Tsa Ya Toh
Bear Clan Open Rodeo in Vanderwagon. The annual Rodeo
Queen Contest for the Navajo Nation Rodeo Association will be
conducted next month; contestants will be judged on horsemanship and personality. These and other listings attest to the social
as well as the economic importance of the pastime for participants.[22]

The size and scale of the big rodeo events would amaze old-
timers. In conjunction with the forty-sixth annual Navajo Nation Fair and Rodeo at the Dean C. Jackson Memorial Rodeo
Arena in Window Rock, Arizona, contestants from the United
States and Canada would vie for about $130,000 in prize money
and awards. Coordinator Mike Etsitty labeled it "the largest
Indian rodeo in the world." "We have a large purse, we have
outstanding awards, and we have excellent stock," he added.
"You can't ask for anything larger. This is it, the show." Harry
Vold Rodeo Company of Avondale, Colorado, provided bareback horses, saddle bronc horses, and bulls. And, yes, they also
have terrific names: saddle bronc horses Bobby Joe Skoal, Wran-
gler Savvy, Bad River, Silver King, Kojax, Gentleman Jim, Grey
Velvet, and Prairie Chick; bareback riding horses Hermie's Worm

and Joe Finn; and the bull, Black Jack Skoal, are among those animals headlining the rodeo. Three rodeo judges, two rodeo announcers, a rodeo secretary, and three rodeo clowns and bullfighters also are part of the cast. The men's all-around champion, Cliff Bruisedhead of Standoff, Alberta, won $2,880 and a horse trailer donated by Rico Motors, of Gallup, New Mexico. Carole Jackson of Tsaile, Arizona, received a trophy buckle in addition to her prize money of $2,877. A total of 581 contestants participated. Spectators could even pick up rodeo coverage on the 50,000-watt Navajo station, KTNN. KTNN also sold "Indian Cowboys," a 14-month calendar, at its booth located next to Corral West, a western clothing store, on the fair midway.[23]

Writing a generation before, Susanne Anderson captured the flavor of the community rodeos that still prevail in smaller locales, including Navajo country.

> Rodeos are the main summer fun on the Reservation, there being no movie houses, golf courses, trout streams, or swimming places. There is usually a rodeo every weekend; people crowd into pickups and drive for a hundred miles, often more, to attend. For the spectators it is a day of dust and candy apples, of ice in your soda pop, . . . a day of watching cousins and friends being pumped and usually dumped by an underfed and angry horse or Brahma bull.[24]

The animals now are better fed, and there is more likely to be a movie theater or two, but the dust and distance are still there.

Anderson also portrays a hero of another time. An Indian from the Northwest, married to a Navajo, Sonny Jim reigned for the moment as The Cowboy. Anderson describes him "with shoulder-length hair and a band of sweatstained leather around his head, . . . wearing a worn leather vest with four ballpoint pens in his pocket." Navajo student Bobby Benally was sufficiently inspired to help create what he and others entitled the "First Book of Sonny Jim." The volume begins, "Sonny Jim is like a hippie. He has long hair with an old headband. . . . He has white old cowboy boots, with spurs. He is a brave man, he is not afraid of all kinds of bull."[25] For those who knew Sonny Jim at this time, that is an apt description.

The romantic appeal of the cowboy can yield a variety of results, as contemporary Indian songs attest. Such subject matter has inspired more than one poem as well. "Raisin Eyes" by Navajo poet Luci Tapahonso reminds us not to get too carried away.

> I saw my friend Ella
> with a tall cowboy at the store
> the other day in Shiprock.
>
> Later, I asked her,
> Who's that guy anyway?
>
> Oh, Luci, she said (I knew what was coming)
> it's terrible. He lives with me
> and my money and my car.
> But just for a while.
> He's in AIRCA and rodeos a lot.
>   And I still work.
>
> This rodeo business is getting to me, you know,
> and I'm going to leave him.
> Because I think all this I'm doing now
> will pay off better somewhere else.
> but I just stay with him and it's hard
> because
>   he just smiles that way, you know,
>   and then I end up paying entry fees
>   and putting shiny Tony Lamas on lay-away again.
>   It's not hard.
>
> But he doesn't know when
> I'll leave him and I'll drive across the flat desert
> from Red Valley in blue morning light
> straight to Shiprock so easily.

And anyway, my car is already used
to humming a mourning song with Gary Stewart
complaining again of aching and breaking,
down-and-out love affairs.

Damn.
These Navajo cowboys with raisin eyes
and pointed boots are just bad news,
but it's so hard to remember that all the time,
she said with a little laugh. [26]

Bad news or not, the vitality of Indian rodeo in Navajo country and elsewhere symbolizes the importance of the cowboy tradition. "I remember as a child growing up," Gabriel Begaye says, "I always wanted to be a cowboy because my father was a cowboy. . . . Some families on the reservation have generations who have participated in Indian rodeo." As Jack Jackson told him, "Some of these kids today, it seems like they were born with their boots on."[27] Crow cowboy and rancher Hank Real Bird linked one tradition and value with another when he spoke of having a sweat bath to pray "before I go out rodeoing."[28]

For Indian cowboys such as Howard Hunter, an Oglala from Pine Ridge, the Indian rodeo circuit has provided many satisfactions in the two decades since he won the South Dakota high-school team rodeo championship all by himself for Pine Ridge High School, taking first in bareback, first in bull riding, second in saddle bronc, and first in the all around. Although he has qualified for the Professional Rodeo Cowboys Association finals on several different occasions, Hunter has had still more success at the Indian National Rodeo finals; he has won the saddle bronc championships there three times. And he admits to liking the inter-tribal nature of the competition. Hunter acknowledges there is still just a bit of rivalry between the Lakotas and the Crows. As for the Navajo rodeos: "They don't like to see me come. They know I'll take their money."[29] Such statements remind us of yet another way that being a cowboy allows you to be an Indian.

FIG. 37. Vern Horse Looking of St. Francis, Rosebud reservation, competes in the South Dakota High School Rodeo, 1993. Photo by Ken Blackbird. Courtesy of *Indian Country Today*.

American Indian Rodeo Cowboy Association president Edison Bisuie concluded recently that "in today's modern setting there's no such thing as Indians and Cowboys." In other words, the old image of the two contrasting symbols is no longer valid. In an article about Indian rodeo, Joan Morrison put it another way: "The cowboys are Indians, the Indians are cowboys—at Indian rodeo there is no difference."[30]

In the summer of 1992, I taught a class at the summer institute of the Buffalo Bill Historical Center in Cody, Wyoming. One day we traveled up to the Little Bighorn College of the Crows. There Dan Old Elk addressed my students and me. In the course of his remarks, he observed: "It's difficult today to be an Indian and it's difficult to be a cowboy." And it is. But his hat, his boots, and his other stories also attested to a heritage that reflected the central place cattle ranching has had in the lives of Indians.[31]

THE COWBOYS ARE INDIANS

"That's it exactly, Sylvester, that's it," noted Pete Fabares to Sylvester Yellow Calf. "Montana is becoming one big reservation and all the people in it are the Indians."[32] This remark by one of the characters in James Welch's novel, *The Indian Lawyer*, addresses the increasing separation of rural states such as Montana from the urban enclaves that now dominate the region. In the past generation, the West has witnessed a continuing increase in its population. That demographic growth has not brought many more folks to Niobrara County, Wyoming, or other comparable locales. Economic expansion appears to be primarily an urban prerogative. In the Pacific Northwest, Californians stream into Oregon and Washington. They flow west of the Cascades; they do not head for the John Day country. Phoenix attracts a slightly larger influx than Fredonia; Las Vegas somehow manages to outdraw Winnemucca, regardless of how clever that town's billboards become along Interstate 80. Indians and others are not drawn to Denver and Los Angeles because they want to see the air they breathe. They come, often with great reluctance, be-

FIG. 38. Profile of the Indian cowboy, Vern Horse Looking, 1993. The use of the image of an eagle feather or other symbols can often be seen in contemporary Indian rodeo attire. Photo by Ken Blackbird. Courtesy of *Indian Country Today*.

cause they need jobs; their home areas, where their families have resided for generations, can no longer yield steady or substantial employment.

Their feeling of loss is considerable, and the move to the city is by no means always a permanent one. Rural people miss their families and their old friends. They miss being people who matter and who are known. They miss the land. They miss the stars. And they have to think anew about choices, about trade-offs, and about how one defines prosperity, security, or wealth. For many non-Indian rural people who return home, there is renewed appreciation for the wisdom of the Indian woman who said, when asked why she would not leave her small home and limited economic circumstances on the reservation, "I am wealthy because I get to see my grandchildren each day."

For all but the wealthiest farmers and ranchers, staying in business today has become a veritable battle for survival. It has been a humbling, at times humiliating, transition for white ranchers who for much of this past century enjoyed considerable power within western legislatures, as well as a generally positive image in the popular media. Today most citizens in the region know little about ranch life. Most of the decisions that modern legislators make concerning water, land use and development, and other matters usually put town and city first. Congressional representatives are increasingly skeptical about ranching claims concerning grazing fees on the public lands. Environmental activists lambaste the livestock owners for desecrating the earth. In sum, the ranchers are more and more like the Indians of old, surrounded by a society that knows little about them and cares less, except when it has other priorities for their land.

Times have definitely changed. Equipment costs continue to rise, the public continues to eat less beef, and more land is not necessarily available. Whites who heretofore espoused smugly a kind of heady mixture of private enterprise, gumption, and agrarian Darwinism now recognize that hard work and virtue are not always enough to make the ranches survive. They see multinational corporate farming entering the picture and wonder if corporate ranching may not be far behind. After all, in a country where R. J. Reynolds Tobacco Company concocts Hawaiian Punch, ITT bakes Wonder Bread, and Dad's Root Beer is brewed by the friendly folks of the Illinois Central Railroad, conglomerate round steak may be the next course on the menu.[33] Is it predictable that the small-scale family ranch may disappear early in the twenty-first century?

Such times inspire reflection. Writing for *Harper's*, Montana rancher Ralph Beer describes his own efforts to hold on to the land and the problems he faces these days from "a commitment to stay on, to invest our loyalty and dreams in the places from which we grew, even as these places changed before our eyes like a conjurer's trick."

He recalls attending a spring conference in Helena at the Colonial Inn. Beer heard a Crow, Jeanine Pease Windy Boy, speak of "the savage process of dispossession that her people still face, emphasizing that today's contracts and agreements are no more binding than those signed in the 1870s." As she spoke, Beer remembered "a story fragment" he had listened to some twenty-five years before. "In the winter of 1909–1910," he states, "my grandfather and his father witnessed on their weekly trips to town a large encampment of Indians on the outskirts of Helena. The Indians were kept under military guard for the duration of that winter, on the ground where the Colonial Inn now stands. These people were en route to reservations, having been forced from land they'd owned for centuries by the governmental processes homesteaders believed would safeguard *their* rights of private ownership." Listening to Jeanine Pease Windy Boy, Beer realized "how many farmers and ranchers I know who feel certain . . . that they are facing the same dispossession that cost those Indians their land only a hundred years ago.[34]

There are many in the West who would not weep for that dispossession. In an essay entitled uncompromisingly, "Healthy Ecosystems and Cows Will Never Mix," Earth First! member Mike Seidman charges that cattle ranchers "seem to live in another world, a pre-ecological world in which life is a struggle for power and the goal of humanity is to grab all we can lest another species takes it." He condemns ranchers as being guilty of "ecological imperialism" and admits "it gratifies me that ranchers are worried these days."[35]

Criticism of cattle ranching these days, to be sure, is not limited to members of Earth First!. The primary, although not sole, target of environmentalists' wrath has been the ranchers' use of the public domain. The public lands are for the most part under the jurisdiction of the Bureau of Land Management. Critics of BLM policymaking perceive bureau officials as under the thumb of the ranching industry. Arizona State University law professor Joe Feller has devoted his spare time over the past several years to monitoring and protesting the decisions of these officials. "The basic motivating factor of any BLM official," Feller concludes, "is to minimize stress in their lives. And in general, they minimize stress by not offending the cattle rancher." Freelance writer Ray Wheeler, in turn, concludes cheerfully, "If this is true, then the way to bring about change, Feller suggests, is to become adept at creating stress for BLM managers. In this Joe Feller has undoubtedly succeeded."[36]

In analyzing and protesting the use and management of one particular grazing allotment of BLM land—the Combs Wash Allotment of about 70,000 acres in southeastern Utah—Feller took the bureau regulations at their word. Public participation is permitted in the management of individual grazing allotments, but one has to go to extraordinary lengths to monitor alleged overgrazing. Imagine Feller in a dry wash, kneeling attentively next to a rancher and BLM employees as they measure the length of a blade of grass. Such participant observation is beyond the realm of the ordinary human's time and patience, but it speaks poignantly to the kind of emotions the issue has prompted.[37]

The very use of the word, "allotment," to be sure, brings to mind Indian reservations. And if we think of pressure for ranchers to decrease the number of cattle as a form of stock reduction, another obvious parallel emerges. Nor are such parallels unique to the contemporary scene. In the 1930s, the American National Livestock Association published its perspective on the matters of drought, land use, and soil erosion. *If and When It Rains*, as Donald Worster observes in a footnote to his essay, "Cowboy Ecology," consisted primarily "of individual rancher's experiences with changing range conditions — the folk's 'wisdom' contradicting the professional's 'mythology.' As the title indicates, the cattlemen blamed dry weather for any range deterioration."[38] Of course, such an assessment is reminiscent of the Navajo and Tohono O'odham response during the same era. In addition, just as certain interests within the United States have sought through the decades to terminate federal trusteeship over Native lands, so, too, have critics of the public lands endeavored to transform these enclaves into private domain. It is not at all surprising that the leader of the so-called Sagebrush Rebellion that erupted briefly in the late 1970s hailed from Nevada, the state with the largest percentage of public land.

Others, of course, do not mind the lands being public. In fact, they would prefer to keep such territory out of private hands. They just want to change who has or does not have access to it and for what reasons. Here one witnesses in microcosm a kind of reflection of a changing West. The old order, so dependent on use of natural resources, is attacked vituperatively by a newer order, buoyed by virtuous assumptions of superiority and not dependent on use of natural resources for their own incomes, let alone their own traditions. Marginal old-time timber interests and marginal old-time ranchers are especially the targets of others who have different notions about how these lands ought to be used. Indians with an eye for history and an appreciation for irony — that is to say, most Indians — must smile at the plight of such individuals. For that matter, they would smile at the use of the word "plight" to describe anybody other than themselves.

If Indian reserves make up an important portion of some of the western states and their water rights figure centrally in the regional future, then the same is even more true of the public lands. Florence Williams of the *High Country News* reports, "The West is literally covered with livestock, from the highest elevation tundra down to the driest sagebrush basins. Domestic animals munch in national forests, national parks, 'recreation' areas, wilderness study areas and river bottoms." The Bureau of Land Management has primary responsibility for this realm, but the National Forest Service also has to keep track of those hoofed locusts as well as cattle. Even the National Park Service and state agencies are involved.[39]

The grazing permits are not always for the full year, and of course many ranchers do not hold grazing permits at all. In the Plains country, extending into the Dakotas, Nebraska, Kansas, Oklahoma, and Texas, the percentage of public land declines. In the Dakotas, as we have seen, the Indian lands became all the more subject to pressure for use by non-Indian ranchers in the absence of public lands. Moreover, in the West where public lands and Indian lands have bordered each other, as is often the case, non-Indian ranchers in the old days tried to combine access to one with access to the other.

The more arid the country, the more vulnerable it is to erosion. More rain or snow will allow for more cows; in sparsely vegetated and watered land, one needs a lot of acres to support even one animal. Historically, the laws and general traditions of the range have allowed ranchers a great deal of influence within the workings of the federal bureaucracy, even as their power at the state and local level continues to plummet. This influence is not necessarily greater than that of the mining industry or the timber industry — to cite two other enterprises with which environmentalists have long done battle. As Charles Wilkinson has said, the environmentalists have jousted against "the lords of yesterday" — the laws and traditions that favor extractive interests. Such contentiousness has resulted in "personal hostility and shallow solutions," and one should not assume that such an atmosphere will be dissipated quickly. Wilkinson predicts, "We are not about to enter an era of immediate, deep, and permanent bonding between the drivers of Volvo station wagons sporting 'Babies can't be cuddled with nuclear arms' bumper stickers and the owners of Ford pickups insured by Smith & Wesson."[40]

In the last several years, letters to the editor and other forms of communication in many western newspapers have illustrated the emotions surrounding the matter. Paul Renfer called the *Arizona Republic*'s "Gripeline" to let the world know how he saw things:

> My gripe is that any time someone proposes a fee hike for farmers or ranchers, whether it be grazing fees or a more realistic cost for water, they say it will drive the small farmer and rancher out of business. Well, pardon my ignorance, but I didn't know our Constitution guaranteed the smaller or less-efficient farmer or rancher a job for life. What about the small restaurants, motels, [and] gas stations that have to compete with the big guy? What about the educated middle-class accountants and engineers and managers and so forth that have to make career changes? Why should the taxpayers have to keep the small ranchers and farmers in business?[41]

A voice resounded from rural Colorado with a contrasting perspective:

> The rancher is the West, as much a part of it as the coyote or elk. You want to fence us out — to make a park or maybe a zoo where righteous eco-saviors shall righteously manage and perhaps even benevolently allow us to trespass as long as we don't disturb anything natural. . . . [I am] hoping that you and your kind who hate what is Western will clear out and rescue, instead, New Jersey.[42]

New Jersey is a favorite example in such epistles not only because of its image in the West as a concrete jungle but also because it is the home of Frank J. Popper, chair in the late 1980s of the Rutgers University urban studies department, and Deborah Epstein Popper, a graduate student in geography at Rutgers. They foresaw "near-total desertion" of the rural Plains over the next generation and thus proposed "deprivatization," not only as an ugly contribution to the English language but as a means to transform most of the region into a buffalo commons.[43] Such a proposal has made it unlikely that either Popper will ever be elected mayor of Murdo, and the additional irony of reclaiming the Plains for bison is hardly lost on some Indian observers. A recent *Nature Conservancy* article about the revival of bison raising lauds the animals as "good for the range and the pocketbook." This kind of circle in time does give one pause.[44]

Despite continuing wrangling, there are some intriguing signs of, if not rapprochement, at least some degree of communication across these cultural lines. The Nature Conservancy has jumped into the ranching business. Wildlife biologist Allan Savory, born in Zimbabwe, has concocted what he terms "holistic resource management." About Savory and his notions there is apparently no middle ground; observers either elevate him to sainthood or sentence him to perdition. He actually thinks that more cattle are better than fewer cattle. More cows will improve the chances for grass seeds to take hold and water to reach the roots, as the cattle hoof and kick the ground. This effect has to take place at the appropriate time, and then the animals must move on. Even if one does not buy Savory's revisionist thinking, the debate itself has encouraged some ranchers to reconsider how they do business and some environmentalists to not automatically make the simple equation, Grazing = Evil.[45]

Another perennial issue is the amount that ranchers who use the public lands must pay in grazing fees. Today as in the 1920s, ranchers fight for the lowest possible rates. Times always seem to be hard, their testimony suggests; no one will voluntarily agree to a more substantial tariff. During the Reagan administration, the Bureau of Land Management set the fee for ranchers at about $1.92 per animal unit month. This perfectly awful term, animal unit month, is the amount of forage consumed by a cow-calf pair in one month's time. A 1992 BLM study revealed the obvious: $1.92 is too low. Everywhere. It is a great deal too low for the Dakotas, where the study concluded $10.26 might represent fair market. It is even too little for the desert Southwest, where $4.68 appeared a more equitable amount.[46]

This inequity has not only earned bad reviews for ranchers who use the public lands but has for decades gained derision from ranchers who do not have access to these lands. One of them now happens to be in Congress. A Democrat from Oklahoma, Mike

Synar, has lobbied for the past five years to boost the fee to over $8 per animal unit month. Synar has not carried the day to date, but with a new administration and a host of new people in the Congress, his day is coming. In 1992, K. Lynn Bennett of the Bureau of Land Management sought a deal with something for everybody, which probably means that all sides will not like it entirely.

Bennett's tentative package included a grazing fee tailored to local fair market value and then a 25 percent discount to a rancher who has a management plan for the grazing allotment, improves the quality of the land on that allotment, and restores that parcel to first-rate condition. Of course, it will be nigh on impossible to judge whether a rancher has met or is meeting said criteria. Nonetheless, a version along these lines probably is going to be tried out, and more cattlemen seem more ready to acknowledge that some fee increase is inevitable, to get the best deal they can and to move on. Montana rancher Jimmie Wilson, the president of the National Cattlemen's Association, argues many ranchers want to work it out. "We have to put this thing to bed. It's costing us too much money and too much adverse publicity. We've just got bigger fish to fry."[47]

At the same time, there are limits to what kind of increase in grazing fees most ranchers will accept, and there remain limits on how much environmentalists and ranchers are willing to listen to each other. When Secretary of the Interior Bruce Babbitt journeyed in late April and early May 1993 to the heart of the West to hold public hearings about grazing reform, he certainly got an earful. Laguna Pueblo rancher David Marmon may have encouraged the two sides to find common ground and "not get sideways with each another," but his counsel went largely unheeded at the packed assemblages in Albuquerque, New Mexico, Bozeman, Montana, Grand Junction, Colorado, and Reno, Nevada. Continuing the fish metaphor, Wyoming rancher Waldo Forbes instructed Babbitt to check out larger agricultural subsidies than grazing fees; at the moment, "you're fishing for the minnow while the shark is eating your lunch."

Even with Babbitt's considerable abilities as a cultural broker, he had to endure the usual tirades about welfare cowboys and socialist environmentalists.

Babbitt's political background as former governor of Arizona as well as his personal background as the son of one of northern Arizona's most prominent families, with ranching an integral part of the family heritage, allowed him to listen and to be heard. He emphasized the need for reform, for improving the condition of the land, and for linking grazing fees and land stewardship.[48]

In August 1993 Babbitt unveiled the latest proposal, labeling it "a reasonable balance between the need to sustain the health of rangeland ecosystems and the need to sustain the economic health of rural western areas." The director of grower affairs for the Arizona Cattleman's Association, Doc Lane, said, unsurprisingly, that the fees would cause up to 80 percent of Arizona's 2,000 ranchers to go out of business in five years. In Arizona the fee would be phased in over three years from the current $1.96 per animal per month to $2.76 in 1994, $3.52 in 1995, and $4.28 in 1996. From that point it could be raised up to 25 percent per year. Although $4.28 still was $1.25 less than the fee for private rangelands, Lane and others protested the amount. By contrast a spokesperson for the Sierra Club, Reana Honan, saw the proposal as "a significant step in the right direction."[49] As one might suspect, more public hearings will be scheduled.

Although Babbitt and others have suggested a need for each party to learn more about why the other saw the world in a particular way, it is difficult for many to be patient. Linda Hasselstrom, for one, has little patience with urban environmentalists who fail the Hereford/Holstein test. Raised in western South Dakota on a small ranch, to which she returned to work for many years, she does not mince her words.

Instead of blaming ranchers and farmers for doing what they were told to do, environmentalists need to show us what's wrong with the way we graze cattle, if they know. Most of the complainers have never been personally introduced to a cow, have no clear idea what's wrong with her grazing habits, and wouldn't know a good stand of native grass if they were lying in it reciting poetry or reading [Edward] Abbey. They're willing to take someone else's word—just as the ranchers took the government's word for how to use the land. Too many environmentalists condemn without knowledge. None of the rhetoric changes the fact that the grasslands are in trouble, and only the people who own the land are likely to resolve the problems.[50]

Peter Blaine, no doubt, would second the motion.

Wilkinson also mentions Savory and argues that ranchers have to be willing to bend and change. At the same time, ranchers deserve "an honest respect," as they are "virtually an indigenous society in the west." Ranchers do feed people, employ people, "and preserve the awesome space that gives the west its identity."[51]

It is not by chance that Wilkinson calls ranchers an indigenous society or that he emphasizes the role of ranchers and Indians as central to the development of an ethic of place. When we move beyond cowboy versus Indian, we see that cowboys are Indians, that Indians are cowboys. We see that both involve, in not identical but not entirely dissimilar ways, elements of tradition, family, place, and homeland that are central to who they have been, to who they are, and to who they will be. There are activities, or rituals, as Gretel Ehrlich calls them, that are associated with specific times of the year.[52] There is work to be done, despite the unbelievable range of temperatures, the wind, the demands on mind and body.

Reading Ehrlich, or better yet, Linda Hasselstrom, gives one a direct, unadorned sense of challenge, with a slight frosting of humor from time to time. It is the last day of November and sleet and freezing rain have left everything on the Hasselstrom ranch "covered with a coat of ice. Fenceposts look as if they've been dipped in wax, and fine casings of ice coat each individual blade of grass, tinkling as we walk through it." Linda Hasselstrom and her husband, George Snell, are out feeding the cattle. "I often think about what our feeding looks like from the air. One of us

drives the pickup, with the other in back shaking out cake or
dropping chunks of hay bales. The cattle follow along trampling
down the snow. George always drives in a great circle or an
S-curve, but I'm always tempted to write a huge message to God
or the pilots flying overhead: SEND HEAT. SEND US TO
ARIZONA."[53]

But, of course, she does not want to be sent to urban Arizona.
A weekend in Scottsdale in January might be a pleasant diver-
sion, but home is elsewhere. In terms of how one defines one's
self, where one finds meaning, where one finds power, it is not
likely to be discovered at a suburban mall. Rather, one returns to
or never leaves a place that carries with it a kind of significance
that some would call sacred.

It is not too much to conclude that American Indians and
western American ranchers are native peoples. Over the past
century Indians on reservations and ranchers on their own
defined plots of ground have become native to their lands — have
known what it is to know and love a particular place, regardless
of its limitations and because of its strengths.

"Once in his life," the Kiowa author N. Scott Momaday has
written, "a man ought to concentrate his mind upon the remembered earth." He continues,

> He ought to give himself up to a particular landscape in his
> experiences, to look at it from as many angles as he can, to wonder
> about it, to dwell upon it. He ought to imagine that he touches it
> with his hands at every season and listens to the sounds that are
> made upon it. He ought to imagine the creatures that are there and
> all the faintest motions in the wind. He ought to recollect the glare
> of noon and all the colors of the dawn and dusk.[54]

That detailed knowledge of the land, nurtured through generations, is part of the collective Indian and white heritage in the
West. Each person who has worked a particular piece of ground,
run cattle on it, stacked hay on it, watched countless sunrises and
sunsets over it, struggled to buy an additional section, tried to

hang on to it in bad times, lost it in worse times, had it passed down to him or her, had a child born upon it, and buried one's own in it has a deep sense of what the land can mean. That is as true for the white rancher on the northern plains as it is for the Apache rancher in central Arizona. They both understand the West as, in Wallace Stegner's memorable words, "the native home of hope."[55] And the West is their native home.

Not much more than a century ago any possibility of shared circumstance or destiny seemed remote. Aggressive white ranchers appeared to have a limitless future, but Indians faced the dilemma of survival. As we have seen, in many instances they turned to cattle ranching as a means toward economic and social well-being. Indian families also, usually with great reluctance, conceded the necessity of the white man's education for their children who would live in a different, rapidly changing society. Richard Henry Pratt's Carlisle Indian Industrial School in Pennsylvania offered one of the early opportunities for that schooling. Those children sent east at the end of the 1870s and for the remainder of the nineteenth century doubtless found the trip a wrenching journey.

When Luther Standing Bear agreed to go east to Carlisle, he "could think of no reason why white people wanted Indian boys except to kill them." Having no idea of what a school was, he felt he was "going East to die." On the long route to Pennsylvania, when the train stopped at railway stations, the children had to get off the cars. "In my mind I often recall that scene — eighty-odd blanketed boys and girls marching down the street surrounded by a jeering, unsympathetic people whose only emotions were those of hate and fear; the conquerors looking upon the conquered. And no more understanding us than if we had suddenly been dropped from the moon."[56]

We now near the twenty-first century, but it often seems as though we have not made much progress since Luther Standing Bear's day. The tradition and heritage of white ranchers who live on or near reservations too frequently includes a dismissal of Indian worth. Images created and stereotypes chiseled have been handed down through time. In a largely ignored study, a social scientist dissected the interaction between Indians and whites in a Canadian Plains community. Whites viewed Indians as "irresponsible, untrustworthy, and childishly impulsive"—as people who could not and would not work hard. Given their value systems and feelings, Indians developed their own perspectives on white society and how to deal with it. They saw whites as stingy and insensitive and as people to con whenever possible. All across the western United States a similar view frequently prevails. Prejudice seems to increase as it is passed from one generation to the next. Indian and non-Indian families who live in the same locale for one hundred years inherit more than land.[57]

In a progressively more urban West, one wonders about what lies ahead for tradition, family, heritage, and dreams. In such a world, can rural people, white and Indian, see commonality as well as difference? Can they, unlike Luther Standing Bear's time, know emotions other than hate and fear? Can they achieve an understanding greater than if one group had suddenly been dropped from the moon? Can they talk to each other about continuity and change—and survival?

The urban West is an environment in which the special enclaves we call reservations or ranches remain on a kind of cultural endangered species list. Publication in July 1993 of a new "Magazine for Western Enthusiasts," entitled, of course, *Cowboys & Indians*, speaks to a common marginality. "Howdy, Friends, We sure hope that you'll enjoy cinching up your saddles and hitting the trail with us," begins the first issue. Although the magazine hopes to touch a number of bases, it is clear that its main audience is the urban West ("A lot of us in our daily lives seem to be caught up in a fast pace of life," say the publishers from their headquarters in San Carlos, 20 miles south of San Francisco) and that the main advertisers are those hawking Indian and cowboy "collectibles." Garland's Navajo Rugs in Sedona, Arizona, claims the back page, but on page four we learn of the upcoming Cowboy Antiques & Collectibles (Bits*Spurs*Saddles) Show & Auction in Cody, Wyoming. Just to drive the point home, a full-page advertisement on page 11 for Santa Fe links the 2d annual Old West Show & Sale, the 10th annual Antique Ethnographic Art Show & Sale, and the 15th annual Santa Fe Invitational Antique Indian Art Show & Sale, all events to be held at Sweeney Center, at the corner of Grant and Marcy.[58] Whatever their taste in collectibles, young and not-quite-as-young urban professionals keep edging into rural lands for housing. Semisuburban, I'd like an acre or two of my own sprawl continues to engulf good farm- and ranchland. Conservationists often seem less anxious about this inexorable process than they do about more pristine and remote areas.[59]

However, just as anthropologists have learned to respect the staying power of ethnic groups throughout the world, we would do well to remember, as Anya Peterson Royce concludes in her study of ethnic identity, "the element of pride is not to be taken lightly." Such an identity "is not a shameful thing; in fact, its absence is." Such pride "is not limited to the group itself; it is the heritage of each and every member. It is the savor and re-membrance of the past. More important, it is the promise of the future."[60]

Joseph Jorgensen has observed in his discussion of the mean-ing of land for ranchers that one cannot restrict that meaning "to the composition of soil, its livestock-carrying capacity, and its monetary value." "Rather," he adds, "vistas, open spaces, the beauty of undulating grassy plains, predators, clean air, clean and sufficient water, physical isolation of houses on the land-scape, and disapproval of blatant trespass are important to this culture." "But surely of equal importance," Jorgensen contends, "are conceptions of family continuity in ranching enterprises on family land centering on the idea that the struggles of one's parents and grandparents to prosper on the land meant some-thing, and one's children and grandchildren should be able to continue the tradition on land already steeped in tradition."[61] Jorgensen's words, of course, apply to Indian ranchers, too.

Even as one applauds Jorgensen's understanding, one is brought back to another reality of the 1990s by a piece on the

Denver stock show by *New York Times* reporter Dirk Johnson. He reminded his readers that environmentalists now outnumbered ranchers and that red meat had become an illicit substance for many people. Moreover, since the 1960s the number of ranchers had declined precipitously. Only a little more than half as many ranchers could be counted today as thirty years ago. The average age of the rancher had increased to fifty-nine. Dan Webster, age thirty, wished he could do something about that statistic. "I'd like to ranch full time, like my dad did," he mused, "but there's just no way." So he worked as a ranch hand in his spare time but had to punch computer keys rather than cows for a living. Instead of being at home on the range, he is employed in Gillette, Wyoming—once described by another *Times* reporter as a place where the entire town is on the wrong side of the tracks.[62]

We should not anticipate more people becoming ranchers or cowboys. That life simply is too hard, demands too much knowledge, and requires too much sacrifice and day-to-day dedication for most of us to muster.[63] Yet each generation discovers new horizons and finds new teachings. There may come a time, perhaps not too far distant, where we in the West realize more fully that ethic of place. We can reconsider what we mean by wealth, by generosity, and by ownership of the land.

Each year aspiring and established bards from the outback congregate in Elko, Nevada, for an annual reading of cowboy poetry. At the eighth annual such gathering in early 1992, a group convened not to recite but to analyze the future of western ranching. Wallace MacRae, author of *The Cowboy Curmudgeon*, Teresa Jordan, author of *Cowgirls*, Paul Stone, a doctoral student in history at Yale but also a Texan who knows the industry firsthand, and, among others, Ian Tyson, the Canadian singer and rancher, spoke to the question, "Ranching Culture: Will It Survive?"[64]

Such a rendezvous would have been as unthinkable as it would have been unnecessary a few generations ago. However, in 1992, the anxiety and concern of the panelists are unmistakable.

Acknowledging that ranchers were under attack from all sides, they accepted the need for new thinking and new approaches. Whether the inspiration came from "Brother Savory," as moderator Jay Dusard termed him, or other sources, one had to be open to change.[65]

Wallace MacRae argued that ranchers had to listen to their critics, for some of the criticism either was true or through repetition was becoming reality. Teresa Jordan spoke of the steady, continuing flow of people off of the land and into town and city. She no longer lives in Iron Mountain, Wyoming, her home community. There each generation has seen a smaller number of people able to hang on and make a viable life for themselves. Her family ranch, held for several generations, has been sold.[66]

In her "western family album," *Riding the White Horse Home*, she would elaborate. Families who had worked as neighbors for three and four generations had gone. Within the past fifteen years, all but one of the old ranches had been vacated by those families. An oil company and an investor who had sought a retreat now own most of the land. "The school is closed," she wrote, "the post office is closed, the teacherage and store and railroad station have burned down, and fewer than thirty people, counting children, live in all those miles and miles." Once tied together as a community "by land and labor and shared destiny," Iron Mountain survives just barely as a community now, "mostly through habit and memory. If the next couple of decades are as hard on the rural economy as the past ones have been," she concluded, "it will not survive at all."[67]

Jordan mourned the loss of tradition—but something more as well. She cited what Wendell Berry has called the home economy, where work and home are integrated. In such an economy older family members teach the younger ones. Knowledge can be passed down from one generaton to the next. Because their work is visible and understood and valued, adults who become elders are people to be respected. It is, she might have said, not unlike American Indian communities.

She also admonished ranchers not to confuse problems with goals. By focusing too much on a current problem, a rancher could easily forget what she or he was trying to create. Environmentalists and ranchers are "not natural enemies but cultural enemies." Both would be better served if they could become "partners in thinking about what we want to create." That, she and Paul Stone emphasized, meant ranchers "have to be flexible in a way that we have never been before."

Ian Tyson addressed the demands of urban people who want to use and share rural lands. Whether in Alberta or in the United States, "in the next ten years we're going to have to learn how to live with those people," he said. Name-calling, tempting though it might be, "isn't going to help." Paul Stone echoed the point about a cultural clash between urban and rural perceptions and priorities. Western history has become urban history. And now, whom do senators from the western states represent today? "They represent articulate urban interests."[68]

Such senators are unlikely to see *Range Magazine*, edited by Caroline J. Hadley. The new publication in its first issue labeled itself a voice for "Cowboy Caretakers on America's Outback." The cover photograph shows a cowboy next to his horse. Linda Duferrena's photograph, taken in the Black Rock Desert of Nevada, may not remind one immediately of James Fraser's statue, "The End of the Trail," the slumped Indian warrior on horseback that so captured the sense of doom and disappearance so many embraced in the early twentieth century. Nonetheless, the photograph is a gloomy one, and the caption reads, "The Disappearing Cowboy."[69]

It did not turn out to be the end of the trail for the Indians, as there are more Indians now than a century ago. Nonetheless, more than half of them have left their old lands and reside now in town and city. All of the ranchers are not going to vanish abruptly, either. Yet they confront unprecedented pressures on their terrain and their way of life. It appears likely that a decreasing number of them will be able to remain on the land. The future seems increasingly fragile and uncertain.

However, the land, these people, and the animals themselves remain symbols for our time and our region. Although contact with and demands by urban society will continue to cause problems, that association may also afford opportunities for the reinforcement of group identity. Rather than seeing native white and Indian ranchers or communities as traditional cultures, frozen in time and devoid of imagination or the ability to change, we must understand them as changing, flexible cultural groups who can play a crucial role in the urban world of the twenty-first century. But the question remains: Will the urban West still afford sufficient room for people who know more than a little about particular landscapes, about generations, about the glare of noon and all the colors of the dawn and dusk?

Notes

PREFACE

1. Joe Medicine Crow, remarks at "The Cowboys Are Indians!" a symposium held at the Buffalo Bill Historical Center, Cody, Wyoming, in conjunction with the annual "Cowboy Songs and Range Ballads" gathering, April 2, 1993.

2. Debra Thunder, "Cowboys Ain't Indians; Buffalo Ain't Cows," *High Country News*, May 31, 1993, 16. An earlier version of the article appeared in the *Salt Lake Tribune*. Debra Thunder is a reporter for the *Casper Star-Tribune*.

3. Ibid.

CHAPTER 1

1. See James Merrell, *The Indians' New World: Catawbas and Their Neighbors From European Contact through the Era of Removal* (Chapel Hill: University of North Carolina Press, 1989).

2. For a more extended discussion, see Peter Iverson, "Native Peoples and Native Histories," the first chapter of *The Oxford History of the American West*, ed. Clyde Milner and Carol O'Connor (New York: Oxford University Press, in press).

3. Discussions of the Indian use of fire may be found in William Cronon,

Changes in the Land: Indians, Colonists, and the Ecology of New England (New York: Hill and Wang, 1983), and Stephen J. Pyne, *Fire in America: A Cultural History of Wildland and Rural Fire* (Princeton: Princeton University Press, 1981).

4. This transition in France is analyzed by Eugen Weber in *Peasants into Frenchmen: The Modernization of Rural France, 1870–1914* (Stanford: Stanford University Press, 1976).

5. For a longer look at western Native North America at the time of the Columbus landing, see Peter Iverson, "Taking Care of the Earth and Sky," in *America in 1492*, ed. Alvin M. Josephy, Jr. (New York: Alfred A. Knopf, 1991), 85–117.

6. Calvin Martin has explored some of these points in his provocative *Keepers of the Game: Indian-Animal Relationships and the Fur Trade* (Berkeley and Los Angeles: University of California Press, 1978).

7. Alfred Crosby, *The Columbian Exchange: Biological and Cultural Consequences of 1492* (Westport: Greenwood Press, 1972).

8. David Dary, *Cowboy Culture: A Saga of Five Centuries* (New York: Alfred A. Knopf, 1981), 5–12.

9. Ibid., 12–26.

10. Aileen O'Bryan, *The Diné: Origin Myths of the Navaho Indians.* Bureau of American Ethnology Bulletin No. 163 (Washington, D.C.: Smithsonian Institution, 1956), 174–77.

11. Ibid, 177–78.

12. Ibid, 178.

13. Ibid, 179–80.

14. This definition of identity is from Anya Peterson Royce, *Ethnic Identity: Strategies of Diversity* (Bloomington: Indiana University Press, 1982), 18. Thomas T. McGuire employs Royce's work in *Politics and Ethnicity on the Río Yaqui: Potam Revisited* (Tucson: University of Arizona Press, 1986).

15. This argument is an old favorite of mine, used in, for example, "Building Toward Self-Determination: Plains and Southwestern Indians in the 1940s and 1950s, *Western Historical Quarterly* 16, no. 2 (April 1985):163–73.

16. Royce, *Ethnic Identity*, 40. She cites the work of A. L. Epstein, J. C. Mitchell, and Abner Cohen.

17. Loretta Fowler, *Shared Symbols, Contested Meanings: Gros Ventre History and Culture, 1778–1984* (Ithaca: Cornell University Press, 1987), 9–10. See Clifford Geertz, *The Social History of an Indonesian Town* (Cambridge: MIT Press, 1965), and Geertz, *The Interpretation of Cultures* (New York: Basic Books, 1973).

18. Royce, *Ethnic Identity*, 146. The quotation is from Abner Cohen, *Two-Dimension Man: An Essay on the Anthropology of Power and Symbolism in Complex Society* (Berkeley and Los Angeles: University of California Press, 1974).

19. Royce, *Ethnic Identity*, 146.

CHAPTER 2

1. See Dary, *Cowboy Culture*, and Richard W. Slatta, *Cowboys of the Americas* (New Haven and London: Yale University Press, 1990). For an

argument emphasizing the southern, Anglo-American roots of ranching, see Terry G. Jordan, *Trails to Texas: Southern Roots of Western Cattle Ranching* (Lincoln: University of Nebraska Press, 1981).

2. See Yasahude Kawashima, *Puritan Justice and the Indian: White Man's Law in Massachusetts: 1630–1765* (Middletown, Conn.: Wesleyan University Press, 1983).

3. William W. Savage, Jr., "Indian Ranchers," in *Ranch and Range in Oklahoma*, ed. Jimmy M. Skaggs (Oklahoma City: Oklahoma Historical Society, 1978), 31–44.

4. R. Douglas Hurt, *Indian Agriculture in America: Prehistory to the Present* (Lawrence: University Press of Kansas, 1987), 98.

5. Ibid., 85–87; see also Reginald Horsman, *Expansion and American Indian Policy* (East Lansing: Michigan State University Press, 1967).

6. Hurt, *Indian Agriculture*, 101–104.

7. Cronon, *Changes in the Land*, 128–38.

8. Ibid., 138–39.

9. Richard White, *The Roots of Dependency: Subsistence, Environment, and Social Change Among the Choctaws, Pawnees, and Navajos* (Lincoln: University of Nebraska Press, 1983), 103–105.

10. Ibid.

11. Edward H. Spicer, *Cycles of Conquest: The Impact of Spain, Mexico, and the United States on the Indians of the Southwest, 1533–1960* (Tucson: University of Arizona Press, 1962), 546–50.

12. Ibid.

13. See Gwyneth Harrington Xavier, *The Cattle Industry of the Southern Papago Districts with Some Information on the Reservation Cattle Industry as a Whole* (Tucson: Bureau of Ethnic Research, University of Arizona, 1938).

14. Slatta, *Cowboys of the Americas*, 22–23.

15. Ibid.; Slatta cites the dissertation of Nora E. Ramirez, "The Vaquero and Ranching in the Southwestern United States, 1600–1970" (Indiana University, 1979). In a new book for children, *The American Indian as Cowboy*, Clifford Trafzer emphasizes the early work of the Indian vaquero in California (Sacramento, Calif.: Sierra Oaks, 1992).

16. The version of the Seattle speech employed here is printed in *Great Documents in American Indian History*, ed. Wayne Moquin with Charles Van Doren (New York: Praeger, 1973), 80–83.

CHAPTER 3

1. Slatta, *Cowboys of the Americas*.

2. Robert F. Berkhofer, Jr., *The White Man's Indian: Images of the American Indian from Columbus to the Present* (New York: Alfred A. Knopf, 1978), 134–54.

3. Richard Slotkin, *Regeneration Through Violence: The Mythology of the American Frontier, 1600–1860* (Middletown, Conn.: Wesleyan University Press, 1973).

4. Fredrick A. Hoxie, *A Final Promise: The Campaign to Assimilate the Indians, 1880–1920* (Lincoln: University of Nebraska Press, 1984). See also Hoxie, "Beyond Savagery: The Campaign to Assimilate the American Indians, 1880–1920," Ph.D. dissertation, Brandeis University, 1977.

5. For a discussion of Nez Perce land allotment, see Elizabeth James, "In Their Best Interests: Allotment and the Assimilation Period on the Nez Perce Reservation," M.A. thesis, Arizona State University, 1992. Fletcher's life and career are the subjects of Joan T. Mark, *A Stranger in Her Native Land: Alice Fletcher and the American Indians* (Lincoln: University of Nebraska Press, 1988).

6. Peter M. Wright, "Washakie," in *American Indian Leaders: Studies in Diversity,* ed. R. David Edmunds (Lincoln: University of Nebraska Press, 1980), 143–49; Loretta Fowler, *Arapahoe Politics, 1851–1978: Symbols in Crises of Authority* (Lincoln: University of Nebraska Press, 1982), 92–96.

7. Hoxie, *A Final Promise.*

8. William Jones Papers, box 5, folder 8, Wisconsin State Historical Society.

9. Ibid. There are several biographies of Muir, and Muir was a prolific writer. See, for example, Frederick Turner, *Rediscovering America: John Muir in His Time and Ours* (New York: Viking, 1985).

10. Jones Papers.

11. Janet A. McDonnell, *The Dispossession of the American Indian, 1887–1934* (Bloomington: Indiana University Press, 1991), 43–70.

12. Bruce Siberts, recorded by Walker D. Wyman, *Nothing But Prairie and Sky, Life on the Dakota Range in the Early Days* (Norman: University of Oklahoma Press, 1954), 4.

13. Ibid., 30.

14. Ibid., 20.

15. Bob Lee and Dick Williams, *Last Grass Frontier: The South Dakota Stock Growers Heritage* (Sturgis, S.D.: Black Hills Publishers, 1969). Lee and Williams include a short epilogue on the Cowbelles, the women's auxiliary unit of the stock growers, established in 1951. Perhaps by coincidence, the discussion is in smaller type.

16. Ibid., 245–47.

17. Ibid., 421–22.

18. Hazel Adele Pulling, *History of the Range Cattle Industry of Dakota* (Pierre: South Dakota Historical Collections, 1940), 504–508.

19. Bert L. Hall, *Roundup Years, Old Muddy to Black Hills* (Pierre, S.D.: The Reminder, 1954), 15.

20. Gladys White Jorgensen, *Before Homesteads: In Tripp County and the Rosebud* (Freeman, S.D.: Pine Hill Press, 1974), 64–75.

21. Hall, *Roundup Years,* 77.

22. Ibid. For a discussion of the leasing controversy at Standing Rock, see Richmond L. Clow, "Cattlemen and Tribal Rights: The Standing Rock Leasing Conflict of 1902," *North Dakota History* 54, no. 2 (Spring 1987):23–30.

23. William W. Savage, Jr., *The Cherokee Strip Livestock Association: Federal Regulation and the Cattleman's Last Frontier* (Columbia: University of Missouri Press, 1973).

24. Ibid.

25. William T. Hagan, "Adjusting to the Opening of the Kiowa, Comanche, and Kiowa-Apache Reservations," and Donald J. Berthrong, "Legacies of the Davies Act: Bureaucrats and Land Thieves at the Cheyenne-Arapaho Agencies of Oklahoma," in *The Plains Indians of the 20th Century*, ed. Peter Iverson (Norman: University of Oklahoma Press, 1985), 11–54.

26. John Wooden Legs, "Back on the War Ponies," *Association of Indian Affairs Newsletter* (1960).

27. E. C. Abbott with Helena Huntington Smith, *We Pointed Them North: Recollections of a Cowpuncher* (Norman: University of Oklahoma Press, 1955), 145.

28. Ibid., 149.

29. William E. Farr, *The Reservation Blackfeet, 1882–1945: A Photographic History of Cultural Survival* (Seattle and London: University of Washington Press), 9.

30. Ibid., 10–12, 97–102.

31. Michael Massie, "The Defeat of Assimilation and the Role of Colonialism on the Fort Belknap Reservation," *American Indian Culture and Research Journal* (1983):33–49, and "The Cultural Roots of Indian Water Rights," *Annals of Wyoming* 59, no. 1 (Spring 1987):15–28.

32. Burton M. Smith, "Politics and the Crow Indian Land Cessions," *Montana: The Magazine of Western History* 36, no. 4 (Autumn 1986):32.

33. Ibid., 32–33; see also Frederick E. Hoxie, "Crow Leadership Amidst Reservation Oppression," *State and Reservation: New Perspectives on Federal Indian Policy*, ed. George Pierre Castile and Robert L. Bee (Tucson: University of Arizona Press, 1992), 38–60.

34. William Kittredge and Steven M. Krauzer, "'Mr. Montana' Revised: Another Look at Granville Stuart," *Montana: The Magazine of Western History* 36, no. 4 (August 1986):14–23.

35. Harry T. Getty, *The San Carlos Apache Cattle Industry* (Tucson: University of Arizona Press, 1963), 14.

36. Henry F. Manuel, Juliann Ramon, and Bernard L. Fontana, "Dressing for the Window: Papago Indians and Economic Development," in *American Indian Economic Development*, ed. Sam Stanley (The Hague: Mouton, 1978), 525–28; Janet Ann McDonnell, "The Disintegration of the Indian Estate: Indian Land Policy, 1913–1929," Ph.D. dissertation, Marquette University, 1980, 34–38.

CHAPTER 4

1. Fowler, *Shared Symbols*, 7–9. It is very easy for the newcomer to a Native community or the student of such a community in any era to misread or misunderstand what she or he sees. One often sees what one expects to see, or one sees things that do not make sense and that are then dismissed or ignored. For a self-deprecating and perceptive example, see Fred McTaggart, *Wolf That I*

230 / NOTES TO PAGES 53–67

Am: In Search of the Red Earth People (Boston: Houghton Mifflin, 1976), which in part describes the author's introduction to the Mesquakie community in Iowa and how he misunderstood what he encountered.

2. Interview with Jack Jackson by Gabriel Arviso Begaye. Begaye, "The Indian Cowboy and Cowgirl in Indian and Professional Rodeo," unpublished paper completed for an undergraduate course at Arizona State University. Copy in possession of the author.

3. Fowler, *Shared Symbols*, 61–65.

4. Ibid., 71–85.

5. Hana Samek, *The Blackfoot Confederacy, 1880–1920: A Comparative Study of Canadian and U.S. Indian Policy* (Albuquerque: University of New Mexico Press, 1987), 73–80.

6. Ibid., 80–81.

7. Ibid., 81–82; Farr, *The Reservation Blackfeet*, 97–111. For a discussion of efforts to promote farming and ranching, see the work of Thomas R. Wessell, including "Agent of Acculturation: Farming on the Northern Plains Reservations, 1880–1910," *Agricultural History* 60, no. 2 (Spring 1986):233–45.

8. Karen Easton discusses this choice in her well-researched study, "Getting into Uniform: Northern Cheyenne Scout in the United States Army, 1876–81," M.A. thesis, University of Wyoming, 1985.

9. Orlan J. Svingen, "Reservation Self-Sufficiency: Stock Raising vs. Farming on the Northern Cheyenne Indian Reservation, 1900–1914," *Montana: The Magazine of Western History* 31, no. 4 (October 1981):16.

10. Ibid.

11. Ibid., 16–17.

12. Ibid., 19–20.

13. Ibid., 19–21; Stan Hoig, *The Cheyenne* (New York: Chelsea House, 1990), 101.

14. Tom Weist, *A History of the Cheyenne People* (Billings: Montana Council for Indian Education, 1977), 177.

15. For a good general discussion of Crow politics at this time, see Frederick E. Hoxie, "Crow Leadership Amidst Reservation Oppression," in *State and Reservation*, 38–60.

16. This material is drawn from the proposal for and eventual film made by Pamela Roberts and Connie Poten on the life and career of Robert Yellowtail. The film, *Contrary Warrior*, provides a good overview of Yellowtail's remarkable story but also sheds light on Crow history on culture in the twentieth century.

17. Ibid.

18. Frederick E. Hoxie, "From Reservation to Homeland: The Cheyenne River Reservation Before World War I," in *The Plains Indians of the Twentieth Century*, 55–75.

19. Harry H. Anderson, *A History of the Cheyenne River Indian Agency and Its Military Post, Fort Bennett, 1868–1891*. South Dakota Historical Society Collections 28 (Pierre: South Dakota Historical Society, 1956), 476.

20. Ibid., 515–16.

21. Ibid., 516; Paul Little, *River of People: A Multicultural History of the*

Cheyenne River Reservation Area (Eagle Butte, S.D.: Eagle Butte Public School District, 1983), 111.

22. Little, *River of People*, 111.

23. Ibid., 112–13.

24. See McDonnell, *The Dispossession of the American Indian*.

25. Cato Sells to James H. McGregor, Superintendent, Cheyenne River, December 24, 1920. General Correspondence Files, 1907–1939, Cheyenne River, file 46573-15-054, pt. 2, National Archives. Copy in University of South Dakota Library.

26. James H. McGregor to Cato Sells, December 28, 1920. Ibid.

27. Memorandum, Grazing, Cheyenne River, December 4, 1920. Ibid.

28. Ibid.

29. Raymond J. DeMallie, "Pine Ridge Economy: Cultural and Historical Perspectives," in *American Indian Economic Development*, 256–57.

30. Ibid., 257–58.

31. John Glover, "History of Washington-Shannon County, 1918–1921," in *Reservation Roundup*, 70.

32. Ibid., 72.

33. Ibid., 69–96; John and Maude Glover, "Reminiscences of Years 1918–1921," ibid., 96–98.

34. Richmond L. Clow, "The Rosebud Sioux: The Federal Government and the Reservation Years, 1878–1940," Ph.D. dissertation, History, University of New Mexico, 1977, 158.

35. Ibid., 158–60.

36. Ibid., 126–138, 161–64.

37. Ibid.

38. William Jordan, "The Jordan Story" and "Indians in the Cattle Business in the Early Days," in *Early Dakota Days*, ed. Winifred Reutter (Stickney, S.D.: Argus Printers, 1962), 88–89. Mr. Jordan presents a more detailed discusion of land allotment, the cattle industry, beef rations, and other subjects in William Red Cloud Jordan, *Eighty Years on the Rosebud* (Pierre: South Dakota Historical Collections, 1970), 323–83.

39. Bess Adrian, "The Life of Yellow Robe" and "Life of Mr. and Mrs. Sam White Horse," in *Early Dakota Days*, 232–33, 241–42.

40. "George Defender: World Champion Indian River," and Bess Adrian, "David Blue Thunder Story," in *Early Dakota Days*, 9, 19–20. Other Indian rodeo performers made their way to New York, including the celebrated Cherokee roper and humorist Will Rogers. The son of Cherokee rancher Clem Rogers, Will Rogers learned firsthand about horses and cattle in eastern Oklahoma.

41. Blanche Kaufman, "Reuben Quick Bear," in *Early Dakota Days*, 167–68; *The Sioux of the Rosebud: A History in Pictures*, with photographs by John A. Anderson and text by Henry W. Hamilton and Jean Tyree Hamilton (Norman: University of Oklahoma Press, 1971). A Swedish immigrant, Anderson lived at Rosebud from 1891 until his death in 1948. The volume includes photographs of many subjects, including "Beef Issues, Domestic Issues, and Annuity

Payments," 91–114, and "The Fourth of July Celebrations," 187–202.

42. Clow, "Rosebud," 165–66.

43. Ernest L. Schusky, *The Forgotten Sioux: An Ethnohistory of the Lower Brule Reservation* (Chicago: Nelson-Hall, 1975), 83.

44. Ibid., 101–10.

45. Ibid., 123–24, 141–54.

46. Ibid., 154–56.

47. Ibid., 156–71.

48. Ibid., 169, 171.

49. Ibid., 171–75.

50. Carolyn Gilman and Mary Jane Schneider, eds., *The Way to Independence: Memories of a Hidatsa Indian Family, 1840–1920* (St. Paul: Minnesota Historical Society Press, 1987), 242. Anthropologist Gilbert Wilson worked with the community from 1906 to 1918, and the book includes much from his observations and collected testimony.

51. Ibid., 242–43.

52. Ibid., 243.

53. Ibid., 244.

54. Ibid., 245.

55. Ibid., 245–46.

CHAPTER 5

1. See, for example, William W. Savage, Jr., *The Cherokee Strip Live Stock Association: Federal Regulation and the Cattleman's Last Frontier* (Columbia: University of Missouri Press, 1973); Donald J. Berthrong, *The Cheyenne and Arapaho Ordeal: Reservation and Agency Life in the Indian Territory, 1875–1907* (Norman: University of Oklahoma Press, 1976); William T. Hagan, *United States-Comanche Relations: The Reservation Years* (New Haven: Yale University Press, 1976); H. Craig Miner, *The Corporation and the Indian: Tribal Sovereignty and Industrial Civilization in Indian Territory, 1865–1907* (Columbia: University of Missouri Press, 1976).

2. William W. Savage, Jr., "Indian Ranchers," in *Ranch and Range in Oklahoma*, ed. Jimmy M. Skaggs (Oklahoma City: Oklahoma Historical Society, 1978), 37–38.

3. Ibid., 38–42; H. Craig Miner, "The Dream of a Native Cattle Industry in Indian Territory," in *Ranch and Range*, 18–29.

4. Berthrong, *The Cheyenne and Arapaho Ordeal*, 57–71.

5. Ibid.

6. Carl N. Tyson, "Ranching and Government Policy in Oklahoma," in *Ranch and Range*, 61–76.

7. Ibid.

8. William T. Hagan, *Quanah Parker, Comanche Chief* (Norman: University of Oklahoma Press, 1993); Hagan, "Kiowas, Comanches, and Cattlemen, 1867–1906: A Case Study of the Failure of U.S. Reservation Policy," *Pacific Historical Review* 40, no. 3 (August 1971):333–55.

9. Hagan, *Quanah Parker*, 50–51. Hagan cites the work of Melissa Meyer and Loretta Fowler on cultural brokers and political middlemen. For a discussion of the limitations of terms such as "progressive" and "conservative" and an intriguing portrait of a Ute cattle rancher, see David Rich Lewis, "Reservation Leadership and the Progressive-Traditional Dichotomy: William Wash and the Northern Utes, 1865–1928," *Ethnohistory* 38, no. 2 (Spring 1991):124–48.

10. See Gerald Betty, "Comanche Pastoralism," M.A. thesis, Arizona State University, 1992.

11. See Hagan, *United States-Comanche Relations*, and Hagan, *Quanah Parker*.

12. Rolf W. Bauer, "The Papago Cattle Economy: Implications for Economic and Community Development in Arid Lands," in *Food, Fiber and the Arid Lands*, ed. William G. McGinnies, Bram J. Goldman, and Patricia Paylore (Tucson: University of Arizona Press, 1971), 80–83; Bernard L. Fontana, "Desertification of Papaguería: Cattle and the Papago," in *Desertification: Process, Problems, Perspectives*, ed. Patricia Paylore and Richard A. Haney, Jr. (Tucson: University of Arizona Office of Arid Lands Studies, 1976), 59–62.

13. Xavier, *The Cattle Industry of the Southern Papago Districts*, 353–58.

14. Ibid.

15. Fontana, "Desertification," 59.

16. See Bauer, "Papago Cattle Economy," 87–101; and Henry F. Manuel, Juliann Ramon, and Bernard Fontana, "Dressing for the Window: Papago Indians and Economic Development," in *American Indian Economic Development*, 522–30.

17. Donald L. Kristoffersen, "Crouse and the Beginnings of the Fort Apache Cattle Industry," M.A. thesis, History, Arizona State University, 1970, 14.

18. Ibid.

19. Ibid., 14–20.

20. Ibid., 21–23.

21. Ibid., 24–54.

22. Ibid., 55–90; see also Thomas R. McGuire, "Mixed-Bloods, Apaches, Economy of the White Mountain Reservation, Arizona," (Tucson: Cultural Resource Management Section, Arizona State Museum, University of Arizona, 1980), 80–84.

23. Ibid., 113–29.

24. Ibid., 129–37.

25. Ibid., 138–47.

26. McGuire, "Mixed-Bloods," 88–91, 137–63, 181–99.

27. Kristoffersen, "C. W. Crouse," 148–62. R-14 has been profiled from time to time in popular journals. See, for example, Raymond E. Maher, "R-14, Apache Cattle King," *Arizona Highways* (October 1940):10, 32–33.

28. Kristoffersen, "C. W. Crouse," 174–201.

29. Harry T. Getty, *The San Carlos Indian Cattle Industry*, 16.

30. Ibid., 27; Superintendent's Annual Report, San Carlos Apache Reservation, 1910. Thanks to Ron Dungan for sharing materials from his research on the development of tribal government at San Carlos.

31. Superintendent's Annual Report, San Carlos, 1910.

32. Ibid.; Superintendent's Annual Report, San Carlos, 1911.

33. Superintendent's Annual Report, San Carlos, 1921.

34. Ron Dungan, "The San Carlos Indian Reservation and Tribal Self Government, 1928–1938," M.A. thesis, History, Arizona State University, 1992.

35. Getty, *San Carlos*, 25.

36. Superintendent's Annual Report, San Carlos, 1925.

37. Ibid.

38. Testimony of Charles L. Davis, June 1, 1925, in Flagstaff, Arizona. "National Forests and the Public Domain," Hearings Before a Subcommittee of the Committee on Public Lands and Surveys, U.S. Senate (Washington, D.C.: Government Printing Office, 1926), 1:1135.

39. Exchange between Charles Davis and Henry Ashurst, ibid., 1144–45.

40. Ashurst, ibid., 1145.

41. Testimony of Fred Bennett, June 4, 1925, in Douglas, Arizona, ibid., 383–84.

42. Testimony of Henry Boice, June 5, 1925, in Tucson, Arizona, ibid., 433–34; testimony of J. M. Ronstadt, June 5, 1925, in Tucson, ibid., 474.

43. Boice testimony, ibid., 434; testimony of A. T. Crocker, June 8, 1925, in Globe, Arizona, ibid., 599.

44. Exchange between T. S. Kimball, June 9, 1925, in Globe, Arizona, and Henry Ashurst, ibid., 667.

45. Testimony of H. W. Shipe, June 16, 1925, in Flagstaff, Arizona, ibid., 1189–90.

46. Exchange between Bowden and Shipe, ibid., 1190.

CHAPTER 6

1. For a thorough study of Collier up to the late 1920s, see Lawrence C. Kelly, *The Assault on Assimilation: John Collier and the Origins of Indian Policy Reform* (Albuquerque: University of New Mexico Press, 1983). Biographical details may also be found in the best study of the Indian New Deal, Kenneth Philp, *John Collier's Crusade for Indian Reform, 1920–1954* (Tucson: University of Arizona Press, 1977).

2. See the above sources and Collier's autobiography, *From Every Zenith* (Denver: Sage Books, 1963).

3. Lewis Meriam (Technical Director), *The Problem of Indian Administration* (Baltimore: Johns Hopkins University Press, 1928).

4. Ibid., 7.

5. Ibid., 430, 476, 488.

6. Ibid., 504.

7. Ibid., 504–507.

8. Ibid., 506.

9. Ibid., 507.

10. John Collier, Jr., "My Father, John Collier: The Missing Dimension in

Recent Historiography," paper presented at the annual meeting of the Organization of American Historians, April 7, 1983.

11. For two perspectives on Navajo livestock reduction, see Donald Parman, *The Navajos and the New Deal* (New Haven: Yale University Press, 1976), and White, *The Roots of Dependency*.

12. See Ron Dungan, "The San Carlos Indian Reservation and Tribal Self-Government, 1928–1938," M.A. thesis, History, Arizona State University, 1992.

13. Getty, *The San Carlos Indian Cattle Industry*, 40.

14. Ibid., 31–44.

15. Ibid., 43–44.

16. Field Report, Santa Fe Office of National Association on Indian Affairs (New York: National Association on Indian Affairs, 1936), 13. John Collier Papers, microfilm edition, reel 31, Yale University.

17. Harry Stevens, "Cattle Raising on the San Carlos Reservation in Arizona," *Indians at Work* (Washington, D.C.: Bureau of Indian Affairs, July 1939), 18–22.

18. "Cattle Sale at San Carlos," *Indians at Work* (Washington, D.C.: Bureau of Indian Affairs, July 15, 1935), 24.

19. Grenville Goodwin, "Report on the San Carlos Indian Reservation," submitted to the Department of the Interior, 1937 (copy in the library of the Arizona State Museum, University of Arizona, Tucson), 120–21.

20. Ibid.

21. Thomas R. McGuire, "Mixed-Bloods, Apaches, and Cattle Barons," 175–76.

22. Ibid., 181–84.

23. "Hard Riding Indian Cowboys Combine Old Time Skills with Modern Methods to Make Cattle Business Pay," *Indians at Work* (Washington, D.C.: Bureau of Indian Affairs, December 1940), 7–8.

24. Ibid.

25. Xavier, *The Cattle Industry of the Southern Papago Districts*, 369, 368–69.

26. Ibid., 373–75; "Hard Riding Indian Cowboys," 8.

27. Peter Blaine, Sr., as told to Michael S. Adams, *Papagos and Politics* (Tucson: Arizona Historical Society, 1981), 87–88.

28. Ibid., 75–77.

29. Xavier, *The Cattle Industry of the Southern Papago Districts*, 370–71.

30. Ibid., 372.

31. Blaine, *Papagos and Politics*, 79.

32. Xavier, *The Cattle Industry of the Southern Papago Districts*, 379.

33. Bauer, "The Papago Cattle Economy," 90.

34. Ernest Nelson, account of livestock reduction, in *Navajo Livestock Reduction: A National Disgrace*, ed. Ruth Roessel and Broderick H. Johnson (Tsaile, Ariz.: Navajo Community College Press, 1974), 159.

35. "Papagos Manage Their Own Fair and Rodeo," *Indians at Work* (Washington, D.C.: Bureau of Indian Affairs, December 1939), 19–20.

36. Gordon Macgregor, *Warriors Without Weapons: A Study of the Society and*

Personality Development of the Pine Ridge Sioux (Chicago: University of Chicago Press, 1975, reprint edition), 39–41.

37. "Cattle Ranching by Indians on Pine Ridge Reservation, South Dakota," (Billings: Missouri River Basin Investigations Project, Bureau of Indian Affairs, May 1964), 4; Macgregor, *Warriors Without Weapons*, 41.

38. Allan G. Harper, "Salvaging the Wreckage of Indian Land Allotment," in *The Changing Indian*, ed. Oliver La Farge (Norman: University of Oklahoma Press, 1942), 93.

39. Ibid., 93–100; Schusky, *The Forgotten Sioux*, 196.

40. John Collier, memo to Harold Ickes, August 24, 1933, Collier Papers, reel 27.

41. Donald Worster, *Dust Bowl: The Southern Plains in the 1930s* (New York: Oxford University Press, 1979), 131–38.

42. "Fort Belknap Shippers," *Indians at Work* (Washington, D.C.: Bureau of Indian Affairs, December 15, 1935), 30.

43. Fred C. Varnum, "The Indian Cattle Association," *Indians at Work* (Washington, D.C.: Bureau of Indian Affairs, May 15, 1936), 42–43.

44. Ibid., 43–46.

45. Fowler, *Shared Symbols*, 98–101.

46. F. A. Asbury and Charles H. Jennings, "The Tongue River Steer Enterprise," *Indians at Work* (Washington, D.C.: Bureau of Indian Affairs, June 1939), 15.

47. Ibid., 15–16.

48. John Herrick, "Arapahoes on Wind River Reservation in Wyoming Are Engaged in an Important Ranching Industry," *Indians at Work* (Washington, D.C.: Bureau of Indian Affairs, January 1941), 17–21.

49. "Arapahoe Ranch, Wind River Reservation, Wyoming," *Indians at Work* (Washington, D.C.: Bureau of Indian Affairs, November-December 1944), 11–12.

50. "Hard Riding Indian Cowboys," 7.

51. As quoted in C. L. Sonnichsen, *The Mescalero Apaches* (Norman: University of Oklahoma Press, 1958), 247.

52. Ibid., 248.

53. Alison R. Bernstein, *American Indians and World War II: Toward a New Era in Indian Affairs* (Norman: University of Oklahoma Press, 1991), 19–21; Richard White, *The Roots of Dependency*, 290–314.

54. McNickle served as the founding director of the Newberry Library's Center for the History of the American Indian, which now bears his name. I had the good fortune to be at the center during the first year it offered fellowships. Newberry Library head Lawrence W. Towner's description of this slightly motley crew of fellows as resembling the Donner Party did not quite do us justice. D'Arcy preferred his home in Albuquerque to living in Chicago—a sentiment that confirmed his place in my eyes as a person of maturity—and he would commute by train from New Mexico to Illinois, spending most of his time in the Southwest, whenever he could. On one of his trips back home to Albuquerque, I took the same Santa Fe train so as to begin research in the

Navajo Nation for my dissertation. He and I sat in the club car and told stories—stories I had heard about the thirties, stories he had lived. "The Emergency Relief Administration (ERA) brand on cattle given to the Indians," he related, "they interpreted to mean, Eat Right Away!" For McNickle's view of Collier and the Indian New Deal, see, among other works, "The Indian New Deal as Mirror of the Future," in *Political Organization of Native North Americans*, ed. Ernest Schusky (Washington, D.C.: University Press of America, 1980), 107–19.

CHAPTER 7

1. Willard W. Beatty, "Land: Primary Resource," in *Education for Action: Selected Articles From Indian Education, 1936–1943*, ed. Willard W. Beatty (Washington, D.C.: U.S. Indian Service, 1944), 20–21.

2. For a good overview of continuity and change in federal Indian policy during this period, see Clayton R. Koppes, "From New Deal to Termination: Liberalism and Indian Policy, 1933–1953," *Pacific Historical Review* 46, no. 4 (November 1977): 543–66.

3. Felix S. Cohen, "The Erosion of Indian Rights, 1950–1953: A Case Study in Bureaucracy," *Yale Law Journal* 62 (February 1953): 390.

4. Arthur V. Watkins, "Termination of Federal Supervision: The Removal of Restrictions Over Indian Property and Person," *Annals of the American Academy of Political and Social Science* 311 (May 1957): 47–55. Cherokee and Creek scholar Tom Holm argues that the Indian experience in the war fueled the fire for termination of federal services and protection. Holm, "Fighting a White Man's War: The Extent and Legacy of American Indian Participation in World War II," in *The Plains Indians of the Twentieth Century*, 149–65. Another useful treatment of the impact of the war years is "The Indian Home Front: A Study in Changes," a chapter in Alison R. Bernstein, *American Indians and World War II: Toward a New Era in Indian Affairs* (Norman: University of Oklahoma Press, 1991), 64–88.

5. E. Y. Berry, statement prepared for the House Indian Affairs Subcommittee, February 6, 1963, box 135, E. Y. Berry Papers, E. Y. Berry Library and Learning Center, Black Hills State College, Spearfish, South Dakota. For a more detailed picture of Berry, see Steven C. Schulte, "Removing the Yoke of Government: E. Y. Berry and the Origins of Indian Termination Policy, *South Dakota History* 14, no. 1 (Spring 1984): 48–67.

6. Schulte, "E. Y. Berry," 67.

7. For a more searching discussion of the idea that the federal policies of the period did not always achieve the goals they sought, see Peter Iverson, "Building Toward Self-Determination: Plains and Southwestern Indians in the 1940s and 1950s," *Western Historical Quarterly* 16, no. 2 (April 1985): 163–73.

8. Sophie D. Aberle to Malcolm S. Major, July 22, 1937; and Major to Aberle, July 30, 1937, file 301.6, Isleta Cattle Trust, Trespass, 1935–1938, Records of the Bureau of Indian Affairs, Federal Records Center, Denver, Colorado.

9. For an overview of the Emmons administration, see Larry W. Burt, *Tribalism in Crisis: Federal Indian Policy, 1953–1961* (Albuquerque: University of New Mexico Press, 1982).

10. Memorandum from T. B. Hall, Acting Director, Gallup Area Office, to General Superintendent, United Pueblos Agency, November 28, 1956, file 930, Isleta Cattle trust, Termination, Records of the Bureau of Indian Affairs, Federal Records Center, Denver, Colorado.

11. Memorandum for the General Superintendent, United Pueblos Agency, February 1, 1956, file 301, Isleta Cattle Trust, 1953–1958, ibid.

12. Memorandum from Woodrow Tiger, United Pueblo Agency Credit Officer, to Charles B. Corke et al., September 5, 1958; Letter from Members of the Isleta Tribe to Carlos Jojola, President of the Isleta Council, October 24, 1958, ibid.; William A. Brophy and Sophie D. Aberle, *The Indian: America's Unfinished Business* (Norman: University of Oklahoma Press, 1966), 81–83.

13. Fowler, *Shared Symbols*, 100–102.

14. Raymond J. DeMallie, "Pine Ridge Economy: Cultural and Historical Perspectives," 280–81.

15. Willard W. Beatty to Lawrence K. Lindley, August 28, 1959, Papers of the Indian Rights Association, microfilm edition, reel 62. Copy in Denver Public Library.

16. Ibid.

17. John Wooden Legs, "Back on the War Ponies," *Indian Affairs*, 1960.

18. LaVerne Madigan, "Indian Survival on the Great Plains," *Indian Affairs* 25 (September 1957). John Collier Papers, microfilm edition, reel 54, Yale University.

19. George Pambrum, comments in the *Congressional Record*, February 5, 1951, ibid.

20. Statement of George Pambrum before the Special Senate Committee on Blackfeet Affairs, April 15, 1952, ibid.

21. See Kenneth R. Philp, "Dillon S. Meyer and the Advent of Termination, 1950–1953, *Western Historical Quarterly* 19, no. 1 (January 1988): 37–59.

22. "Superintendent's Comments," *Fort Berthold Agency News Bulletin* 4, no. 3 (May 18, 1953). John Collier Papers, microfilm edition, reel 54.

23. Ibid. For an analysis of federally sponsored relocation programs and the Indian experiences in the city, see the chapter, "The Relocation Program and Urbanization," in Donald L. Fixico, *Termination and Relocation: Federal Indian Policy, 1945–1960* (Albuquerque: University of New Mexico Press, 1986), 134–57.

24. "Secretary McKay Announces Departmental Decisions on South Dakota Indian Range Lands," news release by the Department of the Interior Information Service, August 12, 1953. Copy in Box 166, "Indian Grazing Leases—Pine Ridge," E. Y. Berry Papers.

25. "Stock Grower Officials Warn on Grazing Fees," newspaper clipping, n.d., ibid.

26. E. Y. Berry to Louis Beckwith, July 7, 1953, ibid.

27. Steven C. Schulte, "Indian and White Politics in the Modern West:

Sioux and White Leadership in South Dakota, 1920–1965," Ph.D. dissertation, University of Wyoming, 1984, 256–59.

28. Ibid., 219–31.

29. See Michael L. Lawson, "The Fractionated Estate: The Problem of Indian Heirship," *South Dakota History* 21, no. 1 (Spring 1991): 1–42, for a discussion of this continuing problem.

30. Among other articles, see Vivien B. Keatley, "Apacheland: Arizona's Finest Cattle Ranch," *Arizona Highways* (July 1950): 14–16; Richard G. Schaus, "Arizona's Apaches Have a Cattle Tradition," *Hereford Journal* (July 1, 1964): 328–45; Terry Burgess, "San Carlos Tribe Cattle Herd Important to Arizona Industry," *Cattlelog* (October 1988): 10–11.

31. Schusky, *The Forgotten Sioux*, 219.

32. Ronald L. Trosper, "American Indian Relative Ranching Efficiency," *American Economic Review* 68, no. 6 (September 1978): 503.

33. Ibid., 503–16.

34. James E. Officer, "Arid Lands Agriculture and the Indians of the American Southwest," in *Food, Fiber, and the Arid Lands*, 70–71.

35. Navajo Cattle Growers Association *Newsletter*, May 24, 1961; "Cattlemen Set Sale," *Navajo Times*, July 14, 1966; both in "Navajo Cattle Growers Association" file, box 15, folder 13, Richard Schaus Collection, Arizona Historical Foundation, Tempe.

36. Henry W. Hough, *Development of Indian Resources* (Denver: World Press, 1967), 75–87. The director of research for the National Congress of American Indians Fund, Hough devotes the second chapter of this study to Indian farming and ranching. See Hough, *Indian Resources*, 71–114.

37. Bernard L. Fontana, "Desertification of Papaguería," 59–62.

38. Ibid., 65.

39. Manuel, Ramon, and Fontana, "Dressing for the Window," 527–29.

40. Ibid., 529.

41. Bauer, "The Papago Cattle Economy," 91–92.

42. Ibid., 93–97. On the changing pattern of cattle distribution by 1962, see William H. Kelly, "The Papago Indians of Arizona," in *Papago Indians III*, ed. David Agee Horr (New York: Garland, 1974), 69–80.

43. Henry F. Dobyns, "Experiment in Conservation: Erosion Control and Forage Production on the Papago Indian Reservations in Arizona," in *Human Problems in Technological Change*, ed. Edward H. Spicer (New York: John Wiley & Sons, Science Editions, 1965), 209–23. Dobyns's article is summarized by Bauer, "The Papago Cattle Economy," 93–95.

44. Ibid.

45. Bauer, "The Papago Cattle Economy," 98.

46. Ibid., 98–100.

47. Telegram from Thomas A. Segundo to Paul Fannin, June 25, 1969, "Papago Drought" file, Paul A. Fannin Papers, Arizona Historical Foundation, Tempe.

48. Open Letter from Augustine B. Lopez to the Congress of the United States, July 5, 1972, John J. Rhodes Papers, box 92:40, folder 9, Arizona

Historical Foundation, Tempe.

49. W. G. Kneeland, "Famed Apache Cattle Raisers to Complete Peak Spring Sales," *Arizona Republic*, May 25, 1952.

50. San Carlos Apache Cattle Growers Association, San Carlos Hereford Feeder Sales Brochure, October–December, 1948, Schaus Collection, box 15, folder 14.

51. Schaus, "Arizona's Apaches," 344.

52. Ibid.; Al Lane and Dick Rice, "The San Carlos Project," *Cattlelog* (October 1988): 14.

53. Schaus, "Arizona's Apaches," 345; Lane and Rice, "The San Carlos Project," 15, 17; "San Carlos Apache Cattle Study Is Being Expanded," *Progressive Agriculture in Arizona* (November-December 1965): 3–6. Copy in Schaus Collection.

54. Carl B. Roubicek, "San Carlos Indian–University of Arizona Cooperative Program of Cattle Improvement," *Indian Programs* (Tucson: University of Arizona, Spring–Summer 1970): 1–4. Copy in Schaus Collection.

55. Getty, *The San Carlos Indian Cattle Industry*, 67–74.

56. Ibid., 76.

57. Ibid., 78.

58. Ibid., 78–83.

CHAPTER 8

1. Ann Nolan Clark, *Singing Sioux Cowboy Reader* (Lakota Pteole Hoksila Lowanksa) (Lawrence, Kan.: Haskell Press for the Bureau of Indian Affairs, 1954), 40–41. This reader, along with others in other Indian languages, was developed initially in the 1930s and early 1940s as part of the effort in bilingual education encouraged by the Indian New Deal. The readers continued in use for many years; the 1954 date represents a reprinted edition. Clark's *The Grass Mountain Mouse* also features a mouse who discovers the appeal of rodeo. "The cousins talked together about which was better—Pine Ridge cowboys or cowboys from Rosebud—and Pine Ridge rodeos or Rosebud rodeos" (39). At the rodeo, "there were more cowboys than there are seeds in a sunflower. There were more horses than there are grasshoppers in a meadow" (57).

2. James F. Downs, "The Cowboy and the Lady: Models as a Determinant of the Rate of Acculturation Among the Piñon Navajo," in *Native Americans Today: Sociological Perspectives*, ed. Howard M. Bahr, Bruce A. Chadwick, and Robert C. Day (New York: Harper & Row, 1972), 284. Downs's article was published originally in 1963.

3. Ibid., 284–87.

4. Donald L. Fixico, "From Indians to Cowboys: The Country Western Trend," in *American Indian Identity: Today's Changing Perspectives*, ed. Clifford E. Trafzer. San Diego State Publications in American Indian Studies no. 1 (San Diego: San Diego State Publications in American Indian Studies), 17–18. Reprinted under the same title in 1985 by Sierra Oaks, Sacramento, California.

5. Russell Martin, *Cowboy: The Enduring Myth of the Wild West* (New York:

Stewart, Tabori, and Chang, 1983), 260–63.

6. Donald L. Parman, "New Deal Indian Agricultural Policy and the Environment: The Papagos as a Case Study." *Agricultural History* 66, no. 2 (1992): 33; Myla Carpio, communication to author.

7. Joseph Medicine Crow, *From the Heart of the Crow Country: The Crow Indians' Own Stories* (New York: Orion Books, 1992), 108–109. Given difficult contemporary economic circumstances, many Indian communities (as well as such rural enclaves as Deadwood, South Dakota) have turned to forms of gambling to bring in needed revenues. The decision to allow gaming has usually been reached with reluctance. Although the early financial returns from such enterprises have generally been considerable, the long-term effects on Indian societies remain to be determined. In addition, there is little doubt about the continuing efforts to try to restrict Indian gaming in the future.

8. Joe Medicine Crow, presentation at "The Cowboys Are Indians!" symposium held at the Buffalo Bill Historical Center, Cody, Wyoming, in conjunction with the annual Cowboy Songs and Range Ballads, April 2–4, 1993.

9. Medicine Crow, *From the Heart of the Crow Country*, 130–131.

10. Barney Nelson, "Ranching on the Reservation—Part 1—The Crows in Montana," *Western Horseman* (April 1993): 94–97.

11. Larry Thompson, presentation at "The Cowboys Are Indians!"

12. Dan Old Elk, presentation at "The Cowboys Are Indians!"

13. Joe Medicine Crow, Larry Thompson, and David Red Boy Schildt, presentations at "The Cowboys Are Indians!"

14. *Navajo Times*, March 28, 1991, 8.

15. Ibid.

16. Avis Little Eagle, "Hobart Pourier: A Legendary Cowboy Memorialized," *Indian Country Today* (February 18, 1993): 3–5.

17. Ibid.

18. Obituary, Dean C. Jackson, *Navajo Times*, August 13, 1992, A-5. See also the tributes to Mr. Jackson by columnist Bill Donovan and speaker of the Navajo Nation council, Nelson Gorman, Jr. Gorman stated that Jackson's name "will be placed among Navajo leaders like Narbona, Manuelito, and Chee Dodge." *Navajo Times*, August 13, 1992, A-4.

19. Marley Shebala, "No Such Thing as Indians and Cowboys," *Navajo Times*, July 4, 1990, B-1. See also the article on Karl Dennison, "Dennison Garners All-Around Award," *Navajo Times*, July 6, 1989, 9; and the article on Carole Jackson, "Jackson Captures Zuñi Tribal Fair Rodeo Top Honor," *Navajo Times*, August 27, 1992, B-1. Carole Jackson is a three-time winner in barrel racing at the Indian National Finals Rodeo world championship.

20. Monty Roessel, "World's Best Indian Cowboys at Fair," *Navajo Nation Today*, September 4–8, 1991, 23.

21. Candi Zion, "A History of the Origins of the Southwest Indian Rodeo Trail," unpublished paper completed for a graduate seminar in American Indian history at Arizona State University. Copy in possession of the author.

22. *Navajo Times*, September 23, 1992, II.

23. Ibid., September 10, 1992, 1 and B-4; September 17, 1992, 16.

24. Susanne Anderson, *Song of the Earth Spirit* (New York: McGraw-Hill, 1973), 55. The book includes some fine photographs, a collection of Anderson's brief essays and several poems by Navajo children. This tradition may be returning in some instances. The community of Sawmill on the Navajo Nation has chosen to return to a local focus, de-emphasizing prize money. Mark Trahant, personal communication to author.

25. Anderson, *Earth Spirit*, 57.

26. Luci Tapahonso, "Raisin Eyes," in her collection of poems and stories, *Sáani Dahataał: The Women Are Singing* (Tucson: University of Arizona Press/ Sun Tracks, 1993), 41–42.

27. Gabriel Arviso Begaye, "The Indian Cowboy and Cowgirl in Indian and Professional Rodeo," paper completed for an undergraduate course in American Indian history at Arizona State University. Copy in possession of the author.

28. Hank Real Bird, statement in the film, *Contrary Warrior*.

29. Joan Morrison, "Indian Rodeo," *Native Peoples* 2, no. 4 (Summer 1989): 22–23.

30. Shebala, "No Such Thing as Indians and Cowboys," B-2; Morrison, "Indian Rodeo," 14.

31. Old Elk, presentation at Little Bighorn College, June 24, 1992.

32. James Welch, *The Indian Lawyer* (New York: W. W. Norton, 1990), 53.

33. These examples of corporate versatility may now be out of date, but they are courtesy of Jim Hightower, *Eat Your Heart Out: How Food Profiteers Victimize the Consumer* (New York: Crown, 1975).

34. Ralph Beer, "Holding to the Land: A Rancher's Sorrow," *Harper's* (September 1985): 62, 64.

35. Mike Seidman, "Healthy Ecosystems and Cows Will Never Mix," *High Country News*, December 28, 1992, 12–13.

36. Ray Wheeler, "One View of Joe Feller: He Doesn't Give Up," *High Country News*, March 12, 1990, 12.

37. Joseph M. Feller, "The Western Wing of Kafka's Castle: After Discovering the Public Range Is Not Very Public, a Law Professor Does Some Ruminating of His Own to Determine Where the BLM West Wrong," ibid., 9–11, and Feller, "A Do-It-Yourself Guide," ibid., 9.

38. Donald Worster, "Cowboy Ecology," in Worster, *Under Western Skies: Nature and History in the American West* (New York: Oxford University Press, 1992), 261.

39. Florence Williams, "Who's at Home on the Range," *High Country News*, March 12, 1990, 8.

40. Charles F. Wilkinson, "Toward An Ethic of Place," in *Beyond the Mythic West* (Salt Lake City: Peregrine Smith Books, 1990), 74–75.

41. Paul Renfer, "Gripeline," *Arizona Republic*, August 25, 1993.

42. Barbara E. Barker, letter to the editor, *High Country News*, January 25, 1993, 16. For a recent exchange of views, see William G. Meyers, "Ranchers Can't Afford Grazing Fee Plans," and Steve Johnson, "Public Lands Belong to All Americans, Pardner," published as letters to the editor in the *New York Times*, September 1, 1993, and September 15, 1993. Meyers represented the

National Cattlemen's Association; Johnson wrote as a public lands consultant for the Humane Society of the United States.

43. Frank J. Popper and Deborah Epstein Popper, "The Fate of the Plains," in *Reopening the Western Frontier*, ed. Ed Marston (Washington, D.C.: Island Press, 1989), 98–113.

44. Greg Breining, "Back Home on the Range," *Nature Conservancy* (November–December 1992): 11–15.

45. Florence Williams, "The West's Time Capsules," *High Country News*, March 12, 1990, 6–7.

46. Steve Stuebner, "BLM May Adopt Grazing Incentive Plan," *High Country News*, December 28, 1992, 5.

47. Ibid.

48. Jon Christensen and Tony Davis, "Bruce Babbitt on Western Land Use: 1993 is the 'Year of Decision,'" *High Country News*, May 17, 1993, 8–9.

49. Steve Yozwiak, "Grazing Fee Hike Proposed: Babbitt Seeks to Double Price, Stiffen Environmental Roles," *Arizona Republic*, August 10, 1993, A-1.

50. Linda Hasselstrom, "The Cow Versus the Animal Activist," in Hasselstrom, *Land Circle: Writings Collected from the Land* (Golden, Colo.: Fulcrum, 1991), 326.

51. Wilkinson, "Toward an Ethic of Place," 82.

52. Wilkinson quotes the following passage from Gretel Ehrlich's book on ranching in Wyoming: "On a ranch, small ceremonies and private, informal rituals arise. We ride the spring pasture, pick chokecherries in August, skin out a deer in the fall, and in the enactment experience a wordless exhilaration between bouts of plain hard work." Wilkinson, "A Sense of Place," 82. Gretel Ehrlich's *The Solace of Open Spaces* (New York: Viking, 1985) is a brief book about sheep, cattle, wind, and space in Wyoming. For another view of ranching, from the perspective of a working cowboy in the Texas panhandle country, see John R. Erickson, *The Modern Cowboy* (Lincoln: University of Nebraska Press, 1981).

53. Linda Hasselstrom, *Windbreak: A Woman Rancher on the Northern Plains* (Berkeley: Barn Owl Books, 1987), 47–48.

54. N. Scott Momaday, "The Man Made of Words," in *The Remembered Earth*, ed. Geary Hobson (Albuquerque: University of New Mexico Press, 1981), 164–65.

55. Wallace Stegner, *The Sound of Mountain Water* (Garden City, N.Y.: Doubleday, 1969), 38.

56. Luther Standing Bear, *Land of the Spotted Eagle* (Lincoln: University of Nebraska Press, 1978), 230–32.

57. Niels Winther Braroe, *Indian and White: Self-Image and Interaction in a Canadian Plains Community* (Stanford: Stanford University Press, 1975), *passim*.

58. *Cowboys & Indians* 1, no. 1 (July 1993). Twelve thousand copies of the first issue were printed and apparently sold out quickly.

59. Beer, "Holding to the Land," 59.

60. Royce, *Ethnic Identity*, 232.

61. Joseph G. Jorgensen, "Land is Cultural, So Is a Commodity: The Locus of Difference Among Indians, Cowboys, Sod-Busters, and Environmentalists," *Journal of Ethnic Studies* 12, no. 3 (Fall 1984): 5.

62. Dirk Johnson, "Big Denver Cattle Show Reflects Sunset on the West," *New York Times*, January 14, 1992.

63. Indeed, there is a shortage of capable ranch hands. See, for example, Guy Webster, "Special Chaps a Rare Breed: Acute Dearth of Cowboys Plagues West," *Arizona Republic*, April 10, 1988, F-1. "Working Cowboys & Buckaroos," says the ad placed by the Cowboy Employment Agency, Inc., in *Cowboy Magazine*, "We'll Find Work For You." Of course there is a 1-800 number to make it easy to contact this "professional cowboy placement service."

64. Panel discussion, "Ranching Culture: Will It Survive?" Eighth Annual Cowboy Poetry Gathering, Elko, Nevada, January 30–February 1, 1992. Discussion taped by World Wide Communications. Thanks to Paul Stone for a copy of the tape.

65. For one view of possible rural responses to an urban West, see Vess Quinlan, "What Ranchers Need to Do Now That the World Has Come Calling," *High Country News*, April 5, 1993, 18. Essay originally published in *Dry Crik Review*.

66. "Ranching Culture."

67. Teresa Jordan, *Riding the White Horse Home* (New York: Pantheon, 1993), 15, 206.

68. "Ranching Culture."

69. *Range Magazine* 1, no. 1 (Summer 1992).

Additional Reading

RATHER THAN OFFERING A TRADITIONAL BIBLIOGRAPHY, primarily composed of sources already cited in the footnotes, I provide below a list of additional readings and sources, drawn from the vast literature of American Indian history and the history of the American West. The varied audience for this book prompts such an alternative. And such a list also speaks to other writers whose work has had some influence on my perspective. I have limited the following to books, as articles in academic journals will be more difficult for many readers to obtain. In a few instances, I have included volumes published in 1993 that emerged too late for direct employment here. Books on the Plains and the Southwest are emphasized. These works combine to give a more complete portrait of Indians, cowboys, and the rural American West.

BIBLIOGRAPHIES AND HISTORIOGRAPHICAL WORKS

Adams, Ramon F. *The Rampaging Herd: A Bibliography of Books and Pamphlets and Men and Events in the Cattle Industry.* Norman: University of Oklahoma Press, 1959.

Bataille, Gretchen M., and Kathleen Mullen Sands, ed. *American Indian Women: Telling Their Lives.* Lincoln: University of Nebraska Press, 1984.

Calloway, Colin G., ed. *New Directions in American Indian History.* Norman: University of Oklahoma Press, 1988.

Etulain, Richard W., ed. *Writing Western History: Essays on Major Western Historians.* Albuquerque: University of New Mexico Press, 1991.

Malone, Michael P., ed. *Historians and the American West.* Lincoln: University of Nebraska Press, 1983.

Markin, Jack W., and Herbert T. Hoover, eds. *Bibliography of the Sioux.* Metuchen, N.J.: Scarecrow Press, 1980.

Martin, Calvin L., ed. *The American Indian and the Problem of History.* New York: Oxford University Press, 1987.

Nash, Gerald D., and Richard W. Etulain, eds. *The Twentieth-Century West: Historical Interpretations.* Albuquerque: University of New Mexico Press, 1989.

Nichols, Roger L., ed. *American Frontier and Western Issues: A Historiographical Review.* Westport, Conn.: Greenwood Press, 1986.

Paul, Rodman W., and Richard W. Etulain, eds. *The Frontier and the American West.* Arlington Heights, Ill.: AHM Publishing, 1977.

Prucha, Francis Paul, ed. *Indian-White Relations in the United States: A Bibliography of Works Published.* Chicago: University of Chicago Press, 1977.

Prucha, Francis Paul, ed. *Indian-White Relations in the United States: A Bibliography of Works Published, 1975–1980.* Lincoln: University of Nebraska Press, 1982.

Smith, Dwight L., ed. *Indians of the United States and Canada: A Bibliography.* 2 vols. Santa Barbara, Calif.: ABC-Clio Press, 1974, 1983.

Smith, Dwight L., ed. *The American and Canadian West: A Bibliography.* Santa Barbara, Calif.: ABC-Clio Press, 1979.

Swagerty, W. R., ed. *Scholars and the Indian Experience: Critical Reviews of Recent Writings in the Social Sciences.* Bloomington: Indiana University Press, 1985.

Walker, Don D. *Clio's Cowboys: Studies in the Historiography of the Cattle Trade.* Lincoln: University of Nebraska Press, 1981.

Wilkinson, Charles F. *The American West: A Narrative Bibliography and a Study in Regionalism.* Niwot: University Press of Colorado, 1989.

AMERICAN INDIAN HISTORY

Bingham, Sam, and Janet Bingham, eds. *Between Sacred Mountains: Navajo Stories and Lessons from the Land.* Tucson: University of Arizona Press/Sun Tracks, 1984.

Carlson, Leonard A. *Indians, Bureaucrats, and the Land: The Dawes Act and the Decline of Indian Farming.* Westport, Conn.: Greenwood Press, 1981.

Carter, Sarah. *Lost Harvests: Prairie Indian Reserve Farmers and Government Policy.* Montreal: McGill-Queen's University Press, 1990.

Deloria, Vine, Jr., ed. *American Indian Policy in the 20th Century.* Norman: University of Oklahoma Press, 1985.

Deloria, Vine, Jr., and Clifford M. Lytle. *The Nations Within: The Past and Future of American Indian Sovereignty.* New York: Pantheon Books, 1984.

Fontana, Bernard L. *Of Earth and Little Rain.* Flagstaff, Ariz.: Northland Press, 1981.

Foster, Morris W. *Being Comanche: A Social History of an American Indian Community.* Tucson: University of Arizona Press, 1991.

Hagan, William T. *The Indian Rights Association: The Herbert Welsh Years, 1882–1904.* Tucson: University of Arizona Press, 1985.

Hoxie, Frederick E., ed. *Indians in American History: An Introduction.* Arlington Heights, Ill.: Harlan Davidson, 1988.

Hurtado, Albert L., and Peter Iverson, eds. *Major Problems in American Indian History.* Lexington, Mass.: D. C. Heath, 1994.

Iverson, Peter. *The Navajo Nation.* Albuquerque: University of New Mexico Press, 1983.

McNickle, D'Arcy. *Native American Tribalism: Indian Survivals and Renewals.* New York: Oxford University Press, 1973.

Nabokov, Peter, ed. *Native American Testimony: A Chronicle of Indian-White Relations from Prophecy to the Present, 1492–1992.* New York: Viking, 1991.

Noyes, Stanley. *Los Comanches: The Horse People, 1751–1845.* Albuquerque: University of New Mexico Press, 1993.

Olson, James S., and Raymond Wilson. *Native Americans in the 20th Century*. Provo, Utah: Brigham Young University Press, 1984.

Olson, Paul A., ed. *The Struggle for the Land: Indigenous Insight and Industrial Empire in the Semiarid World*. Lincoln: University of Nebraska Press, 1990.

Perry, Richard J. *Apache Reservation: Indigenous Peoples and the American State*. Austin: University of Texas Press, 1993.

Philp, Kenneth R., ed. *Indian Self-Rule: First Hand Accounts of Indian-White Relations from Roosevelt to Reagan*. Salt Lake City: Howe Brothers, 1985.

Prucha, Francis Paul. *The Great Father: The U.S. Government and the American Indians*. 2 vols. Lincoln: University of Nebraska Press, 1984.

Ross, Thomas E., and Tyrel G. Moore, eds. *A Cultural Geography of North American Indians*. Boulder, Colo.: Westview Press, 1987.

Snipp, C. Matthew. *American Indians: The First of This Land*. New York: Russell Sage, 1989.

Sutton, Imre, ed. *Irredeemable America: The Indians' Estate and Land Claims*. Albuquerque: University of New Mexico Press, 1985.

Svingen, Orlan J. *The Northern Cheyenne Indian Reservation, 1877–1900*. Niwot: University Press of Colorado, 1993.

Swan, Madonna, as told through Mark St. Pierre. *Madonna Swan: A Lakota Woman's Story*. Norman: University of Oklahoma Press, 1991.

Tiller, Veronica E. Velarde. *The Jicarilla Apache Tribe: A History, 1846–1970*. Rev. ed. Lincoln: University of Nebraska Press, 1992.

Trimble, Stephen. *The People: Indians of the American Southwest*. Santa Fe: School of American Research Press, 1993.

Vecsey, Christopher, and Robert W. Venables, eds. *American Indian Environments: Ecological Issues in Native American History*. Syracuse: Syracuse University Press, 1980.

Wilkinson, Charles F. *American Indians, Time, and the Law*. New Haven: Yale University Press, 1987.

RANCHERS AND COWBOYS

Alderson, Nanny T., and Helena Huntington Smith. *A Bride Goes West*. Lincoln: University of Nebraska Press, 1969. Reprint.

Atherton, Lewis E. *The Cattle Kings*. Bloomington: Indiana University Press, 1961.

Beckstead, James H. *Cowboying: A Tough Job in a Hard Land*. Salt Lake City: University of Utah Press, 1991.

Bennett, John W. *Northern Plainsmen: Adaptive Strategy and Agrarian Life*. Chicago: Aldine, 1969.

Breen, David H. *The Canadian Prairie West and the Ranching Frontier, 1874–1924*. Toronto: University of Toronto Press, 1983.

Brooks, Connie. *The Last Cowboys: Closing the Open Range in Southeastern New Mexico, 1890s–1920s*. Albuquerque: University of New Mexico Press, 1993.

Clawson, Marion. *The Western Range Livestock Industry*. New York: McGraw-Hill, 1950.

Collings, Ellsworth. *The 101 Ranch*. Norman: University of Oklahoma Press, 1957.

Dale, Edward E. *Cow Country*. Norman: University of Oklahoma Press, 1942.

———. *The Range Cattle Industry*. Norman: University of Oklahoma Press, 1930.

Durham, Philip, and Everett L. Jones. *The Negro Cowboys*. New York: Dodd, Mead, & Co., 1965.

Frederiksson, Kristine. *American Rodeo: From Buffalo Bill to Big Business*. College Station: Texas A&M Press, 1984.

Frantz, Joe B., and Julian Choate. *The American Cowboy: The Myth and the Reality*. Norman: University of Oklahoma Press, 1955.

Frink, Maurice, W. Turrentine Jackson, and Agnes Wright Spring. *When Grass Was King*. Boulder: University of Colorado Press, 1956.

Hadley, Caroline J. *Trappings of the Great Basin Buckaroo*. Reno: University of Nevada Press, 1993.

Jordan, Teresa. *Cowgirls: Women of the American West*. Garden City, N.Y.: Anchor Press, 1982.

Jordan, Terry G. *North American Cattle-Ranching Frontiers: Origins, Diffusion, and Differentiation*. Albuquerque: University of New Mexico Press, 1993.

Kramer, Jane. *The Last Cowboy*. New York: Harper & Row, 1977.

Lawrence, Elizabeth Atwood. *Rodeo: An Anthropologist Looks at the Wild and the Tame*. Chicago: University of Chicago Press, 1984.

LeCompte, Mary Lou. *Cowgirls of the Rodeo*. Champaign: University of Illinois Press, 1993.

Osgood, Ernest S. *The Day of the Cattleman*. Chicago: University of Chicago Press, 1957. Reprint.

Pearce, W. M. *The Matador Land and Cattle Company.* Norman: University of Oklahoma Press, 1964.

Pelzer, Louis. *The Cattlemen's Frontier: A Record of the Trans-Mississippi Cattle Industry from Oxen Trains to Pooling Companies, 1850–1890.* Glendale, Calif.: Arthur H. Clark, 1936.

Remley, David. *Bell Ranch: Cattle Ranching in the Southwest, 1824–1947.* Albuquerque: University of New Mexico Press, 1993.

Roach, Joyce Gibson. *The Cowgirls.* 2d ed. Denton: University of North Texas Press, 1990.

Sands, Kathleen. *Charrería Mexicana: An Equestrian Folk Tradition.* Tucson: University of Arizona Press, 1993.

Savage, William W., ed. *Cowboy Life: Reconstructing a Myth.* Norman: University of Oklahoma Press, 1975.

Savage, William W. *The Cowboy Hero: His Image in American History and Culture.* Norman: University of Oklahoma Press, 1979.

Schlebecker, John T. *Cattle Raising on the Plains, 1900–1961.* Lincoln: University of Nebraska Press, 1963.

Sonnichsen, C. L. *Cowboys and Cattle Kings: Life on the Range Today.* Norman: University of Oklahoma Press, 1950.

Steiner, Stan. *The Ranchers: A Book of Generations.* New York: Alfred A. Knopf, 1980.

Wood, Charles L. *The Kansas Beef Industry.* Lawrence: Regents Press of Kansas, 1980.

Worcester, Don. *The Chisholm Trail: High Road of the Cattle Kingdom.* Lincoln: University of Nebraska Press, 1980.

Young, James A., and B. Abbott Sparks. *Cattle in the Cold Desert.* Logan: Utah State University Press, 1985.

GRAZING AND THE PUBLIC LANDS

Alcock, John. *The Masked Bobwhite Rides Again.* Tucson: University of Arizona Press, 1993.

Calef, Wesley. *Private Grazing on Public Lands: Studies of the Local Management of the Taylor Grazing Act.* Chicago: University of Chicago Press, 1960.

Carstensen, Vernon, ed. *The Public Lands: Studies in the History of the Public Domain.* Madison: University of Wisconsin Press, 1968.

Clawson, Marion. *The Bureau of Land Management.* New York: Praeger, 1971.

Foss, Philip O. *Politics and Grass: The Administration of Grazing on the Public Domain.* Seattle: University of Washington Press, 1960.

Gates, Paul W. *History of Public Land Law Development.* Washington, D.C.: Public Land Law Review Commission, 1968.

Libecap, Gary D. *Locking Up the Range: Federal Land Controls and Grazing.* Cambridge: Ballinger, 1981.

Robbins, Roy M. *Our Landed Heritage: The Public Domain.* 2d ed., rev. Lincoln: University of Nebraska Press, 1976.

Rowley, William D. *U.S. Forest Service Grazing and Rangelands: A History.* College Station: Texas A&M Press, 1985.

Russell, Sharman Apt. *Kill the Cowboy: A Battle of Mythology in the New West.* Reading, Mass.: Addison-Wesley, 1993.

Voight, William J. *Public Grazing Lands.* New Brunswick: Rutgers University Press, 1976.

HOMESTEADING, FARMING, AND THE RURAL WEST

Blew, Mary Clearman. *All But the Waltz: Essays on a Montana Family.* New York: Viking Press, 1991.

Blouet, Brian W., and Frederick C. Luebke, eds. *The Great Plains: Environment and Culture.* Lincoln: University of Nebraska Press, 1979.

Doig, Ivan. *This House of Sky: Landscapes of a Western Mind.* New York: Harcourt Brace Jovanovich, 1978.

Fink, Deborah. *Agrarian Women: Wives and Mothers in Rural Nebraska, 1880–1940.* Chapel Hill: University of North Carolina Press, 1992.

Fite, Gilbert C. *American Farmers: The New Minority.* Bloomington: Indiana University Press, 1981.

———. *The Farmer's Frontier, 1865–1900.* New York: Holt, Rinehart & Winston, 1966.

Frazier, Ian. *Great Plains.* New York: Farrar, Strauss, & Giroux, 1989.

Gregory, James. *American Exodus: The Dust Bowl Migration and Okie Culture in California.* New York: Oxford University Press, 1989.

Hargreaves, Mary W. M. *Dry Farming in the Northern Great Plains: Years of Readjustment, 1920–1990.* Lawrence: University Press of Kansas, 1993.

Harris, Katherine. *Long Vistas: Women and Families on Colorado Homesteads.* Niwot: University Press of Colorado, 1993.

Hart, E. Richard, ed. *The Future of Agriculture in the Rocky Mountains.* Salt Lake City and Chicago: Westwater Press, 1980.

Jensen, Joan. *Promise to the Land: Essays on Rural Women*. Albuquerque: University of New Mexico Press, 1991.

Kittredge, William. *Owning It All*. St. Paul: Graywolf Press, 1987.

Nelson, Paula M. *After the West Was Won: Homesteaders and Town Builders in Western South Dakota, 1900–1917*. Iowa City: University of Iowa Press, 1986.

Opie, John. *The Law of the Land: 200 Years of American Farmland Policy*. Lincoln: University of Nebraska Press, 1987.

Sandoz, Mari. *Old Jules*. Lincoln: University of Nebraska Press, 1962. Reprint.

Schlebecker, John T. *Whereby We Thrive: A History of American Farming, 1607–1972*. Ames: Iowa State University Press, 1975.

Stegner, Wallace. *Wolf Willow: A History, A Story, and a Memory of the Last Plains Frontier*. New York: Viking, 1962.

Stewart, Elinore Pruitt. *Letters of a Woman Homesteader*. Boston: Houghton Mifflin, 1914.

Wessel, Thomas R., ed. *Agriculture on the Great Plains, 1876–1936*. Washington, D.C.: Agricultural History Society, 1977.

West, Elliott. *Growing Up with the Country: Childhood on the Far Western Frontier*. Albuquerque: University of New Mexico Press, 1989.

HISTORY OF THE AMERICAN WEST

Abbott, Carl. *The Metropolitan Frontier: Cities in the Modern American West*. Tucson: University of Arizona Press, 1993.

Armitage, Susan, and Elizabeth Jameson, eds. *The Women's West*. Norman: University of Oklahoma Press, 1987.

Athearn, Robert. *The Mythic West in 20th-Century America*. Lawrence: University Press of Kansas, 1986.

Chen, Sucheng, Douglas Henry Daniels, Mario T. Garcia, and Terry P. Wilson, eds. *Peoples of Color in the American West*. Lexington, Mass.: D. C. Heath, 1994.

Cronon, William, George Miles, and Jay Gitlin, eds. *Under an Open Sky: Rethinking America's Western Past*. New York: W. W. Norton, 1991.

Dorman, Robert L. *Revolt of the Provinces: The Regionalist Movement in America, 1920–1945*. Chapel Hill: University of North Carolina Press, 1993.

Hall, Thomas D. *Social Change in the Southwest, 1350–1880*. Lawrence: University Press of Kansas, 1989.

Hundley, Norris, Jr. *The Big Thirst: Californians and Water, 1770s–1990s*. Berkeley and Los Angeles: University of California Press, 1992.

Kittredge, William, and Annick Smith, eds. *The Last Best Place: A Montana Anthology*. Helena: Montana Historical Society Press, 1988.

Lang, William L., ed. *The Centennial West: Essays on the Northern Tier States*. Seattle: University of Washington Press, 1991.

Limerick, Patricia Nelson. *The Legacy of Conquest: The Unbroken Past of the American West*. New York: W. W. Norton, 1987.

Limerick, Patricia, Clyde A. Milner II, and Charles Rankin, eds. *Trails: Toward a New Western History*. Lawrence: University Press of Kansas, 1991.

Lowitt, Richard. *The New Deal and the West*. Bloomington: Indiana University Press, 1984.

Luebke, Frederick C., ed. *Ethnicity on the Great Plains*. Lincoln: University of Nebraska Press, 1980.

Luey, Beth, and Noel J. Stowe, eds. *Arizona at Seventy-Five: The Next Twenty-Five Years*. Tempe and Tucson: Arizona State University Public History Program and Arizona Historical Society, 1987.

Malone, Michael P., and Richard W. Etulain. *The American West: A Twentieth-Century History*. Lincoln: University of Nebraska Press, 1989.

Milner II, Clyde A., ed. *Major Problems in the History of the American West*. Lexington, Mass.: D. C. Heath, 1989.

Morgan Neil. *Westward Tilt: The American West Today*. New York: Random House, 1963.

Nash, Gerald D. *The American West Transformed: Impact of the Second World War*. Bloomington: Indiana University Press, 1985.

Paul, Rodman. *The Far West and Great Plains in Transition, 1859–1900*. New York: Harper & Row, 1988.

Robbins, William G., Robert J. Frank, and Richard E. Ross, eds. *Regionalism and the Pacific Northwest*. Corvallis: Oregon State University Press, 1983.

Stein, Howard F., and Robert F. Hill, eds. *The Culture of Oklahoma*. Norman: University of Oklahoma Press, 1993.

Walton, John. *Western Times and Water Wars: State, Culture and*

Rebellion in California. Berkeley and Los Angeles: University of California Press, 1992.

Webb, Walter P. *The Great Plains.* Boston: Ginn and Company, 1931.

Weber, David J. *The Spanish Frontier in North America.* New Haven: Yale University Press, 1992.

White, Richard. *"It's Your Misfortune and None of My Own": A History of the American West.* Norman: University of Oklahoma Press, 1991.

Wiley, Peter, and Robert Gottlieb. *Empires in the Sun: The Rise of the New American West.* Tucson: University of Arizona Press, 1985.

Worster, Donald. *Rivers of Empire: Water, Aridity, and the Growth of the American West.* New York: Pantheon, 1987.

THE RURAL AMERICAN WEST THROUGH FICTION

Abbey, Edward. *The Brave Cowboy: An Old Tale in a New Time.* Albuquerque: University of New Mexico Press, 1977. Reprint.

Alexie, Sherman. *The Lone Ranger and Tonto Fistfight in Heaven.* Boston: Atlantic Monthly Press, 1993.

Anaya, Rudolfo. *Bless Me, Última.* Berkeley: Tonatiuh-Quinto Sol International Publishers, 1972.

Borland, Hal. *When the Legends Die.* Philadelphia: J. B. Lippincott, 1963.

Cook-Lynn, Elizabeth. *From the River's Edge.* New York: Arcade Publishing, 1991.

Cushman, Dan. *Stay Away, Joe.* New York: Viking, 1953.

Erdrich, Louise. *Love Medicine.* New York: Holt, Rinehart, and Winston, 1984.

Garry, Jim. *This Ol' Drought Ain't Broke Us Yet (But We're All Bent Pretty Bad): Stories of the American West.* New York: Orion Books, 1992.

Gish, Robert Franklin. *First Horses: Stories of the New West.* Reno: University of Nevada Press, 1993.

Harjo, Joy. *Secrets from the Center of the World.* Tucson: University of Arizona Press, 1989.

Martin, Russell, and Marc Barasch, eds. *Writers of the Purple Sage: An Anthology of Recent Western Writing.* New York: Viking, 1984.

Mathews, John Joseph. *Sundown.* New York: Longmans, Green and Co., 1934.

McNickle, D'Arcy. *The Surrounded.* Albuquerque: University of New Mexico Press, 1978. Reprint.

Momaday, N. Scott. *House Made of Dawn*. New York: Harper & Row, 1968.

Mourning Dove. *Cogewea: The Half-Blood (A Depiction of the Great Montana Cattle Range)*. Lincoln: University of Nebraska Press, 1981. Reprint.

O'Brien, Dan. *In the Center of the Nation*. New York: Atlantic Monthly Press, 1991.

Ortiz, Simon. *Woven Stone*. Tucson: University of Arizona Press, 1992.

Silko, Leslie Marmon. *Ceremony*. New York: Viking, 1977.

Stegner, Wallace. *The Big Rock Candy Mountain*. New York: Doubleday, 1938.

Welch, James. *Winter in the Blood*. New York: Harper & Row, 1974.

Work, James C., ed. *Prose and Poetry of the American West*. Lincoln: University of Nebraska Press, 1990.

Index

Women, Indian: contemporary perspectives on: 65, 192–94, 196, 202–203, 208; involvement in ranching, 74, 93–94, 99, 101–102, 119, 135; involvement in rodeo, 192, 194–96, 199, 201; marriage to non-Indians, 40–41, 45–46, 73, 99; participation in college basketball, 54
Wooden Legs, John, 45, 158–59, 161
Work, Hubert, 116–18
Worster, Donald, 142–43, 210

Xavier, Gwyneth Harrington, 94, 133, 136

Yakima Reservation, Wash., 147
Yellow Robe, Sam, 73
Yellowstone County, Mont., 48
Yellowtail, Robert, 65

Zia Pueblo, N.M., 167
Ziebach County, S.Dak., 42
Zuni Pueblo, N.M., 167